THE OLD WILD WEST

ADVENTURES OF ARIZONA BILL

BY

RAYMOND HATFIELD GARDNER

(ARIZONA BILL)

In Collaboration With

B. H. MONROE

Illustrated by GRADY SOWELL

THE NAYLOR COMPANY

SAN ANTONIO, TEXAS

1944

RAYMOND HATFIELD GARDNER
(ARIZONA BILL)

CONTENTS

(over)

CONTENTS— (*Continued*)

CHAPTER I Captured by Indians

WHEN THE INDIAN stuck his head inside the flap of our old covered wagon and stared at me, I was only a year old. I don't remember whether I laughed or howled. My father and mother had started across the plains with a wagon train of pioneers to seek fortunes for themselves in the Far West. But while my parents were off on their horses to get some buffalo meat, our wagon got separated and was left behind and a roving band of Indians came up to see what they could kill or steal.

There was something about me, which I will explain shortly, that bothered those painted redskins a whole lot. Instead of sinking a tomahawk into my skull, they picked me up and carried me off to an Indian village. They were Comanche Indians, a bad outfit. An Indian squaw adopted me and I became her papoose; I didn't know I was a white boy until many years later. Then I found out that my parents' name was Gardner and my own rightful name was Raymond Hatfield Gardner.

About all that most people know about the redskins is that they tortured to death all the palefaces they captured. Yes, the Indians sure did torture them, even the children and babies. When they got a white woman and her baby they would tie up the mother and torture her baby to death where she could see it. And the first thing I remember as a small boy running around in the redskins' camp is how I and other boys watched the white men, women and youngsters being tortured to death.

I was a white boy, about three years old, by that time, but I thought I was a redskin and I thought it was all right to torture all the white captives. The squaws, old braves and the young warriors all took a hand. The small boys liked to see the captives squirm and hear them yell.

My tribe massacred as many as 600 in a year and nobody in my hearing ever said there was anything wrong about it. The poor palefaces, "spread-eagled" on the ground, must have wondered at seeing a little red-headed white child toddling from one to another according to which screamed the loudest. They were brave pioneer emigrants, on their way to California and unknown parts of the West in their covered wagons, just like my own father and mother who happened to have joined up with that hard-luck Donner expedition.

"Spread-eagling," Comanche style, meant throwing the prisoner on his back, with his legs and arms outstretched and holding him that way until he could be nailed to the ground by long, sharp stakes driven through the hands and feet. This held them quiet and put them in a handy position for the real torture.

In addition to being staked out like this all the men were scalped. The Indians didn't figure scalping was a part of the torture. It was just picking up a souvenir and something of an honor to the captive. Only a rare and remarkable woman was thought worthy of it. An Indian warrior always wore a tuft of hair on his head called the scalp lock, so that his conqueror would have something to pull his scalp off with. After death, in the Happy Hunting Ground, his spirit would never live down the disgrace of being left unscalped with the women. For this reason, baldness, very rare among Indians, was much dreaded. When the Indians came to a bald-headed man they had killed they were plenty mad—couldn't scalp him.

A favorite kind of torture was to drive splinters under fingernails and toenails and into other specially sensitive parts of the body and set them on fire. From some they slowly cut off one at a time, the toes, fingers and other projections.

Now and then they would put a rattlesnake beside the body of a prisoner and then tease the snake into striking. I still remember seeing a pretty girl of fourteen, just my mother's age when I was born, who was put to death that way. Most folks shudder more at hearing about that rattlesnake death than any of the others but really it was an easy way out, compared with some, that the Indian didn't figure it was torture at all.

The best kind was the one that allowed the victim to live the longest and kept him screaming to the end. When Indians were tortured, even squaws, they almost never made a sound. That was partly because in the old days before they were softened up with sweets and easy living, they did not feel pain so much. But mostly it was because they knew that the more signs of suffering they showed, the longer and more unpleasant would be their experience. The way to make the torturer lose interest and put him out of his misery was not to show so much as a change of expression. After what I had seen, I am sure I would not have whimpered under torture. I would not have dared. All of us boys in camp were brought up to this idea.

For variety, the Comanches would sometimes pull up the "spread-eagled" man's stakes, tie him to a horse and drag him around by the heels through the brush and over rocks until nearly dead. They would then revive him, nail him down again and try something else. A scared and nervous person usually got the worst dose of all while an enemy who had won their admiration by putting up a fearless fight might be rewarded by a fairly easy death.

The fun the redskins got from all of this was not entirely cruelty. They were in a life-and-death struggle with this strange new race of palefaces and believed that the white man's weakering under torture was a sign that the Indian was a better man and would win out in the end. Some of the old frontiersmen took their "last medicine" so quietly that it shook their torturers' confidence in themselves.

I remember once out on the Kansas plains, the Comanches captured a wagon train and took its leader alive, after a brave fight in which he made many a squaw a widow. They tied him to a tree, scalped him, shot him full of arrows, disemboweled him, and then, still alive, threw him into a fire so that he passed out of his pain pretty quick.

The man may not have known it, but the Comanches did not consider that torture, but a special honor and favor, due such a brave and effective fighter. They did not want his spirit to have any real hard feelings against them. That was this man's good luck.

There were lots of things going on in an Indian camp besides torturing the captives. At the time I had been stolen and adopted by the redskins there were plenty of buffaloes ranging over the plains. The red-skins followed the buffalo herds and the hunters kill-ed them in large quantities so that we had all of the buffalo meat we needed all of the time and now and then some antelope and fish. Pretty tough that buf-falo was for my young teeth, but nobody complained. Chasing after buffalo meat kept us moving most of the time. But that was all right. The Indians I lived with were a restless bunch. As long as there was plenty of buffalo meat easy to get they were able to keep on the warpath, one tribe fighting another or all hands fighting the palefaces.

The best part of the buffalo was his tongue because it was juicy and tender. The squaws would dry thin strips of buffalo meat until it was as hard as board and this is what the warriors took with them when they went on their raids. It didn't weigh much, took up little room and would keep for weeks.

The Indians ate meat three times a day, mostly always raw. Besides the buffalo meat we had sometimes antelope, wild turkeys and other game and sometimes horse and dog meat. If meat was scarce we could get along on rattlesnakes and lizards. But buffalo was the mainstay.

I have eaten worse things since I left living with the Indians than I ever did with them. A hungry man on the desert isn't fussy. He will eat anything. I have enjoyed fricassee of snake meat, have eaten with relish of roasted Gila monster, although it was pretty greasy and strong-flavored. I have held out my plate for a second helping of alligator flesh and, of course, dog stew and roast horse were nothing uncommon.

Most people don't understand what the buffalo did for America. If it hadn't been for these animals, we might now just be settling the plains. There were millions, maybe billions of them and it is wicked the way they were killed off until hardly any were left. There were so many buffalo skulls and bones on the plains that in some places a man could jump from carcass to carcass for fifty miles without once touching the ground.

Indians never saw a horse until the Spaniards came and when they got hold of horses, that completely changed the redskins' life. They could then ride along the herds and kill buffalo in big numbers. Soon the white men came along and hunted them. That opened trails for the covered wagon emigrants who never could have got across the plains had it not been for buffalo meat.

Lots of people don't know that the white man did a lot of scalping in those days too. They hated the Indians as bad as the Indians hated them. The whites called the Indians "war-whoops" and "paintshops" on account of their war paint, and "feather dusters" because of their war feathers, and other pet names.

When a rancher came home from riding the range and found his wife with her throat cut and his babies chopped to pieces, he wasn't likely to forget it. The next time he and his neighbors started after a raiding party of redskins, they usually scalped them, if they caught any prisoners, and were likely to give them a dose of the same kind of torture the Indians used. The torture made the red man respect the white man, as being serious and hard, like himself, but the scalping he took as a compliment.

Even scalping could be done in a mean sort of way. One day a Cherokee Indian came into our camp, very soon after his tribe and ours had gone on the warpath. His errand was to open peace negotiations but the Comanches despised the Cherokees and showed it by tying the prisoner to a tree and shooting him full of arrows until he bristled with them.

Because he hadn't been killed in fight and was looked on as a rather no-good Indian anyway, no brave wanted to spoil his scalp collection by adding this one. So the women were told they could scalp him.

Now it happens that my scalp was worth more to me than my eyes. I was born a long time ago but that would not have done me much good if I had not also been born a redhead. But for that I would have lasted just about one year.

I was born when my mother was about 14 years old and my father only a few years older. Nobody thought anything of that because it was common for girls to be married and have children at that age, and, if a boy wasn't able to play a man's part in life by the time he was 18, his family was ashamed of him. Because I, their first-born, came along just before the adventure across the plains was to start, did not interfere with their plans.

It turned out to be an unlucky expedition. The main party got lost in the desert and the mountains and most of them starved to death at Donner's Lake, in the Sierra Nevada Mountains of California. Father showed such ability as a scout and hunter, that most of the time he was sent ahead to find the way or off to one side to forage for food, which finally resulted in his becoming separated from the main body. This let my parents and me out of sharing in the starvation at Donner's Lake but it ran us into some special adventures of our own and made me an Indian papoose.

One day Father and Mother both galloped away from the wagon, hoping by a quick dash to cut off part of a distant herd of buffalo. They were not gone very long but when they got back they found the wagon had been robbed of most everything worth stealing and myself. Of course they knew it was the work of Indians but the mysterious thing was that the redskins had taken me along.

I was no treasure. A white baby was of no more value to an Indian than would have been a baby rattlesnake. White babies were usually knocked in the head to prevent them from growing into white men and women. Father had to make a quick decision. The fact that the wagon was not being attacked was evidence that the theft had been made by a scouting party, one of whom with me in his arm, would be at that moment riding as fast as he could go back to the main body while one or two others would most likely be watching the wagon from cover.

If father followed the kidnaper's trail he would run into ambush, my mother would then be captured and both tortured to death without doing me any good. Until dark they pretended to be hunting for me in the vicinity of the wagon. Then, under cover of darkness, father, wide-awake scout that he was, managed to get away from the Indians, wagon and all.

When the Comanche scout peered into the wagon and saw a one-year-old baby, he must have had every intention of doing his duty to his race, by tapping me with a tomahawk on my skull.

But he saw that the skull was covered with as bright a covering of red hair as ever came West, and that stopped him. Pure-blooded Indians, at least Comanches, never had red hair but some of their gods did. I was a curiosity, maybe with a touch of the divine about me. At any rate too interesting to be killed. So, resting in the naked arm of a savage in war paint, riding bare-back, I was carried to the Comanche camp.

I soon forgot my parents and became a real Indian in most everything but my skin and hair.

I was well treated and had more fun and excitement than an ordinary white child. It was some sight to see a band of our Comanches, in all their war paint and war bonnets, ride down onto a party of immigrants letting out bloody warwhoops.

I was small for my age but compactly built. By the time I was nine years old, I was such a good rider that the Comanches were thinking about making me a brave. But something happened which made me become a Sioux instead of a Comanche.

One day after a powwow with the Comanches, a party of Sioux caught sight of me on a horse and they decided they ought to have my red head in their tribe. There was another powwow in which they gradually raised their offer for me until it stood at nine ponies, nine blankets, and two girls, one of them white.

The two girls were not worth much but nine blankets certainly were and as for nine ponies, they were real wealth. It was a big offer, too big to be refused. I was very proud and the Sioux respected one who had cost so much. Maybe they could have gotten me at a more reasonable figure but the Sioux were always the dead game sports of the Indian outfit. They were known as the "Monarchs of the Plains," the finest and bravest of the plains Indians, a bit less cruel than the Comanches and not devils like the Apaches.

My training with the Sioux went on rapidly. I was taught the use of bow and arrow, the rifle, the lance, the tomahawk and the scalping knife. I was adopted as a foster-son by the chief, John Gall, who treated me with severe kindness and training me in every art of hunting and killing. My foster-mother must have been fond of me but, according to Indian customs, never showed it in public because it would have disgraced me, nor much in private for fear it would soften me. The Indian never shows much affection for his wife, though he may sometimes feel it, nor the son for his mother. It seems to be part of the ancient custom to keep the squaw in her place.

Of course I had a name when I was with the Sioux. The Comanches had called me by a name meaning "Red Head." But Chief Gall, my adopted father in the Sioux tribe, changed it and I was called "Mant-i-has-tas-i-looha," which means "The Man Who Loves To Go Alone."

Although the Indians pretend to hold a low opinion of women and never let the squaw have any say in important matters, I noticed that women of strong character made their influence felt.

There was a Pawnee woman who fought so like a tiger against the Sioux that they showed their respect and approval by scalping her. After this and all sorts of ill-treatment, she refused to die, so they buried her to the neck in sand for three days. Finding her still alive, they dug her up and gave her something useful to do in the tribe. They must have thought there was something supernatural about her to live through all that and they had better quit trying to kill her for fear the Evil Spirits might bring a severe curse on them.

She got well after a while and escaped to her own people.

In Indian fighting no mercy was given or expected

Ordinarily a warrior was dead when he was scalped but sometimes in the hurry and confusion of battle, they failed to make a thorough job of it. There were quite a number of men who had been scalped and left for dead but recovered and lived the rest of their lives with a queer looking red spot on the back of their heads to remember the incident by. The amount of scalp taken varied but in most cases it was not bigger than a silver dollar. I have seen hundreds of scalps and have run across a few men who were scalped and got well.

At the age of ten, I became a Sioux buck, was proud, happy and might have remained one all my life but for the words of a high-minded American army officer. At the time I was made a Sioux brave my tribe and other Indians were fighting mad at the American prospectors who were swarming into the Black Hills Basin, following a gold strike.

Every wagon train that came along was attacked, but many of them were escorted by soldiers and most of the emigrants were first class gun-fighters, causing plenty of redskins to "bite the dust." But death seemed to have no terrors for the Sioux. In attacking, the Indians learned better than to surround a train which would cause heavy losses. Their tactics were to spread out fan-shaped, constantly shifting backward and forward, ready without warning to dash close enough to pick off a man or an animal.

Considering that the Indians had never seen a rifle or a pistol until the white men used them on them, they certainly learned quick to make the best of both. The Indians schemed out the trick of riding past the wagons, hanging on the far side of the horse, with only part of one leg exposed and firing under the horse's neck. I had to become an expert at this ingenious style of fighting. Of course the redskins didn't use saddles. They rode bareback or on a blanket.

During all this warfare certain traders, with their wagons, went wherever they pleased, without danger of attack by the Indians. No wonder. They were selling the white man's enemy better rifles than the United States cavalry and infantry carried at the time. The whites ought to have attacked them.

When the Sioux captured a wagon train, they killed and scalped all of the men but took a few women as slaves. Only in a few rare instances did they subject the white women to the "last indignity."

The reason for such restraint was the not very flattering one; they did not think the white women worth that much attention but, if one was exceptionally strong and handsome, they might give her the opportunity of raising some warriors.

There was a fine looking girl of about sixteen from Pennsylvania captured by the Sioux on her way to California. I thought she was as pretty as a statue and was sorry to see the Indians pestering her with their nasty attentions. After a while her character and ability gained her a respected position in the tribe Finally she escaped to the Mission School at Pine Ridge, South Dakota, and became a nurse in the Union Army during the Civil War.

Many years later when I was at the Sesquicentennial at Philadelphia, a quiet, elderly woman walked up to me and said:

"I am Jane Dunning. I was captured by the Sioux on my way to California and you were traded by the Comanches to the Sioux. Don't you remember me?"

Another who got a good break was a tall and well-built Negress from Kentucky. My tribe had never seen a colored person before and figured that divine favor or good luck was attached to her. Many of the most powerful chiefs paid her attention and until she finally escaped, her black skin outranked my red head.

The real truth about the "noble red man" is that he was not very "sexy" in the old, brave days when he hunted and fought. Now that he has grown fat, lazy and round-shouldered it may be different.

The family habits of the Indian were based on leadership and discipline. They lived dangerously and, to survive at all as a tribe, everyone had to be absolutely obedient to the chief and tribal rules. Indians say that women are naturally unruly, would play petticoat politics if given a chance, filling the tribe with confusion and squabbles. To prevent any such thing they kept the squaws in a constant state of subjection, maintaining a cold, contemptuous attitude even in courtship.

If an Indian girl noticed that a young brave seemed to be scowling at her longer and harder than at other girls, she might expect a proposal. It would come with about as much delicacy as when a farmer enters his chicken coop to drag out a pullet for dinner. The buck just walked into the herd of girls and yanked out the girl of his choice. The rougher he was about it, the better she liked it because it was supposed to mean he really wanted her.

She knew it meant doing all the hard work for her husband, not merely the cooking, but cultivating the soil, making baskets and pots and even burying the dead. A wife knew she was valued lower in her husband's estimation than a good horse but I never heard one complain. It wouldn't have done her much good if she had.

The husband devoted his valuable time to the noble arts of fighting, hunting and fishing. The few hours given to raising a future generation he thought the least important of his life.

Indians, however, seldom ill-treated their wives and were expected to be faithful. Most always they were. For the Indian felt all women were alike and hardly thought any of them worth the trouble of an affair. But I believe some of those bucks were not able to hide from their wives their respect and affection, though all the torture in the world would never have made them say so.

If a Sioux husband was unfaithful to his wife she had a certain way of getting even. She could hang his hunting outfit outside the tent and bob her hair. This meant that she had divorced him and nobody doubted but that she had plenty of cause because the price she must pay for the divorce was high. She could never marry again, but must be a slave to other squaws who were hardly better than slaves themselves. It was something of a disgrace to the buck to have everyone know that he had driven his wife to leave him. The Navajos still follow this custom.

When the Indian family was growing up the mother had charge of the boys until they were about

eight years old. Then the father took them over and
they paid almost no attention to her afterward, but
she kept right on teaching the girls to make blankets,
tents, clothes and do all the hard work she could put
onto them, so that they in turn would make good
wives.

There was almost no immorality among the Indians
until the whites came along. I remember a young
Indian girl whose name meant "Little Prairie Flower."
It was found out by her tribe members that she had
been too friendly with one of the young white scouts
at a nearby army post. A tribal countil was held and
it was decided that she must be banished from the
tribe.

When the girl entered her wigwam that night there
was no sign of trouble, but in the morning when she
arose, she found her blankets and pony with an eagle
feather in its forelock tethered outside the lodge.
Hung also on the forelock of the pony was a white
weasel skin. That meant that the girl was banished
from the tribe and barred from its privileges.

As she stood thinking about her problem, she was
met by the chief of the tribe who told her with a gesture to the East, where the rising sun glowed:

"Go, and never return. Woman, go to the palefaces and live among them for the rest of your days.
If you return to the wickiup the Evil Spirit and Bad
Medicine will destroy you—the Angels of Death hover
over your trail all of your days. Go, and never return."

Thus the girl knew she was an outcast and was no
longer wanted by her tribe. She accepted the order, as
she knew she must, and went to the padre at the mis-

sion and asked for care until she could find some way to live. After a time, Prairie Flower had the good fortune to find a young white scout who sincerely loved her and whom she loved too. This scout took her under his care and sent her to the medical school at the mission on her reservation where she became a nurse.

The Indians never slept in a house, if they could avoid it, being happy and healthy lying on the bare ground. As long as the redskin could do this, follow the buffalo herds and get plenty of meat, he was a fine, healthy creature. The killing off of the buffalo put him on a largely vegetarian diet, tied him to his cultivated land, where he learned to stay more or less in a house and got tuberculosis, but, perhaps, most important of all, it knocked him out as a military danger, for the buffalo was the Indian's food on the warpath and without it he could not go very long or far.

Life was much the same among the warriors, the women and children in most of the tribes scattered over the West. Indian boys were all aiming to become braves and. at the age of fourteen or fifteen, they could be full-fledged warriors if they could prove they were tough enough. They had to be able to stand exposure to all kinds of weather, to go for a long time without food and to take severe pain without a whimper.

In some tribes a boy could not call himself a warrior until he had gotten for his head-dress the plume of a full grown eagle that had lost its life without shedding any of its blood—in other words, an eagle the boy had captured with his bare hands and

strangled. To do this the youngster had to fix his decoy and a blind to hide in, on some mountain peak or
canyon crag where eagles rested, and wait there for
days without shelter until an eagle came. During this
time the boy could eat no food. When the eagle finally did come and pounce on the meat left there for bait,
a fierce fight followed as the boy tried to throttle the
giant bird. His flesh would be torn by the eagle's
talons and beak, and he might be so weak from hardship and exposure himself that the eagle would kill
him. Often the young Indian lost his life in this test
of endurance and bravery.

Every Indian brave collected as many scalps as possible. He kept a "coop-stick" on which he cut a notch
for every scalp taken which may have given the idea to
the frontiersmen to cut one on the butt of his gun every
time he killed anyone. One of my Indian friends took
14 scalps in one day and 200 in one season. They were
dried in the sun and hung in the entrance to the tepee.
When they had a Scalp Dance every warrior brought
out his string of scalps, and they were all hung on a
pole, and the braves danced around them. The Indian
with the biggest bunch of scalps was reckoned the
bravest warrior. These grim treasures were willed to a
man's most respected relatives.

I well remember what a gloomy lot the Indians
were. They thought they never would get what they
wanted, this side of the Happy Hunting Grounds.
They believe in only one god, which they called the
Great Spirit, and they thought he was always a good
god. But there were all sorts of evil gods or spirits
working against them, and they had to make sacrifices

to these. They always fasted and had other ceremonies before going on the warpath or just before a big hunt for game, and sometimes they did penance by burning their flesh and slashing themselves with knives. And, of course, we children looked on with eyes wide open at these ceremonies.

It was the Indians' gloomy nature that made them such drunkards when the white man came with his whisky. They found it was a quick way to work up excitement and forget their troubles. Before they knew about whisky, they couldn't get warmed up about anything except in the heat of a bloody battle. But when they drank liquor, they found they could get quick excitement and it gingered them up in fighting. too. But the white man's whisky cost many a white man's life when drunken Indians went on the warpath.

The Indians showed greater love for the dead than they did for the living and they often went back to visit the burial places of their dead, even if the tribe had wandered two hundred miles away, and a year or more had passed. Then they would carefully gather up the bones, take them away to the new territory where they had settled and solemnly bury them.

Many tribes left their dead wrapped in buffalo robes, on platforms high in the air. They usually wrapped a fighter's rifles and knives with his body for they believed the departed would need these articles in the Happy Hunting Grounds. They often left blankets, pots and bowls for cooking and eating purposes, and much other property for a dead warrior to use. Greedy white men, curious to see if anything valuable had been left under the buffalo robes, often brought whole tribes on the warpath when the Indians discovered things were stolen from their dead.

The white men of the frontier trading posts always cheated the Indians. I have seen Indian women bring bundles of fine buffalo hides and other furs, which they had worked hard curing and dressing, and trade them for a cup of dirty, brown sugar. They had no idea of the sugar's value. They only knew it was something they had never tasted before, and something that tasted good. As if this sort of bargain was not mean enough the white trader would stick his big finger in the cup when he measured the sugar in it. Many a swindling white trader got a tomahawk in his skull sooner or later and I couldn't feel very sorry for them.

I visited among the Hopi Indians who live in a country where the chief worry is shortage of rain. Being accepted as fellow redskin, I probably know as much about their famous Snake Dance as any white man that ever lived. The idea of the dance is to cause the gods to send rain but the interesting part is that the dancers hold live rattlesnkaes in their teeth. Many people have tried to explain why the snakes do not bite the dancers. They are all wrong because the snakes do bite them over and over.

The Hopis always say that their gods protect them from the poison, but there's nothing in that. The bite doesn't often kill a healthy man in his full vigor of life and each time he is rebitten increases his immunity until finally a snake-bite hardly bothers him more than a mosquito. The Hopis make themselves thoroughly immune and that's the secret of their harmless Snake Dance.

While I was with the Sioux nobody asked me to fight against the white man, but I would have had to if we had ever been cornered. My jobs were mostly hunting and taking care of livestock. I took part in all the war dances and was treated in every way as an honored warrior. At my initiation as a brave, they put on me a war bonnet of eagles' and roosters' feathers and showed their expectation of my future by giving me an extra large helping of dog soup which is supposed to put strength into a warrior. My face was painted black and scarlet, like all Sioux warriors, giving them that terrifying appearance they were famous for.

Several other white children were adopted by the Indians at various times. One, I will never forget, was a boy from Kentucky who grew up more bloodthirsty and cruel than the worst of the Sioux. He took a delight in torturing both white and red captives and in tearing off their scalps.

When I saw this white youth, working with joy on his own kind. I felt sort of sick and began to realize that something was wrong. I found myself dreading that I might get to be so much of an Indian that some day I too would enjoy torturing people, as this paleface did.

I made many good friends among the leading Indian chiefs: Chief Rain-in-the-face and American Horse of the Sioux, Two Moons of the Cheyennes, Joseph of the Nez Perces, the famous Geronimo of the

Arizona Apaches, the wily Nocona and Lone Wolf of the Comanches.

At the age of 12, I was a red-headed white Indian, who could not speak a word of English but between then and my 14th year I came in contact with white people at Fort Sill and other army posts where soldiers were posted to watch the Indians and keep them in order. From them I quickly picked up some English and soon realized that I was really a white man. But this, at first, gave me no notion of quitting my Sioux friends.

One day Major Elliot, an officer everyone admirerd at Fort Sill, spoke a few words to me. They were in English but brief, the kind of speech an Indian likes. He said:

"My boy, you are really an American and you ought to live with us. What would your Sioux friends think of a Sioux who preferred to live with white men instead of his own race? You know they would despise him. Do you want your people to look upon you as a deserter, a kind of squaw man?"

My answer was probably a grunt, and I am sure my expression did not change but his words hit hard. I remembered that bloodthirsty white boy and returned for other pow-wows with the major with the final result that I left the Sioux and became a scout for the United States Army at $15 a month. My redskin foster-parents and my Sioux friends said goodbye to me without showing any feelings, but I never knew what was passing behind their grave faces.

I often wonder if they realized what they had done. By their training they had turned out a far better scout for leading soldiers against them than any white man the army itself could possibly have trained. I could crawl on my belly, silently as a snake, knew all their methods, their tricks, what they expected the white man to do under all circumstances and could think as they thought.

If necessary I could walk into a camp of hostiles, sit in the war council disguised as an Indian from a distant tribe, learn all their plans and give them bad advice. I actually did this with Sitting Bull and got away with it.

When the Civil War broke out, for a while instead of stalking the red man, I found myself working for the Northern whites against the Southern ones. That was not what I had expected.

After the Civil War there came many Indian battles in the campaigns out West. There were the Battle of Wounded Knee and The Little Big Horn. I was a scout continuously down to 1883. Then I joined Buffalo Bill's outfit for a time.

During my long life with the Indians and the white men of the West and especially when I was scouting I got to know nearly all the famous and notorious characters of the Western Frontier. I stopped for a time at Tombstone in Arizona when life there was at its wildest and deadliest and struggled through Death Valley and Skeleton Gulch when there were no railroads and only a trail marked by skeletons.

All those wild people and the sudden and violent things that happened then seemed strange now but I can't remember them as anything but natural then. They belong to the times that have gone forever.

And looking back in memory shortens it all up. I now see the winning of the West, like a sort of moving picture with a plot that was always getting somewhere. But while it was happening before my eyes, it seemed just one thing tumbling over another. No sooner did somebody get something all set and working right than somebody or something came along and upset it. There were plenty of cases like old Sutter who had set himself up and was slowly getting rich and making sense out of the crazy West when they discovered gold. Instead of making him ten times richer, it ruined him.

CHAPTER II — Scouting Days

WHEN THE SOLDIERS took me away from the Indians and I went to live at an army post, I was a bow-legged, red-headed boy of fifteen. I didn't know one letter of the alphabet from another and couldn't speak English very well, but I knew the Indian lingo and all the redskin's tricks. So I got a job as a scout for the army at $15 a month.

I reckon I couldn't have had a better training for the job of army scout. I was naturally fitted for this kind of life because my father was the chief scout of the Donner Party. My mother was a Hatfield of the old Kentucky fighting family that almost wiped itself out in the Hatfield-McCoy mountaineer fights that went on for years and years. So it was in my blood on both sides and it came easy for me to pick up the fine points of scouting, trailing and reading sign.

I learned a lot from the Indians I had lived with and I had the good luck to learn a lot more from the best white men scouts on the plains. The old-time frontier scout had to have mighty sharp eyes, ears, nose and a special kind of memory. He was able to ride all day and remember how every foot of the trail looked. A day or a month later he ought to know if a pebble had been shifted, a twig broken, or a piece of dead wood moved from where it was the first time he passed it. A good scout would stop right there in his tracks until he figured out what any change meant. If he came across the cold ashes of a camp fire he could tell how old it was, how many had been in the party and whether they were Indians, cowpunchers or miners.

When his eyes spotted one of these signs, his knowing how to read its meaning depended again on memory. By remembering the date and hour of the last shower on the dusty plain or the last thaw in winter he could often tell exactly when a man or animal made a certain track. I have just that sort of memory. Even now before going to sleep at night I often see in my mind long stretches of trail I covered as a scout more than 75 years ago.

Of course the Indians and the frontiersmen were matching their wits against each other all the time. Some things they did in just about the same way. The plains were long and level and stretched hundreds of miles in all directions without a tree as a guide post.

A tenderfoot would get lost just as quick as he would in a thick forest in the middle of the night. But the redskins could go right along at night by watching a star, and in daytime they went by the sun and the "trade winds." The frontiersmen traveled the same way. Nobody but the soldiers and the emigrants carried a compass.

A sharp eye open not to miss anything and memory made it possible for the scout to get the information he was hired for. But his own life depended on his being the most suspicious man in the world. About like a fox, he figured most anything might be a trap or ambush until he had examined it on all sides. This habit of suspicioning everything got such a hold on us that we often amused people and sometimes annoyed ordinary white people.

I happened to be present when an old scout came in to make his report to General Harney in command at old Fort Randall in the Dakotas. He stopped in the doorway, his sharp eye taking in every person and object in the room and his nostrils quivering. It was just the way a cat acts before going into a strange house.

At last, when the General spoke up and said, "Come in," he stepped in but went sidling over to an open window and stuck his head out. While studying the view he kept snapping his head around like an owl, for quick glances at what we were up to behind him.

I knew what was on his mind. He was taking note of every tree or other object that a man could hide behind and take a pot shot at him through the window. Also he was sizing up what cover there was in case he had to jump out that window and run for his life. Yet that scout knew perfectly well that he was in the safest possible place, a government fort, full of soldiers. It annoyed General Harney, who invited him to sit down. The scout knew it was a command and he obeyed, squatting on the floor, with his back against the wall, in a position where he could watch the door and the open window.

"What the devil do you want to sit on the floor for when there are three empty chairs?" the General snapped at him. The old fellow got up and took one of the chairs but he kept looking under it and over his shoulder. His mind would have been at ease and probably he'd have given a better report, if they had let him stand with his back against the wall.

The way he acted did not seem funny to me because I felt the same way. I had not slept in a house since I was old enough to remember and a room always seemed like a trap to me. None of us was afraid to sleep in the open because we knew we would wake quick if a twig snapped anywhere around. If we didn't, our horses would hear it and wake us up with a whinny.

I was suspicious enough, had the right kind of memory and the best training in the world but I did not know it all at that, as I soon found out when some of the old-timer scouts at Fort Sill and elsewhere took me in hand. One of my first lessons was following some hoofprints for about a mile. Then the old scout said:

"Well, Bub, what do you make of it?"

"A stray horse," I told him.

"It is a stray black horse," he said, "with a long bushy tail and nearly starved to death. It has a split hoof on the left fore foot and goes a little bit lame. It passed through here early this morning."

I knew it was a stray because the animal had not gone in a a direct line but I saw my carelessness when he told me the rest. He said:

"Its tail was long because it dragged over the snow and it left a couple of black hairs on a bush back yonder. Didn't you see where it had snapped at those, high, dry weeds that a horse won't touch unless it is near starved to death? I saw that one hoof mark seemed a bit lighter than the others, and, by watching it carefully, saw the crack in it. The tracks were made this morning when the ground was hard with frost."

We went back and I read it all as clear as print, as you would say, though to me print meant nothing at all. The trouble was that I hadn't been paying attention, a thing that never happens to a scout when he is really on the trail.

Nothing made a tenderfoot from the East wonder so much as the way we old trailers followed tracks that they couldn't see. There was an army doctor at Fort Randall who never could quite figure out how scouts could "read sign" that meant nothing to him.

He was out with a scout one day and they came across some prints of an Indian moccasin. That didn't mean much to the doctor, but the scout said right away:

"It was an old Yangton Indian, who came across the Missouri late evening to look at his traps. In com·

ing over he carried in his right hand a trap, and in his left a lasso to catch a pony which he had lost. He returned without finding the pony, but had caught in the trap he had out, a prairie wolf, which he carried home on his back and a bundle of kinni-kinic wood in his right hand.''

Then, he gave his reasons:

"I know he is old by the impression his gait has made and that he is a Yangton by that point of his moccasin. He is from the other side of the river, as there are no Yanktons on this side. The trap he carried struck the snow now and then, and in same manner as when he came, and that shows that he did not find his pony. A drop of blood in the center of his tracks shows that he carried the wolf on his back, and the bundle of kinni-kinic wood he used for a staff for support, and catching a wolf shows that he had traps out.''

"But," the army doctor asked, "how do you know it is a wolf; why not a fox, or a coyote, or even a deer?''

The old scout chuckled and said:

"If it had been a fox, or coyote or any other animal—small game—he would have slipped the head of the animal in his waist-belt, and so carried by his side, and not on his shoulders. Deer are not caught by traps but if it had been a deer, he would not have crossed this high hill, but would have gone back the easier way through the ravine, and the load would have made his steps still more tottering.''

Another Indian track which they saw twenty miles west of this, the old-timer figured out this way:

"He is an upper Indian— a prowling horse thief— carried a double-barrelled shotgun, and is a murderer who has killed some white man lately, and passed here one week ago, For," said he, "a lone Indian in these parts is on mischief, and generally on the lookout for horse. He had on the shoes of a white man that he had in all probability killed, but his steps are those of an Indian. Going through the ravine, the end of his gun hit into the snow. A week ago we had a very warm day, and the snow being soft, he made these deep tracks, ever since it has been very cold weather, which makes very shallow tracks."

The doctor said that maybe he bought those shoes.

"Indians don't buy shoes, and if they did they would not buy them as large as these were, for Indians have very small feet," the scout answered.

One of the greatest trailers of all time was Paul Daloria, a half-breed. Once I asked him to tell me about a very faint elk track. He followed it a few hundred feet and then said:

"It is one month old and was made at 2 o'clock in the afternoon."

His memory told him when we had our last rain and just at that hour he had taken pains to note that the ground was at its softest. We followed the trail over a mile, now and then seeing where a wolf, a fox and other animals had practiced their trailing and hunting skill along the elk's tracks. Here and there he would show me where a snake, a rat and a prairie dog had crossed the trail. There was nothing that had crossed the track that the quick eye of Daloria did not spot. He described the habits of all the animals that had left their footprints, also the state of the weather since the elk passed and the effect of sunshine, winds, dryness, sand-storms, and other weather that had added to the story.

At the age of fifteen, I could still learn a lot about the art of "reading sign" because after all, much of that skill comes only from long experience. My chief value to the army lay in the fact that I understood the Indian better than most anyone else because I had just stopped living as one of them. Also I could not only act as a scout but, if necessary, as a spy. A spy caught during war is pretty sure of being shot. If I had been caught I would have been scalped and tortured to death.

When soldiers and Indians or two tribes of Indians are on the warpath, their scouts groping around in between are likely to run afoul of each other. In that case, the most prudent thing to remember is the old saying that dead men tell no tales, also that the only good Indian is a dead Indian. But, unless the rival scout can be killed without the sound of a shot or giving him time to utter his death screech, it is better to get away as quickly and quietly as possible.

Once when I was crawling on my belly, with rifle poked ahead of me, I peeped around the corner of a high ledge and saw not twenty feet away a Sioux Indian scout doing the very same thing. We saw each other at the same instant, stiffened for a few minutes, then saying nothing, inch by inch, ready to fire at the slightest hostile move of the other, we backed out of each other's view.

I ran for my horse and put as much land between

me and that hedge as I could because I did not know how much support he might have close at hand. He did not know that about me either and probably did the same thing. But the closest call I have had to death in scouting was when I was doing it for the Seventh Cavalry, in Dakota.

They saw smoke rising from the valley and thought it was a party of white emigrants, but sent me out dressed as an Indian scout. I found they were a band of Comanches on the warpath. I had ridden far ahead of the seventh Cavalry and turned back to carry the information. But the cavalry got onto the fact also and as I turned back they came charging on the Comanches. The bullets flew around me and my horse was shot dead.

I jumped up, yelled who I was and made peace gestures but the bullets only came thicker, one clipping a moccasin and several going through the feathers on my headdress. That gave me the idea that saved my life. Tearing off the headdress I showed them the reddest head of hair that ever emigrated to the West, something you don't see on an Indian. The cavalry, not a second too soon, knew me for their own boy scout and saved their bullets for the real enemy. Soldier humor is grim. After the battle their only apology was to say:

"Anybody who can look so much like a damn warwhoop ought to be shot anyhow."

That Indian-fighting Seventh Cavalry was famous, not only in the East but many parts of Europe and the thrill of shooting Indians lured the sons of wealthy families from both sides of the Atlantic. Out West, in those days, everybody, even the few called "rich," lived lives of hardship. They thrived on it but most of them yearned for the ease and luxury they had heard about. Most of those who tried it, disliked it almost as much as I did having to learn to sleep in a bed, inside a house. That was a natural enough mistake but it is not so easy to understand why young fellows who had been tenderly raised, should enlist for hardships they were not fitted for.

Those tenderfoots did not know that to get within gunshot of a redskin meant weeks of riding in the zero cold or under a burning sun, often without enough water and no food but tough, dry jerked beef. Sometimes when these boys lay down at night on the bare ground, they prayed that an Indian would sneak up and tomahawk them in their sleep. It was no fault of the Indian that those prayers were not answered.

In scouting I was easily enough able to tell whether footprints were made by Sioux, Comanches, Arapahoes, Cheyennes, Apaches, Blackfeet or any other of the Plains Indians. Of course all Indians were mounted fighters but usually one would get off his cayuse now and then for various reasons, long enough to leave a few footprints.

But I could tell plenty from just the horses alone. Any number of horses traveling abreast across the prairie leave marks that a child could count. If they follow each other along a trail single file, most people could not say whether the party was 50, 100 or 500, but a good scout would come pretty close to the mark. I could tell how much food they were carrying by how deep the hoofs sank in the ground.

Sioux and Arapahoes were easy to spot because they

put a carryall, called a "travois," on some of their horses which hung down on both sides and left tracks.

The size and number of the campfires confirmed other signs. Sometimes the ground was so hard, especially if the trail was old, that the hoofs left no dent even to the trained eye of the scout. That would not deceive a good tracker who knew other things to look for and, what was more important, where to look. He would hunt for a shaded spot where it might be damp enough for moss or sand, soft enough to be disturbed by a hoof.

If these were not handy then there were other signs. He would find a place where horse and rider must squeeze between bushes or a rock and a tree. At such places he would stop and examine every inch, for the smallest sign of a broken twig, which might mean only that a bear or some other heavy animal had crashed through or, what would be better, a hair of a horse's tail, caught on the rough bark of a tree as the animal swished at a fly in passing.

Even the hard, dry surface of a barren ledge on which a hoof could make no scratch, may leave something just as good. A large, juicy insect, squashed on a rock may tell the scout all he wants to know—that is whether it was done by a paw or by the hoof of a horse.

Once I got off my horse because I saw an ant staggering along with the wing of a butterfly. When I found the rest of the butterfly it did not mean anything but by that time I had a presentiment that there was an old campfire nearby, and, following another line of ants into a thicket near the ledge, found the remains of a carefully hidden fire where two enemy scouts had slept the night before.

With this clue I was able to find where the pair had gone slowly on to a high hill and then turned back, riding in a straight line and at top speed. At once I returned with the information that our soldiers had been sighted and there was no hope we could make a surprise attack.

I have had plenty of these presentiments and usually they were right when I had time enough to look into them. At first I used to wonder where they came from, but before long I figured it out. It is not a sixth sense or anything mysterious like that, but just one of the regular senses that has been tickled so gently. that it does not wake up quite but sort of dreams in its sleep. A dead fire has a heavy bitter smell, when it is covered with dirt, like this one, but there was mighty little of the smell. Just the faintest whiff must have gotten to my nose and suggested "campfire maybe."

I learned more from Kit Carson than any man I ever met. When I was young I may have known a thing or two more about Indian life than he did but in everything else he was the finest scout and all-around frontiersman in the country. Besides polishing up my education in reading sign, he gave me some good advice that I needed even more. It was a tough civilization where every man did as he pleased unless he thought it would make someone take a shot at him, and often even then, if he thought he was quicker on the draw. My Indian bringing up was a little too rough he figured, and the rules of health and behavior he gave me have never been forgotten.

Nobody was Kit's equal as hunter, trapper and scout. He killed plenty of Indians but never did a mean act in his life. Carson was the son of a frontiersman who apprenticed him to a saddle-maker. Kit, a born scout, wouldn't work in a shop and at the age of fifteen joined a hunting party of 18 headed for the Sacramento Valley to hunt animals, but never suspecting that it was full of gold.

One night when he was in a trapping camp on the San Joaquin River, Indians crept up and stole more than half their horses. In those days horse-stealing was one of the worst crimes of all and there was no dispute about death being the punishment. On the other hand, for killing another man, often as not, nothing would be done.

"We had an argument, he drawed and I drawed. He missed and I got him," was usually considered sufficient explanation and defense so that there was not even the formality of a trail. But a horse was the only way a man had of getting around, a man's life depended on it all the time, yet a lot of the time the precious animals had to be left unguarded. So a horse-thief was shot or hung pronto.

The head of the camp asked Uncle Kit, as some of us got to call him later, to take 12 of his best men and get the horses back because without them they were doomed. There was no need of telling him what to do with the redskins when he caught them. It is surprising that this young man should be able to catch a band of skilled Indian horse-thieves, Apaches and Comanches, and take their booty away from them.

But Kit did it. He had to travel faster than the thieves
and not let them know it.

Many a time he outwitted them, not just by following their trail, but by reasoning out the direction
they were taking and making a shorter cut. The chase
went on to the Sierra Nevada Mountains, a couple of
hundred miles away. There the Indians looked back
over the plain and satisfied themselves that there was
not pursuit. Feeling quite safe, they sat down and enjoyed a big meal of roast horse, which they relished
more even than buffalo or deer. In the midst of their
feasting and merry-making came a frightful series of
yells and whoops. A dozen horsemen headed by Carson swept down on the thieves. The redskins bit the
dust right and left, and those who escaped death scattered and ran. Every horse stolen, except those killed
for the feast, were recovered and Carson took them
back to camp without the loss of a man.

The trappers then worked their way down the
Colorado River and then to the Gila until they reached
the mouth of the San Pedro. They had collected a pile
of furs and needed lots more horses to carry their
goods. Just then they saw a large herd of horses and
mules in the care of a few Indians. The white man was
not supposed to steal Indian horses either, but Kit
figured that these had been stolen, and, anyway, it was
a chance to even up the balance, so they took them all.

That night all the men slept the sleep that only the
just are supposed to get, except Uncle Kit, who was
awake wishing he had a bit more evidence. About
midnight it came in a sound like distant thunder. Kit's
ears told him it was the thunder of hoofs. Waking his

men they went out and waited for it. It was a drove of about 100 horses being guided headlong through the night by half a dozen Indians. Somehow Carson knew that these were some more stolen horses.

The boys opened fire, dropping a few redskins and causing the surviving Indians to gallop off. They now had more horses than they wanted, so after eating a couple of the fattest, they turned the rest loose to breed.

The expedition brought back so many pelts that when it cashed in at Santa Fé, Carson had a lot of money to spend. He spent it in what was the usual manner of the times, a long drunken debauch ending with empty pockets and an awful headache. It was his first and his last. Once was enough to teach him that it was a poor way to fool away his money.

The redskins had given me something of their own foolish idea of the value of fire-water and it was Kit who convinced me that it was a mistake. Yet at his funeral I saw an Indian, solemnly and reverently put a quart of whisky in the grave with this man who had so often talked against it. The priest and I made no protest because we knew that a beautiful sentiment was behind the sacrifice.

One winter while Carson was trapping on the Laramie River, a party of Crow Indians called in a snowstorm on night and silently removed nine of the party's best horses. In the morning it was still snowing and most of the men didn't see what could be done about it.

"Reckon we shore have to do something," said Kit, "or they'll come back for the rest."

With a few men mounted on what few good horses were left, he took the trail now covered by heavy snow and crossed by several buffalo herds. Kit followed that trail more with his mind than his eyes, figuring out what the thieves would do. After 40 miles they came upon the Indians fortified in the woods. They not only outnumbered Kit's outfit but had built a rough fort of logs and stone. Inside they were holding a feast in celebration of what they had done to the white man.

After they had stuffed themselves the redskins went to sleep. They must have thought they were safe from pursuit, but an Indian always sleeps with both ears open, so Kit and a couple of others crept very quietly into the wood where the cayuses were tethered. They dared not lead them all away in a bunch because the noise would surely have waked the red sleepers.

Cutting one tether at a time, Kit directed each horse's wanderings by an occasional snowball until it was far enough away to be safely lassoed. They got back not only their own but all the others the Indians had. Knowing that there would be no pursuit, they rode leisurely home, feeling sure they could not hear the howl when the Indians found that they were in a midst of a snowy wilderness without a single horse. Many a time I laughed to myself as I rode along alone, over the plains or the deserts and remembered how Kit left those warhoops on foot in the snow miles and miles from their village.

It took a lot of lessons to teach the Indians that horse-stealing is bad medicine and in some of these brushes it was only Kit's quick hand and eye that saved his life. There are lots of crack pistol and rifle shots today if they have plenty of time to draw a bead on the target. But Indians, animals and white badmen were kind of stingy about giving you time to aim.

Once on his way to California, an Indian paid one of those silent calls and got away with all but two of Kit's best horses. As always he went right hot after him, his only companion a reliable Indian buck. After 100 miles the buck's horse went sick and Carson kept on alone. Just then the thief slowed up so suddenly that Kit came in sight of him without warning.

Knowing that he was spotted, the thief jumped from his horse and started on a run for a clump of trees where he could find shelter and shoot his pursuer when he pleased. The Indian was as fast on foot as a deer, but as he leaped for the nearest tree he was caught by Carson's bullet. Without checking his horse in the least Carson had aimed and shot the redskin through the heart.

The death screech of the savage rang out as he leapt into the air and tumbled to the earth. He was so near shooting Kit that his gun was fired after he was shot and the bullet whizzed over the head of the scout. Another second's delay would have been the end of Carson, for this warwhoop was as good a shot as Kit.

Among the trappers at the base of the Big Snake River was a very husky Frenchman called Captain Chounin. He was smart and quick in the use of arms and the most quarrelsome man in camp. He seemed to spend all his time trying to stir up quarrels with those around him. His strength was so great that nobody could handle him, and he could only be overcome with a gun. He knocked down several inoffensive persons and swaggered around the camp bragging that he could wallop anybody there. In the midst of his bluster Carson walked up to the Frenchman and said in a loud voice:

"Captain Chounin, there are plenty here who could kill you, but they would rather put up with your insolence for the sake of peace. Now we've had enough of you, and I'm tellin' you to behave yourself right now or I'll kill you."

These seemed surprising words from a man six inches shorter and many pounds lighter than the blustering captain and they took his breath away. Then without a word he walked back to his quarters. Kid did the same and came out of his lodge carrying an out-of-date single-barreled pistol. He was so anxious to be in time that he caught at the first weapon he found.

Almost at the same moment Captain Chounin appeared with a rifle. The other trappers gathered gaping, pretty sure from what they kne wof the two men that one of them was going to be killed.

Each man mounted his horse and rode toward the other. When they stopped, Carson looked the other in the eye and asked coolly, "Are you lookin' for me?"

"No," said the Frenchman.

As he spoke, Chounin brought his rifle to his shoulder, and, pointing it at the chest of Carson, pulled the trigger. But Kit had expected treachery and before the gun could be fired he fired his pistol across the barrel of the other's weapon. The bullet broke the forearm of Captain Chounin at the very moment that he fired his gun. The shock upset his aim so that the bullet grazed Carson's scalp, causing only a trifling wound. The men were so close that the powder of the rifle scorched Kit's face.

Captain Chounin recovered and afterwards became a model of good behavior.

In battle Carson saw everything and thought for everyone. Once when the white men he was with were attacking a party of Blackfeet at the headwaters of the Missouri, he knew that the Indian opposite him was getting ready to shoot at him. This was just what Kit wanted because in so doing the Indian would expose himself and get a bullet from the lightning-quick scout.

To encourage him, Carson looked away for an instant and as he did, saw another Indian aiming at one of his friends who was examining the lock of his rifle. Instantly Carson turned and shot that one, at the same time dodging to avoid the bullet he knew would be coming his way. But the bullet grazed his neck and buried itself in his shoulder, shattering the head of one of the bones. During the long journey back through the wilderness Carson's wounds continued bleeding and then froze under the rough dressing. His agony must have been hard to stand but he never complained and took his part in guiding the party back. His wonderful constitution and good habits made him recover quickly.

On these long, hungry trails we used to make ourselves big promises of what we would do the next time

we got into a good restaurant. Once Kit drove a herd
of sheep from New Mexico to California, gaining a
profit of a few thousand dollars and one of those ap-
petites. Stepping into one of the best restaurants in
San Francisco, he ordered a hearty meal for six persons
and then ate every crumb of it all himself.

The waiter told the proprietor, who thought the
stranger must be the world's best single-mouthed customer and offered him his family rates.

"I ain't so good as you reckon I am. Only do this
about once a year when I come in off the trail," mut ·
tered Kit as he started slowly and sleepily back to his
hotel.

My pay as an army scout varied from $15 to $30
a month. Kit, with the Fremont expeditions, got $100,
which was about the record. A good scout was worth
whatever the lives of the party were worth; a poor
scout was worse than none at all. The three exploring
expeditions of the famous John C. Fremont that were
guided by Kit, went successfully through all sorts of
risks. The fourth, led by a scout who should have
been something else, got lost in the mountain snows.
After eating their mules, and according to some reports each other, the survivors, more dead than alive,
stumbled onto Kit's ranch where he nursed them back
to health.

During the Mexican War he helped capture Los
Angeles. When General Kearney was surrounded by
a strong force of Mexicans, he and Lieutenant Beal
crawled on their faces, all night through the lines,
sometimes taking an hour to creep around one sentry.
Once a Mexican officer was so close that when he

tossed his cigarette away it fell on Kit's head. He had to keep quiet and let it burn right down into his scalp, hoping that the smell of singed hair would not make the "Greasers" investigate.

They did the creeping barefoot and when finally through the lines found they had lost their shoes. They reached Commodore Stockton, at San Diego with feet in terrible condition from thorns and cactus, but General Kearney and his men were saved.

Uncle Kit got the injury that cost him his life after years of suffering while on an errand of mercy to rescue a Ute Indian squaw and her six children from being tortured to death by a band of Arapahoes that her tribe was at war with. On the way he went down a mountain so steep that he led his horse by a lariat. The cayuse fell, but though Kit threw the lariat from him he was caught in it and dragged some distance. He was badly hurt and his heart strained.

He lived through the Civil War, where he did splendid service in keeping down the Indians of New Mexico and was made Brigadier-General. At first he did not suffer much from his injury, which never stopped his work, but as years went by, he developed a heart trouble which couldn't be cured.

The Indians knew that Kit had killed plenty of them but that these had all been bad Indians. They also knew that he always kept faith with them and was ready at the risk of his own life, to help a good Indian. In appreciation of these things the Indians presented him with a $600 ring, which he thought more of than anything else he ever had.

Wandering back from a long trapping trip through

Wyoming and Idaho, in 1868, I paid my old teacher what turned out to be a last visit. I found him lying under a tree, suffering as the lines in his face showed, but smoking a pipe and making no complaint.

"How are you Kit," I asked.

"Oh, pretty well, son," he answered, "but I don't think I shall live long."

Then he ordered his men to give me a liberal supply of jerked beef, sugar and beans for my journey and he handed me his precious ring. Kit wanted it preserved as a memento of himself but especially of the fact that the redskin appreciates honest treatment.

I attended his strange but impressive funeral. Uncle Kit was a Roman Catholic and a priest officiated at the burial, but Indians in great numbers traveled day and night to be present, showing the deepest grief on their faces, usually as changeless as the stony face of a mountain. Such sincere feeling could not be slighted, so the priest, in addition to the church rites, permitted such Indian ones as satisfied the redskins that the man they loved had been properly started on his journey to the White Man's Happy Hunting Ground

A bugler from Fort Marcy sounded "Taps" over the grave. Before it was filled in, the Indians came forward and placed in the grave a liberal supply of bear meat and bread. Last and most reverently of all, they added a quart of whisky.

The old warriors he had known did not want the great white scout to be hungry or thirsty on his last long trail. Before this they had all passed the body and given it a last farewell kiss on the forehead.

When the grave had been filled in, the Indians marched past it again. Then without a backward look, they climbed onto their ponies and turned their stony faces in the various directions they came from.

The priest and I agreed that sometimes the Indian is the most dignified man in the world.

CHAPTER III   Scouting For the U. S. A.

EVERYBODY KNOWS ABOUT "The Custer
Massacre." General Custer was surrounded by
the redskins and he and every soldier in his command
was killed. It stirred up an awful fuss to think an army
general and his troopers could be wiped out by a
bunch of naked, yelling redskins.

It was just a piece of good luck that I didn't happen to be in that fight. I was one of General Custer's
scouts and had been sent away to deliver a message
when the warwhoops in big numbers rode up and
completely wiped out Custer and his part of the
famous old Seventh Cavalry.

Sitting Bull, the big chief of the Sioux, was on the warpath with a good many more braves than the soldiers figured he had. Joining up with Sitting Bull were some other redskin chiefs like Red Cloud, Spotted Tail and Crazy Horse. This was in 1876, and the Government knew that the redskins were on the warpath. Word was sent to Sitting Bull to behave himself or the soldiers would teach him a lesson, but the old chief was itching for a fight and he thought he could clean up the palefaces.

Three columns of troopers were sent out to surround the Sioux, and General Custer, who was in command of the Seventh Cavalry, was hungry to get into the fight and maybe capture the big chief. As Custer and his men began to get near where he suspected the Indian camp was, he sent out scouts and soon I saw tracks, dead campfires and other signs easy for a scout to read, that showed that there were more braves on the warpath than Custer had any idea of. The trails all aimed toward one point, and the way the hoofs of the cayuses sunk deep in the ground showed they were loaded with provisions and ammunition.

I camped on what was a fresh trail and knew I was not very far behind the bunch of redskins I was tracking. My horse was tethered and hidden in a bunch of chaparral, and as I lay rolled up in my blanket under the stars a crazy notion came to my young head. I would do more than scout; I would be a spy and walk right into Sitting Bull's camp and come back with the plans and numbers of the Indians. Of course, if I was caught, I would not just be shot as a spy. I

knew I would be killed by inches, tortured to death
the way I had seen it done often enough when I was
a little boy running around the Comanche and Sioux
camps.

But I was better fixed than most any white man
that ever lived to get away with it because I had been
raised among these Sioux, knew their language and
ways. It might be all right if some of the hundreds
of them who knew me were not in the gathering, and if
so, did not see through my disguise.

I cut off most of my red hair except a scalp-lock and
I blackened what I kept. Over this I placed a war
bonnet made of furs and turkey feathers. My face I
painted yellow and black and pretended that I was
from one of those hardly-known Indian tribes of
Northwestern Canada. No white man had ever seen
them at that time and I had never met an Indian who
had either. But I knew that as far south as Mexico the
Indians managed to communicate with these far-
northern ones by that mysterious "wireless teleg-
raphy" of the wilderness.

Well satisfied with my disguise, I followed one of
the sets of tracks into the biggest Indian camp I had
ever seen. It was my idea, if everything went well, to
dare talking with Sitting Bull himself. I had that risky
piece of luck sooner than I liked. Hardly had I got to
camp when I was brought straight to the chief.

He squinted his eyes and looked at me with a poker-
face like a frog sitting on a rock. I drew my hand
across my face to show that my errand was friendly.
He kept on looking me over for a while, then he said:

"Where does the brother come from?"

"Oh, Great Chief," I replied, in a frontier jargon of Sioux and broken English, "I come from the land where the sun shines at midnight. I come from the land where the fires burn in the skies, the home of the night-fires of the North, the land of the Dog Ribs and the Clouds (two very distant Canadian tribes)."

"How many moons has the brother traveled?"

"Three moons," I answered promptly, though I had calculated it with great care.

"What has the brother seen on the journey?"

"I have seen the big rivers run in circles (meaning Lake Athabasca and the Mackenzie River area), I have seen the caribou shovel snow with his nose. I have seen Chief Long Nose (the moose) hunt in the snow."

The chief nodded his head and almost pleasantly he said:

"Then the brother comes from the land of the Kodiak bear."

I was a young man standing before a big and powerful chief. If he did not like what I said he would not hesitate to put me to death by slow torture. But if I pleased him he could make it easy for me to get back after a successful adventure that might make me a famous scout. The way he spoke would make most anyone figure he was showing off his knowledge and so my cue would be to flatter him by agreeing. But I had heard my Sioux Indian foster-father tell, as we sat in front of a tepee fire, how old Sitting Bull trapped liars in just that way. So, when he asked about the Kodiak bear I answered with what looked like I knew what he was up to and said:

"No, not as far as that."

It was the right answer and put an end to that part of my test. He turned to something else.

"What has the brother seen over on Little Big Horn?"

"More dog soldiers (Indian word for United States soldiers) than the hairs on your head. More than you could count."

That was the most important information he could hear, if true, and I was ready for him to follow it up with many more questions. But Sitting Bull always fooled everyone. He started talking about something else. Looking at the wolverine skin I was wearing, he said it was a bad devil, worse than a dog soldier. The redskins hated the wolverine because it chewed up the things they thought the most of such as hides and ropes.

The chief stopped his questions, which I didn't like, because I figured I hadn't answered enough to satisfy one of the smarest and most suspicious redskins that ever lived. He was still suspicious but would wait until he could find out more about me or thought up some sort of trap like getting a real Dog Rib Indian to face me.

The old chief acted friendly and ordered the squaws to bring me something to eat. It was first-class food, a big bowl of stew, mostly dog meat. He watched me eat, not my table manners, which were perfectly good Sioux Indian style, but what I would think of my bowl, which was a cracker bowl from the United States Quartermaster Department, and the spoon, a silver one from the officers' mess. I tried to show natural curiosity as if such things were new to me.

When I put the bowl down, Sitting Bull offered to trade a rifle for the two sacred white weasels on my war bonnet. It was more than they were worth, so I grunted and handed them over. He had them put a piece of buffalo hide on a tree 500 feet away and told me to shoot at it. I was pretty good and the chief said so. I told him that we Dog Ribs were too poor to waste powder. That pleased him, and he shouted that his braves should remember it.

Then he took me on a long ride up on a high plateau and showed me the body of a big chief, wrapped in a blanket lying in his funeral lodge. I wondered why he did this and after a while Sitting Bull spoke:

"Long Hair killed him," he said, "and I will kill Long Hair."

Long Hair was the Indian name for Custer, and I didn't like Sitting Bull telling me this because it struck me that he felt I was on the white man's side. Coming back, he took a path that let me see all the camps and gave me an idea of how big his forces were. I didn't like that either—looked too much like a cat playing with a mouse. But after that he had me sit down in a circle with a lot of other chiefs. He got a stone pipe filled it with mullen tobacco, passed it around, and we all smoked.

This made me an honored guest, but I could see all the time that I was being watched, and, as time passed, I grew more doubtful of ever seeing my regiment again. I passed a whole week in the camp, watching the Indians working themselves up to a kind of crazy fury. with dancing, yelling and drinking. The drinking did not amount to much because there was not enough liquor for such a big crowd of braves.

"Listen, white man, you'd better get out of here tonight!"

A scout has to learn not to jump at any surprises and I have looked over the top of a log and into the face of a rattlesnake without a quiver. I have been shot three times and had lots of things happen to me, but I don't think anything ever startled me more than when a girl's voice whispered that in my ear, the last day I was in Sitting Bull's camp. She was a prisoner from the Maricopos, a civilized tribe of Pueblo Indians in Arizona, and had been badly mistreated by the Sioux.

Many a time I have known squaws to see through the disguise of a stranger when the sharpest braves were fooled. I grunted indifferently, but she went on telling me that an evil old squaw was telling everyone that I was a disguised white man and that next morning they were going to look me over carefully and find out.

She might have been sent to test me, but I took that chance and told her she was right. That night she scratched the earth away from the back of my tent while a brave sat on guard in front. We had to crawl on our stomachs for nearly a mile to get out of camp, and only an Indian girl and a boy who was trained like one could have done it.

At one place we had to creep past where some horses were tethered. Just then one of the horses shifted his weight and placed a hind foot on my left hand. It was not very hard earth and did not hurt much, but I did not dare to startle the horse, so we had to wait what seemed an hour until he shifted again and released me. In the dark we followed the trail hurriedly back and at last reached Custer's camp.

I was in such a hurry to tell the news and what I had done that I came right up to the sentry on a run. Seeing what he supposed was an Indian in war paint running at him he shot and missed me. Before he could shoot again I managed to tell him who I was. That shot brought me to Custer even quicker than I got to Sitting Bull. The General was in council with other officers.

It was the proudest moment of my life when I told him what I had done and seen. I thought they would crowd toward me, shake my hand and pat me on the back. But instead, General Custer's face turned red, he was so mad, and he roared:

"I ordered you to go out in front and reconnoitre, not to live with the enemy. I will have you court-martialed."

Well, I was struck so dumb that anybody could have walked up and scalped me without my noticing it. Didn't the man want to know? The fact is he didn't want to hear anything except where the enemy was. When I told him there were 7,000 of them, it made him mad because he was already having an argument with his officers, who wanted him to go cautiously. General Custer, as brave a man as ever lived, believed that numbers didn't count. He figured that with his reputation, the sight of "Long Hair" charging at the head of a handful of cavalry should be enough to make all the Indians in the world turn tail. So it was

usually, but not this time, because Sitting Bull had
made his Sioux believe that he was a better man than
Long Hair, even than the Great White Father at
Washington, President Grant. One of the officers suggested quietly:

"If you will permit it, Sir—the man may have
some useful information. Would it not be well to get
it all out of him before you discipline him?"

General Custer's anger never lasted long. He soon
forgot me and the unpleasant news I brought him.
He went right ahead with his plans to attack the big
Indian camp without waiting for General Terry and
General Crook who were advancing from different
directions to surround the redskins.

Custer had command of the Seventh Cavalry and
he split up his force into three parts. One part he led
himself and the other two divisions were commanded
by Major Reno and Captain Benteen. I was sent off
to find General Terry and deliver a message and then
Custer started forward.

It was a mistake for General Custer to divide up his
troops in the face of such a big bunch of warwhoops.
He paid no attention to warning and so he hurried
on to his death. I was about two miles away on my
errand to General Terry when I heard firing. I knew
Custer's force was in trouble because I heard volley-
firing. In that sort of Indian fighting you don't fire
volleys—everybody shoots when he sees a chance. I
knew those volleys were signal calls for help. Indians
seemed to be everywhere. I managed to catch up with
Major Reno's detachment. We were just able to hold

our own until General Terry relieved us next day. Captain Benteen held out a few miles away.

I won't tell the strategy that led up to that battle, but there were one or two queer things I noticed after the battle. Every one of the 265 men in Custer's command was scalped except the leader. Long Hair's scalp would have been the biggest trophy an Indian could possibly have had. Sitting Bull was entitled to it, but he forbade anyone to scalp his fearless enemy.

Also it is true, except in a few cases, that the men were not mutilated except for the scalping. After their great victory the Sioux ran off in such panic that they even abandoned their funeral lodges of the dead. Those Indians, from the chief down, felt that they had killed a sort of god. They did not dare to scalp a god, and the scene where he had been killed became "bad medicine" for them.

It turned out to be "bad medicine" for old Sitting Bull too, who was captured some years later and killed when some of his warwhoops tried to rescue him from the soldiers. With him died the last real hope of getting the better of the white man. The redskins saw that fighting the paleface soldiers wouldn't work. And that left most of us Indian scouts out of a job. But small bands kept up their deviltries, so for some time I picked up a few odd jobs, such as fighting Indians for the Union Pacific Railroad, because the laborers who were building it were fussy about keeping their scalps.

When the railroads began to push across the plains the Indians didn't like the idea. They suspected the palefaces were somehow going to fence them in and they were superstitious about what they called the "iron horse." So the work gangs had trouble with roving bunches of redskins now and then. The warwhoops would ride up and shoot at the track-layers and now and then kill an outfit and ride off with their scalps and provisions. Sometimes the track-layers would put up a fight and beat off the redskins.

On the section of the road where I had my job as guard nothing very exciting happened. We had some skirmishes, drove the braves away, and killed a few. But I knew of some cases which were quite exciting on sections near mine.

One Sunday one of the railroad men went out fishing and as he sat on the banks of a little stream an arrow zipped by his ear and stuck in a tree nearby. He hadn't seen or heard anything and before he could get up and reach for his gun, his arms were grabbed and tied behind his back and he found himself in the middle of a bunch of yelling redskins who were jumping around him. They lifted him up on a cayuse and drove off with him to an Indian camp.

Those Indians were a bad lot and most always tortured any paleface they got their hands on. They tied the fisherman to a stake and the braves, squaws and papooses danced and yelled around him for hours. First they drove little wooden needles into the man's flesh and then set fire to them. As he screamed and writhed they danced and shouted.

Next they piled some wooden shavings around his feet and set fire to them. But they seemed to have forgotten that heat makes a man perspire and that moisture makes a deerskin rope soft and stretchy. So while the man was twisting about he found he could free his hands and suddenly seizing an old squaw who stood near him with a papoose, he pulled her into the flames. The old woman's clothes caught fire and the redskins ran to help her. This was just the chance the white man was looking for, and while they were busy trying to pull the old woman and the baby out of the flames, he jumped away and ran down the hill like a scared coyote. He said he ran for a day and a half before he dared stop.

Finally the Indians, or most of them all over the West, had been rounded up and put on the reservations where the soldiers kept watch over them. There were outbreaks now and then by restless bucks who raided the ranches in little war parties. And there was a habit of giving permission at times for Indians to go off the reservation to hunt game. More often than not, if these "hunters" passed a ranch they couldn't resist killing and scalping everybody in sight and stealing a bunch of horses.

There was one outfit of Indians led by a crafty chief that the soldiers couldn't seem to get their hands on. They were Apaches and their chief was the famous Geronimo. They raided around near the Mexican Border and when hard pressed went over into Mexico and hid in the mountains.

At last orders came from Washington to get Geronimo—to keep after him and not let up until he and his braves were killed or captured. He had tormented Mexican towns and the Mexicans were glad to let our soldiers come across the border and get the thieving, murdering redskins if they could.

They were a wicked bunch. The Apaches were

almost as wild as coyotes. They never did any farming
never raised anything, and lived by hunting and raiding the settlers. They were always roving around like
a pack of wolves, went almost naked and lived in
wickiups, little shelters made of boughs of trees and
bushes. They were about the most cruel of all the redskins.

Nobody knew for sure how many Geronimo had
with him—some said there were 500 warriors besides
squaws and children. So quite a big force of soldiers
were rounded up from half a dozen forts in Arizona
and Texas, mostly cavalry. General Miles and General Crook were in command; the redskins called General Crook "The Gray Wolf," because of his long,
thick, bushy, gray beard. I was sent for to join two
other scouts, Tom Horn and Al Sieber. We were all
friends and had been together on many a scouting trip
for the troops.

In the little army was a young doctor in the medical
corps, Leonard Wood. He had the rank of lieutenant
and took just as much interest in the fighting end of
things as he did in his bottles and pills. Later on he
got to be Major General, was made Governor General
of Cuba and then of the Philippines. Young Wood
had charge of one of the medical units with the cavalry
division.

Our expedition started out in the hottest summer
weather. The heat was terrible in the deserts of Arizona and Sonora, Mexico. We had word that Geronimo was across the border and pretty soon the three
of us scouts picked up the trail. We figured the warwhoops were about five days ahead of us.

The soldiers were not used to desert campaigning. They suffered a lot from the blazing sun and lack of water. The Apaches and us scouts were used to it and it didn't bother us.

Geronimo knew we were after him and kept on until they got into the rough, rocky canyons of the Sierra Madre Mountains in Sonora. These mountains had a heavy growth of trees, were hard for troops to travel in and had no end of good grazing for the cayuses and game for the braves to shoot. It looked to us like these Indians could stand off the whole United States Army as long as they wanted to.

Well, one afternoon following a two weeks' march, I was ahead scouting the foot of the hills when about four o'clock I thought my eye caught a thin wisp of smoke rising up in a mountain. I faded quick into a clump of trees and got out my field-glasses for a careful look. It was smoke all right and I believed I had located old Geronimo's camp—but as I watched that smoke through the glasses I could see the dot-and-dash of a heliograph signal about a quarter of a mile to one side. I sure was puzzled. Redskins don't signal that way.

I couldn't read the code so I signaled with my handkerchief to the troops about three miles away to send along a signal man. Pretty soon he came galloping up and this was the signal he read:

"We have the renegade surrounded in a thicket of timber and are awaiting reinforcements. Please advise us.   Signed, WOOD."

It turned out that young Lieutenant Wood and

Lieutenant Gatewood with a small party of cavalry, unknown to the rest of us, had gone ahead early that morning. By that time it was almost dark and the column of smoke was nearly ten miles away up on a mountain shelf. So when the advance guard came up, we had supper and made camp for the night. We built our campfires with screens of brush so the redskins couldn't locate us and posted night scouts well in advance of the camp. I rolled up in my blanket, rifle and Colts at my side when one of Lieutenant Gatewood's scouts rode into camp and said Geronimo was ready to pow-wow with the big white chief, Miles.

Captain Lawton, who was in command of the advance guard, shook his head. Geronimo had no intention of surrendering, he said—it was only a stand-off. As Captain Lawton had contradicted the scout, nothing more was said. Next morning General Miles ordered an advance to find out the strength of the enemy which had been reported at about 300. Some of the officers said there couldn't be that many because the Mexican troops had given the band quite a battle on the border and they knew Geronimo had lost a lot of braves.

As soon as daylight came, an advance party was sent ahead on a reconnoitering expedition. I was at the head of the main column and rode up into the Sierra Madre Mountains about four miles. Within hailing distance of Wood's camp, one of the outposts called to me and told me Geronimo had been captured by Lieutenant Wood and his party and that there were only about seventy Indians in the band. I knew then that Captain Lawton had made a mistake and that there had been a lot of exaggeration concerning the strength of the Apache war-party.

Geronimo acted surprised at the way things had turned out. He signaled Tom Horn that he wanted him to interpret for him. Tom rode forward and Geronimo shook hands with him and called him "Amigo!" (friend).

Tom got off his cayuse and lit his pipe and commenced to draw circles in the dirt which meant Peace. The Indians squatted in a circle and the pow-wow was on.

Geronimo said he wanted to see Big White Chief Miles, but he wouldn't talk to Gray Wolf (Crook). General Miles was back in camp resting after the rough march and we had our doubts whether he would want to be disturbed right then. But I knew General Miles well, having been in a number of campaigns with him, and I said the least we could do was to try and fix up an interview. So I went to his headquarters and asked if I might give some news to him. He said to come in and I stepped into the tent. I told him that Geronimo had surrendered and that he asked for a pow-wow with Great White Chief. General Miles got up and said he would go back with me and see what the chief had to say.

We arrived at the campfire and Geronimo came forward and shook hands with General Miles. Geronimo seemed much pleased at the sight of the General. A council of war was soon going on and it was finally decided that the surrender was unconditional. The terms of the surrender were forwarded to the War Department in Washington for confirmation and we waited for further orders as to what we should do with Geronimo and his Apaches.

At last orders came from Washington that we were to take Chief Geronimo and his Indian band to Fort Marion at St. Augustine, Florida. The idea of taking that outfit of wild Indian prisoners over the deserts and then by rail clear to Florida struck us as a big undertaking. But we started. The trip up Sulphur Springs Valley to Fort Bowie, Arizona Territory, was a distance of about 400 miles. It took us twenty-one days to make this lap of the trip. It was a tough trip across the desert through the Valley, but we got safely to Fort Bowie.

The seventy-one Indians we had under our care were both old and young men, their squaws and some papooses. Two of the squaws gave birth to Indian babies on the march and made an interesting addition to our flock. We put the mothers and the babies in the ambulance and took care of them until we were able to reach Fort Bowie.

The Indians, as well as ourselves, seemed glad to reach the end of the desert trip for at the fort we had comfortable quarters for them in the guardhouse. And once more we waited the next orders from Washington. In about ten days, orders came to load our Indians in railroad cars (these were of the old wooden passenger kind) and go along on our journey.

On this lap of our trip two stops were made. One at Fort Bliss, El Paso, Texas, and at Fort Sam Houston, San Antonio, Texas. At that time San Antonio was a town scattered in all directions over considerable territory.

The well known quadrangle at Fort Sam Houston was our unloading point. And here we camped with our Apaches when they finally were unloaded. A strong military guard was furnished to escort them to the quadrangle. These troops expected the Indians to run and lead them a chase, perhaps give their famous war-cry. Nothing of the kind happened but a few funny things did.

As the caravan taking the Indians to the quadrangle moved forward, Chief Geronimo peeked from behind the curtains of his wagon, which was drawn by army mules. He grinned and wiggled his fingers at his nose and cursed in Spanish. One of the soldiers on horseback grabbed one of the chief's plaits of hair with a yank. Geronimo let out a roar and the mule team nearly ran away. As the wagons rattled along, the Indians began to chant and make warwhoops and the old army mules, not used to redskins with war-cries, decided to bolt. One of the wagons broke a king-bolt and scattered a bunch of the bucks out over the road. The Indians were not as much hurt as they were scared at the galloping mules and the yelling soldiers. But we finally got them all quieted down and went on to the end of the quadrangle in military formation.

Uncle Sam treated these Indians mighty good. He ordered fine tents pitched in the shade of large trees and provided cots and a regulation army cook and mess-fed them. The Indians looked at their clean dishes, the plates, cups, knives and forks, at the Government black coffee, and they seemed well content to settle down.

The squaws soon found out that favors were to be

had for the asking and they called for wagons to go
to town. They got them and they went to a store on
the Plaza in San Antonio and bought all the red calico
in the shop. The sight of those Apache squaws with
their papooses rigged out in all of the gaudy finery,
with an escort of cavalry parading around the old
military plaza in front of the store, brought a big
crowd.

Besides the raid on the red calico counter the squaws
bought knick-knacks and posed for their photographs
in front of the store and with their shopping done, the
pictures taken, accompanied by grunts and grins, the
happy shopping party climbed into Uncle Sam's Government wagons and headed back for Fort Sam Houston. Most of these squaws had never seen a store before but they acted like old shoppers.

I did not go to town that day. I stayed at the fort
with Chief Geronimo to keep him quiet and satisfied,
and with Tom Horn, played dominoes, of which the
chief was very fond. The chief was a real player and
would play for hours. Geronimo was great for any
gambling game. He had little to say, but if in the
mood, would talk to Tom Horn and myself. He had
sense enough to know his raiding days were over and
that the palefaces were going to treat him right.

Our stop at Fort Sam Houston lasted about eighteen days when orders came to load our Indians on the
train and go on to Fort Marion. This move brought
out a lot of grumbling objections from our copper-
colored charges. They had enjoyed life at the quadrangle and wanted to stay there.

We stopped on our way at Houston, Texas. There

at the Grand Central Station we allowed our Indians to stretch their legs. Houston also turned out to see Geronimo and his Apaches. The scene was more like a comic opera road show than that of a band of wild Indians that had terrorized the Southwest.

Our arrival at Fort Marion in Florida marked the end of our trek from the mountains in Old Mexico to Florida. Chief Geronimo and his band of murderous Apaches were tame now and were gruntingly glad to be out of those railroad cars and be able to stretch their legs once more.

But the damp climate and malaria killed off quite a lot of them and the Government moved what were left to Fort Sill, Indian Territory. There they were kept in a military prison until old Geronimo died. He was converted by the missionaries at the post and was given Christian burial.

People have asked me why the Indian wars lasted so long—couldn't understand why the United States Army didn't clean up the redskins pronto. Well, it wasn't so easy. A few years ago General Pershing with a big army and heavy guns and airplanes marched down into Mexico to get Villa, the bandit, and his outfit. He wandered around and came back never having even caught a glimpse of Villa.

The redskin warriors had a big advantage over the army cavalry. The warwhoops traveled light, but the soldiers were loaded down with equipment. The Indian brave usually wore a red bandana handkerchief to hold back the black, wiry hair, and he dolled himself up with a few glass beads or strings of dried berries or various trinkets he got from the palefaces. He

traveled pretty well naked, except a G-string around
his middle and buckskin moccasins on his legs to keep
the thorns and cactus needles from scratching him.
On the warpath he wore a war bonnet of feathers and
painted his face with two or three colors.

The soldiers loaded their horses with a 40-pound
saddle and blanket roll and canteens of water. The
soldier himself was quite a load for his horse, with his
cavalry boots and army clothes and accoutrements.
Besides this the troops had to have camp and cooking
equipment. So the warwhoops could outride the slow
moving, heavily loaded cavalry, and the Indians knew
the soldiers couldn't catch them. They were more
afraid of the cowboys. These ranchers were just as
good riders as the redskins, and they did not carry
heavy equipment. The cowpunchers were well armed
and good shooters with their long-range rifles.

The Indians could get along with very little water.
In desert fighting they could fill up a strip of horse
intestines with water and sling it across their pony's
back. The warrior also carried a hunk of roasted ma-
guey, a kind of stringy food that didn't turn sour.
This was known as mescal bread, made from the ma-
guey root by roasting it under cover until it softens
up into a white, sticky sweetish mass. It held a lot of
nourishment. Then they had some hard bread baked
from mesquite seeds and a few hunks of dried horse
meat.

So it was that the Indians could travel faster, un-
hampered by equipment and could eat when they needed food while traveling along in the saddle. If a war
party was out longer than was expected, the Indians

could stop and kill a few rattlesnakes and lizards, eat them, and go on again. Neither the Indians or the cow-punchers needed to carry a watch. They could tell time very well by the shadow a cactus or tree threw on the ground.

The Indian was well armed. Most of them had Winchesters, repeating rifles that fired a moderate-sized bullet and were good up to about 1,800 feet, but many of them had the Sharps Special, a one-shot, .45-calibre rifle, that used a cartridge about four inches long and threw a bullet much further and with greater accuracy than the Winchesters. So the Indians were not so much afraid of the cavalry except in a stand-up fight, and that was the kind of fighting they never figured to be caught in. But the cowpunchers, they were different—the redskins didn't like those hard-riding, straight-shooting ranchmen.

CHAPTER IV Bad Men of the Old West

THE MAN WHO named and founded Tombstone was a prospector hunting for gold and silver, named Ed Schiefflin. One day he said he was planning on prospecting out in the Arizona desert and mountain country where nobody had been because everyone knew that it was full of Apache Indians. The 'Paches, as the cowpunchers called them, were a bad lot of killers. As Ed started off, one of the old-timers called after him:

"Reckon what you're most likely to find is yore tombstone."

Ed was still thinking about that when he came upon two human skeletons, bleaching on a hillside.

Schieffelin thought he would take time to see if **they** were any of his missing friends and found **between** them a pile of fine samples of silver ore. A few **hun-** dred feet away he located the ledge the silver had **been** taken out of. Ed jumped the dead men's claim **and** named it the Tombstone mine. The silver rush **that** followed quickly built the settlement up to a **town** of not far from 15,000 people in no time. And in **the** next six years more than $30,000,000 in silver **and** gold were taken out of those mines around Tomb- stone.

Everybody liked Ed Schieffelin, and when he **died** his friends built him a monument of rock and **cement** out on the hill where he had his camp and put **this** sign on it—

Ed Schieffelin

Died May 12th, 1897

Aged 40 Years

A Dutiful Son—A Faithful

Husband—A Kind Brother

—A True Friend.

Many a day I spent in Tombstone while it **was at** its richest and wildest. Talk about prosperity! **Every-** body and every business was making money **fast.** Saloons, dance halls and gambling joints thrived **and** everywhere with their hands out for gold dust **were** the painted-up vamps. In those days no decent **woman** would any more think of painting her face than a sky- pilot (clergyman) would think of putting on **Indian**

war-paint. The undertakers did big business too, laying out the gents who died with their boots on and
burying them in Boot Hill Cemetery. They called it
Boot Hill because they were in such a hurry to bury
the dead badmen they didn't bother to take their boots
off.

The editor of the town's newspaper called it the
"Tombstone Epitaph." He had plenty of front page
war stories and printed paid obituaries of the fallen.
All night long came sounds of hell-raising in the dives
in each of which a man, always called "the professor,"
pounded a piano without rest. Now and then he would
carry the tune with his right hand while his left neg-
lected the bass long enough to take a drink offered by
a customer for playing his favorite piece.

Most any minute the professor and everyone else
would throw themselves on the floor while some of
the customers argued it out with their Colts. At the
first crack even the people out in the street dived for
cover or dropped on the ground because as like as not
the shooting would be kept up out there in a few
seconds. It was considered unlucky to shoot a minister,
but even the sky-pilots walked the streets like cats, not
leaving one cover until they had fixed their eyes on
the next one.

When cowboys came to town and decided the night
had been too quiet, they used to ride out of town in
the morning shooting through the windows of the
saloons and dance halls as they passed. Glass was expensive, and bartenders, customers and the painted
women now and then got shot. So window-shooting
was decided to be a nuisance and the sheriff was ordered

to stop it. But it was some job to make a drunken cowboy believe he mustn't blaze away with his shooting irons any time he felt like it.

Tombstone had courts and judges but the court proceedings were as queer as everything else. Life was dear to the judges so when a well-known killer had given the undertaker a job, the judge usually declined to hold him for trial on one excuse or another. Otherwise the killer's friends might overrule him with a bullet.

Billy Claiborne got into a gun-fight one day with Frank Leslie, usually called "Buckskin Frank," a sure-shot killer, and was found dead. The jury decided that the deceased met his death by getting in the way of a gun. Several years later Leslie killed his sweetheart, Diamond Annie, which was a serious offense as women were scarce and were regarded as priceless treasures. He was sentenced to 25 years in Yuma Penitentiary.

Frank had broken the unwritten law that: "You shouldn't shoot a woman—not nohow."

In those days it was dangerous for the sheriff to catch up with the boys he was after but sometimes it might be just as bad if he didn't. Bisbee, the copper city, 26 miles away, probably would have been the toughest town in the West if it hadn't been for Tombstone. Its street named Brewery Gulch was about as tough as anything we had.

One day near Christmas in 1883, two gents named Dan Dowd and Red Semple started to shoot up and down the main street while their friends Tex Howard, Bill Delaney and Dan Kelly went through the stores where the best citizens were doing their Christmas shopping. Shopkeepers and customers were lined along the walls with hands in the air while the bandits carried off the cash and looted the showcases in jewelry stores. Dan Dowd and Red Semple were spreading death all around them. John Tapinrer was a little slow getting into a saloon and a bullet dropped him dead at the undertaker's door. Mrs. Anna Roberts, a restaurant keeper, was killed accidentally, as the bandits would not have intentionally killed a woman.

D. T. Smith and his wife had just come down town and he was eating breakfast in a restaurant. When he heard the firing, he ran out into the street and called.

"I'm a deputy sheriff."

"You're the kind we're looking for," replied one of the robbers and shot him dead with a bullet in the center of his forehead.

Castañeda's general store was the first one invaded by the robbers, but the owner was lying in a back room sick with rheumatism. So the bandits covered Joe Goldwater, his assistant, with their Colts, and ordered him to open the safe and empty the contents into a sack held by one of the robbers. Joe was kind of nervous and spilled a drawer full of Mexican dollars. After he had picked them up and put them in a sack he got his nerve back and started to get funny. Rubbing his hands softly together, Joe said:

"Can I do somedings more for you, schentlemen? Ve haf some very fine clodings, vich I would be pleased to show you and some sbledit ofergoats—"

But the cold muzzle of a revolver pressed against

the back of his head and a voice saying, "None of your guff, shut up!" cut Joe's words short.

The robbers then went through the other shops, killing three more citizens and rode out of town with their booty, firing as they went. This little excitement was known as the "Bisbee Massacre."

Tombstone, county seat, and not far from Bisbee, was thrown into great uproar by this occurrence and Deputy Sheriff Johnny Heath set out to hunt down the murderers with a posse of sixteen crackshot gun-fighters.

"Have no mercy on them murderers," said Johnny savagely, "hang 'em to the nearest tree."

He looked and talked fierce enough, but on the way it seemed to the posse that Johnny was not following the murderer's trail, but was leading them in an opposite direction. In one place they came into Sulphur Springs Valley, Heath told them that the trail turned one way, when they saw clear enough that it ran the other way. They argued awhile and set off in the direction the posse figured was the right one, and before long had proof that Johnny was wrong. They found the five dead horses of the robbers who had stolen fresh ones and had them scattered in different directions.

The posse had lost a lot of time and pursuit was now useless, and so they came back in a bad frame of mind towards Deputy Sheriff Heath. On the way home a ranchman named Frank Buckles told them that the bandits had stopped at his ranch two nights before the crime and that Deputy Sheriff Heath was with them. This confirmed their suspicions.

Tombstone was then hollering to punish someone

for the crime and so Heath was arrested by his own posse and locked up in jail. The other murderers were all caught and condemned to death, but Heath was only sentenced to life imprisonment. Good and mad at this miscarriage of justice 150 men, mostly miners from Bisbee, rode into Tombstone and took Heath out of jail and led him to a telegraph pole near the Courthouse in Tough Nut Street.

Jailer Billy Ward, a brother of the sheriff I think, was on duty at the Courthouse jail when somebody knocked. It was about 8:30 in the morning and Ward reckoned it was the Chinaman bringing in breakfast for the prisoners. But when Billy opened the door he looked into the muzzles of seven Colts and he gave up the keys pronto.

They had Johnny Heath out of his cell in no time and first it was planned to string him up right there in the Courthouse, to the banister of the stairs. But the crowd said no; they wanted a hand in it. Just then the sheriff came up and holding up his hands, told everybody to go away in the name of the law. The sheriff was quickly picked up and moved out of the way.

The crowd put a rope around Johnny's neck and about twenty men had hold of it and started down the street on a run. The rope never got taut during the run because the prisoner kept up with the crowd. They reached the telegraph pole. One of the party climbed up and passed the rope over the cross-bar.

Johnny Heath being an officer of the law, wanted to be hanged right. He pulled a handkerchief from his pocket and tied it around his head so that it covered his face, taking the place of the usual black mask. He gave them such expert advice as:

"Wish you'd be careful to put the knot under my left ear."

"Anything else to say?" asked the leader holding the end of the rope in his hands.

"Just one thing," replied the crooked Deputy Sheriff, "wish you boys would promise not to riddle my body with bullets after you swing me up."

"O. K. That goes," said the leader, and up went Johnny along the pole.

Johnny Heath was left hanging a dozen feet in the air from the telegraph pole with a sign under his feet which said that John Heath had been hanged to the pole by the citizens of Cochise County for having a hand in the Bisbee Massacre. The body was cut down in about an hour and identified by Emma Mortimer, the girl Johnny had been living with.

The coroner's jury were puzzled to frame their verdict. The usual verdict of "death at the hands of parties unknown" would have been silly 'cause they all knew who the executioners were. Doctor Good-fellow offered a suggestion which was accepted. So they recorded their verdict that "John Heath came to his death from emphysema of the lungs which might have been, and probably was, caused by strangulation, self-inflicted, or otherwise."

I wasn't in Tombstone at the time so I missed the hanging. But I read in a Tombstone newspaper how the ticket on Johnny's body read and how the coroner's jury got out of its fix.

Johnny Heath was strung up by the necktie party

on February 22, and the rest of the outfit that did the
"Bisbee Massacre" job were hanged by Sheriff Ward
about five weeks later. Everybody was invited to the
hanging, and this was the invitation card printed in a
black border:

```
+---------------------------------------------+
|                                             |
|               Execution Of                  |
|                                             |
|       Daniel Kelly, Omar W. Semple,         |
|                                             |
|         Jas. Howard, Daniel Dowd            |
|                                             |
|            and William Delaney              |
|                                             |
|    At the Courthouse, Tombstone, Ari.,      |
|                                             |
|      March 28, 1884, at 1 o'clock p. m.     |
|                                             |
|                      J. L. Ward, Sheriff.   |
|                                             |
+---------------------------------------------+
```

The five outlaws met their death without a whimper. As the noose was fitted to his neck Dowd said,
"This is a regular choking machine." And Kelly
shouted through his mask in a muffled voice, "Let her
go boys!" The bodies were allowed to hang thirty
minutes. Then they were cut down and the crowd
wandered away.

At that time the law in Arizona ordered sheriffs to
send out invitations to all hangings. But the law did
not say just what words should be used. Over in Navajo County, Sheriff Watson, when he came to his
first hanging, puzzled over what to say. It is said his
invitations read this way:

"You are hereby cordially invited to attend the hanging of one George Smiley, murderer. His soul will be swung into eternity on December 8, 1889, at 2 o'clock P. M. sharp. Latest improved methods in the art of scientific strangling will be employed and everything possible will be done to make the surroundings cheerful and the execution a success."

Life in Tombstone was not entirely shooting and bloodshed. This is shown by the fact that during the liveliest period several churches prospered there. The parsons were always ready to preach at the burial of the victim of a gun-fight and did so in a way that brought tears to the eyes of many a hardened frontiersman. Church sociables and afternoon tea parties were very popular and social life was gay.

Like everybody else ministers made good money there. Even prohibitionists did well in Tombstone and nobody hurt them unless they went into one of the saloons and bothered somebody too much. So the righteous and the unrighteous got along together side by side without interfering with each other.

Stagecoach robbers did a big business too and even the Apaches used to swoop down on a stagecoach once in a while, butcher the driver and passengers and ride off with the pokes of gold dust and other valuables It was almost impossible to find out which Apaches happened to do any particular crime and if the whites had known, there was no way they could have proved it in court. They didn't bother to try.

Instead, a posse would ride around until it had shot down enough Apaches to make the others remember that Tombstone didn't like such doings. Since any

Apache would gladly have robbed the stagecoach, it
didn't matter which ones were punished for it. Old
Geronimo, their chief used to fuss about this but the
policy worked, finally making the Indians give the
game up.

When the robbery was pulled off by some of the
Tombstone badmen, the punishment was not so
simple. It was one of these cases that brought on the
battle between the famous Earp Brothers and Doc
Holliday, one side more or less represented by Tombstone's idea of law and order and the McLowery-
Clanton gang on the other side. The Bisbee stage had
been stuck up on the way to Tombstone which prided
itself on being the county seat. The passengers had
been robbed and the Wells-Fargo Express box with
$3,000 in it was taken.

Frank Stillwell and Pete Spence, two old-time hold-
up men with a long and bad record, were picked up for
the job by Wyatt Earp with his brother Morgan, and
much later on, convicted by a jury of miners and sent
to prison. This made their friends mad. The Mc-
Lowerys and Clantons, a gang of swaggering gunmen with a long list of killings and other crimes, all
unpunished, seemed to have Tombstone terrorized.
They didn't care if everyone knew pretty well that
they were partners with the stage robbers and they had
a lot to say around the saloons.

Just before this robbery, another stage had been held
up and robbed of a much larger sum, and "Bud"
Philpot, the popular express messenger, was killed.
The citizens at Tombstone figured hold-ups had gone
beyond a reasonable limit and said somebody must be

shot or hanged. Wyatt Earp was Federal Marshal in Tombstone, and with his brothers, who were town marshals, undertook to execute justice. Ike Clanton, leader of the gang rode into Tombstone, and so confident was he that everybody was scared of him, that he left his Winchester rifle and six-shooter behind the bar at the Grand Hotel and went out to enjoy himself in the saloons and other joints.

The trouble began when Doc Holliday, a friend of the Earps, ran into Ike Clanton enjoying a little liquid refreshment in the Alhambra Saloon.

Doc started right in saying that Ike had lied to Wyatt Earp about him and then called him all the fighting words they knew in Tombstone. Finally Doc ran out of fighting words and then he said:

"You've been tellin' everybody you were goin' to kill me. Now is a right good time to do it. Pull yore gun and get to work."

As Doc spoke, his long, delicate fingers were on his six-shooter which came out like a flash. All Ike did was to look at it gloomily and say he had no gun on him. Holliday was calling him a liar and a coward when Virgil Earp came up and stopped the quarrel for the time being, but it only put things off.

Ike Clanton ran around to the hotel to get his shooting irons. Many a gun-fighter at this period carried two six-shooters, one on each hip, usually a smaller one under the left arm and a sawed-off shotgun with a charge of large buckshot with the wad spread to do more damage. These buckshot would almost blow a man to pieces. Doc always wore his shotgun strapped

to his right shoulder beneath his coat and he put it
on in the morning when he dressed.

On his way back from the hotel to find and finish
Doc Holliday, Ike met Virgil Earp, also a duly appointed representative of the law, like his brothers.
Ike Clanton started to point the rifle at him, but Earp,
pushing the barrel aside, hit him on the head with his
own revolver, doing what was known as "bending a
six-shooter over his head." It knocked him down.
Wyatt and Morgan Earp came running up, disarmed
Clanton and took him to Judge Wallace's court. The
poor judge was in a fix. It would be dangerous for
him to decide against the bandit but also bad for him
to decide against the Earps who had the substantial
business men and the churches behind them. So he adjourned the case. Outside the court Wyatt Earp ran
into Tom McLowery who was more vicious and hot-
headed than Ike Clanton.

"You dirty coyote!" said McLowery, "you honing
for a fight? Now is the time."

For reply Wyatt Earp punched McLowery in the
nose with his left hand and with his right pulled his
Colt. McLowery had a gun handy with the butt sticking up at the right hip, but it was too late to use it.

McLowery slunk away bleeding from his battered
nose. Of course Tom wasn't through; he started making his plans to kill Wyatt Earp and it wasn't long
before things began to happen.

Soon afterwards Wyatt Earp, while sitting on the
bench in front of Hafford's saloon saw Tom and
Frank McLowery and young Billy Clanton pass by,
all with their six-shooters buckled around them and

eased up in the holsters ready for quick use. Frank
McLowery had left his horse standing on the sidewalk in front of a gunsmith's shop. This was a viola-
tion of a city ordinance. Wyatt took hold of the horse's
bridle and ordered Frank to take him off the sidewalk
and Frank did so.

Just then along came Ike Clanton who for some
reason had gone back to the court and offered to pay
a fine of $25 and not be bothered any more, a proposi-
tion which the judge was glad to accept. Ike took a
scowling look at Wyatt Earp and stepped into the
gunsmith's shop. The Earps had taken Clanton's
hardware away from him so he was disarmed. Nobody
doubted that he would step out in a minute bristling
with firearms but the gunsmith, not liking the prospect
of a shooting match right on his doorstep, refused to
sell him anything. But everyone figured that a fight
was not far away.

The McLowery-Clanton outfit, joined by Billy
Clanton, met in an open lot on Fremont Street. Opening out of the lot was the rear gate of the O. K. Corral
a livery stable running through to another street.
Nearby was the office of the "Tombstone Epitaph"
whose editor looking out the window foresaw a big
story and hoped to be able to report it in person without having his own obituary printed. I was sitting
comfortably behind a nice thick door, heard all the
shots and stayed right there until it was all over. Then
I looked the battlefield over and it had all happened so
quick nobody could figure it out.

After that famous battle of the O. K. Corral, Wyatt
Earp gave his version of it. Wyatt and his two

brothers, Virgil and Morgan, backed up by Doc Holliday, had been walking along the street with steady
steps, their faces set and their eyes fixed on their ene-
mies. They were all well heeled with shooting irons.

As the Earps and Holliday came to the vacant lot
the guns suddenly began to roar and here is Wyatt's
story:

"Frank McLowery fired at me and Billy Clanton
fired at Morgan, and both missed." Wyatt Earp said.
"I had a gun in my overcoat pocket and I jerked it
out and fired at Fronk McLowery, hitting him in the
stomach at the same time that Morgan shot Billy
Clanton in the breast. So far, we had gotten the best
of it, but just then Tom McLowery who had gotten
behind a horse, fired a shot under the animal's neck
which bored a hole through Morgan sideways, having
entered one shoulder and coming out through the
other.

"I've got it," said Morgan.

"Then get behind me and keep quiet," said I, but
he didn't.

"By this time the bullets were flying fast, and I
couldn't keep any track of them. Frank McLowery had
given a yell when I shot him, and made for the street
with his hand over his stomach. Ike Clanton and Billy
Clanton were shooting fast, and so was Virgil. Ike
and Billy made a break for the street. I fired a shot
into Tom McLowery's horse and made it break away
and Doc Holliday took the opportunity of pumping a
charge of buckshot out of a Wells-Fargo shotgun, into
Tom McLowery, who promptly fell dead. Doc Holliday in the excitement of the moment did not know

what he had done and flung the shotgun away in disgust, pulling his six-shooter instead.

"Then I witnessed a strange spectacle. Frank McLowery and Billy Clanton were sitting in the middle of the street, both badly wounded, but emptying their six-shooters like lightning. One of them shot Virgil through the leg and then Virgil shot Billy Clanton, then Frank McLowery staggered to his feet and across the street although he was full of bullets. On his way he came face to face with Doc Holliday and said:

" 'I've got you now, Doc.'

" 'Well, you're a good one if you have,' said Holliday with a laugh, and with that they both aimed. But before you can understand what happened next, I must carry you back half a minute.

"After the first exchange of shots in the lot, Ike Clanton had gotten into one of the buildings from the rear and, when I reached the street, he was shooting out of one of the front windows. Seeing him aim at Morgan, I shouted:

"Look out, Morg, you're getting it in the back."

"Morgan wheeled around and, in so doing, fell on his side. While in that position he caught sight of Doc Holliday and Frank McLowery aiming at each other and, with a quick drop, shot McLowery in the head at the same instant McLowery's pistol flashed and Doc Holliday was shot in the hip. That ended the fight."

A lively fight! And it was all over in a minute or two—less time a good deal than it took Wyatt Earp to tell about it. Nobody in the saloons had time to run out and see what was happening and I reckon nobody wanted to.

After the fight Sheriff Johnny Behan, who had such a kindly way with bandits that lots of people thought he was closer to them than to the peace officers, sauntered up and said he would have to arrest the Earps. Wyatt Earp said they might let him arrest them the next day. He had an idea that while disarmed and in jail, Ike Clanton and some others of the gang that were still alive might be allowed to get in and polish them off. A month later the Earps and Holliday were tried and acquitted on the ground that they were performing their duty as peace officers.

But they had some opposition. Sheriff Behan, who hated the Earps and their friends, swore the Clanton outfit were unarmed and were shot while they were holding their hands up. Judge Spicer didn't pay much attention to this testimony and in his decision said:

"I cannot resist the firm conviction that the Earps acted wisely, discretely and prudently to secure their own self-preservation; they saw at once the direct necessity of giving the first shot to save themselves from certain death. They acted; their shots were effective, and this alone saved the Earps from being slain. I concluded the performance of duty imposed upon me by saying in the language of the statute: there being no sufficient cause to believe the within named Wyatt Earp and John H. Holliday guilty of the offense mentioned within, I order them released."

Ike Clanton and plenty of his relatives and members of the gang still lived. They were set on revenge but from now on it was to be a war of assassination, **the** way modern gangsters work.

As Virgil Earp stepped out of the Prairie **Queen** Saloon one evening, there was the roar of several **shot**-guns going off at once. Wyatt Earp and Doc **Holliday** ran out, guns in hand, to find Virgil riddled **with** buckshot fired from an unfinished house across **the** street. He was soon out of the hospital but one **arm** was useless and he was condemned to crutches the **rest** of his life.

The next attempt was more successful .Pete **Spence** and Frank Stillwell, out after a brief visit to **prison,** had a half-breed named Indian Charlie enter one **saloon** after another and give them a signal when all **was** ripe for getting one of the Earps. In Campbell **and** Hatch's saloon and billiard parlor, this scheme **gave** them a chance to catch Morgan Earp bending over **to** make a billiard shot. They fired through the **window** from outside and killed him with bullets through **the** back. One of the bullets went on and killed a **by**-stander, George Berry.

Wyatt and Virgil Earp and the always **faithful** Doc Holliday left town with Morgan's body. **When** the train stopped at Tucson, Wyatt and Doc **stepped** out on the platform to take a look at the other **cars** and saw Frank Stillwell hiding behind a box car. **They** knew what he was there for and just before the **train** started, let him have it. His thoroughly peppered **body** was found on the tracks.

When they got back to Tombstone, Sheriff **Behan** told Wyatt that he was going to arrest him for **the** murder of Frank Stillwell. Placing his hand on the butt of his Colts, Wyatt said softly:

"It can't be done. Sheriff, I'm saying you're the partner of crooks and besides, you ain't half man enough."

The sheriff must have thought there was some truth in his words for he made no attempt to take him. But soon after that the remaining Earps and Doc Holliday, figuring that Tombstone was no longer a healthy place for them, rode out one morning with rifles across their saddles. After they had passed Spence's ranch, Indian Charlie's body was found with four bullets in it.

A little later Wyatt, riding in front, caught sight of Curly Bill, one of the Clanton gang, skulking in a ditch, and blew him to Kingdom Come with a couple of charges of buckshot.

Sheriff Behan went after them with a posse made up of Ike Clanton and 15 other badmen. Somebody asked the sheriff why he picked such a bunch of badmen and Behan said they were "honest ranchmen," which made everyone laugh. This stirred up Wyatt to write this letter to the Tombstone Epitaph:

"We have kept a careful track of the movements of Sheriff Behan and his posse of honest ranchmen. If they possessed even average trailing ability we might have had trouble with them, which we are not seeking. Neither are we avoiding those honest farmer boys. We thoroughly understand their intentions."

Wyatt never came back to Tombstone. I believe he was a square man and just the kind of police officer the town needed. He died in Southern California eight years ago, past 80 years old and he died with his boots off.

Doc Holliday never had much to say about himself and nobody knew where he came from. He had been a dentist and he had a good education, but got lung trouble, and came West hoping to get cured.

It was in Fort Griffin that Wyatt Earp ran across Holliday and they got to be great pals. Earp was a Deputy United States Marshal at Dodge City at that time and was trailing a bunch of cattle thieves when he met Holliday.

Doc was a great gambler, and was in a poker game with several more men one evening when a man named Ed Bailey, who was sitting on the right of Doc, insisted on holding post-mortems over the discards. This is a dangerous pastime because when a hand is thrown into the deadwood, it is so dead that it cannot be resurrected, and flirting with the discard is positively barred in all well-regulated poker games.

Doc had advised Bailey several times, according to Wyatt's account, to "play poker," which was about the same as telling him to "stop cheating." Bailey didn't pay any attention to these warnings but kept right on pawing over the dead hands and turning them face up and making remarks on their value or the way their owners ought to have played them.

Finally there developed a good-sized pot and all of the players dropped out but Doc and Bailey. As Bailey had been fumbling the discard Doc reached out and gathered in the pot without going through the formality of showing down his hand, which was playing good poker, according to poker etiquette. When a man is found trying to handle too many cards all at one time he forfeits his claim to the pot.

Bailey made a move to get his gun into action but Doc beat him by flashing a bowie knife, which he had concealed under his arm and, to use Doc's own words, he caught Bailey "just below the brisket." Bailey passed on to the next world.

The poker game was broken up right away and Doc was arrested by the city marshal and placed in charge of two policemen, to prevent a hundred or more drunken miners and gamblers from stretching his neck on some handy tree. Doc had not been in Fort Griffin very long and had no friends, but Bailey was very popular among the crooked element.

Big Nose Kate, Doc's sweetheart, saw what was going on and decided that quick action was necessary or she would lose her meal ticket. There was a horse stable in a shed behind the hotel where they were holding the prisoner. Kate took a horse out and tied him in the alley, then set fire to the shed. As the fire blazed up, Kate shouted, "Fire! Fire! Fire!" Everyone except Doc's guards rushed out.

Kate, armed with two Colts, walked boldly into the hotel and covered the officers before they knew what it all meant. Handing one of the six-shooters to Doc, she said with a laugh, "Come on Doc." They backed out of the hotel keeping the officers covered until they were clear of the door and then faded away into the darkness of the night on that horse, riding double. They kept in hiding all night among the willows and in the morning a friend brought them two horses and some clothes which he managed to sneak out of Doc's room.

Kate dressed in a suit of Doc's and together they rode 400 miles to Dodge City, Kansas and there they met up with Wyatt Earp again. Shortly after Doc's arrival in Dodge City he chanced to save Wyatt's life. A man had sneaked up behind Wyatt and had his six-shooter on him, but before he could use it, Doc shouted, "Look out Wyatt!" and, with a motion that baffled the eye, he pulled his own gun and shot the would-be killer dead. This friendly and timely act on the part of Doc bound the ties of friendship more strongly than ever between them.

At last Doc and Big Nose Kate decided to play quits and she left him. Later in the year Wyatt and Doc planned to go to Tombstone which was getting to be a lively town. They came by the way of Las Vegas, New Mexico, where they found Big Nose Kate and she and Doc soon patched up their differences and she went along to Tombstone. But again Kate became peeved at Doc after they were settled in Tombstone and one day she went before the District Attorney and told how Doc Holliday had shot Bud Philpot, the driver of the Fairbanks stage. Doc Holliday, she said, was implicated with three others.

On the strength of Kate's information, a warrant was issued for the arrest of Doc Holliday on a charge of murder and he was seized and held for trial. But in a day or two, Kate, once more with a change of heart, went to the District Attorney and made a sworn statement that at the time she filed the murder infor-mation against Doc, she was both drunk and mad and did not know what she was doing. She had no trouble in proving that she was drunk so the charge against Doc was dropped.

There was always something unexpected happening in those days. Shortly before the battle between the Earps and the Clantons I had occasion to be riding into Tombstone from over at the Old Contention Mine. I was an Arizona Ranger at the time—kind of mounted police. My stopping place was always at the O. K. Corral where I put up my cayuse. I had just got inside the gate of the corral when Holliday pulled a double-barrelled shotgun and covered me as I slid off my horse. About the time he had me covered I walked around my pony and quick-pulled my carbine from its scabbard. I walked over to Holliday and told him to put up his hands. One of my pals made Holliday unbuckle his six-shooter belt and drop it to the ground. I told him to eject the shells in his sawed-off shotgun, which was his favorite weapon, and drop them to the ground. And I said: "Don't try any funny work or I'll bore you through."

I asked Holliday what he was aiming to do, pointing his shotgun at me. He said I was a suspicious character and he was rounding up all such. One of my pals told him that I happened to be an Arizona Ranger and we were looking for a couple of Mexicans from below the line who had been mixed up in a holdup in the Whetstone Mountains, north of Tombstone.

While we were talking Wyatt Earp came up and wanted to know what all the trouble was about. I told him.

Earp told Doc to go and lie down and sober up.

Then Earp suggested we go over to the Chin-Chan Chink beanery and moisten up with some Java.

While we were at the table waiting for our meal, Holliday came in and seated himself at the end of the table and ordered coffee. He looked at me with a staring scowl. The City Marshal came over and tapped Holliday on the shoulder and told him to shuffle the hardware and leave it with the Chink at the counter. The rest of us had observed the Law's commands as we knew we didn't need guns to eat dinner with.

Holliday got up grumblingly and took his artillery off and gave it to the Chinaman to keep until the meal was over. As he sat down I noticed he had a bowie knife stuck in his belt. I told him to get that off too and when he cussed at my suggestion, I jerked it off him and handed it to the Chinaman. And I told Doc if there was any fighting to be done we'd do it the old style of knock down and drag out basis.

The City Marshal told Doc when he got sobered up he could have his weapons.

As we left Tombstone, on our way to Benson, we got word of the hold-up of the Benson-Tombstone stagecoach, which had been stopped over at the Ironside Mine, west of Benson. It had been held up at a point called Dragoon Station. We cut across the Cochise trail and from there north to the Tucson-Phoenix Road where the hold-up had taken place.

We found the driver of the coach who was wounded but not to death. The Wells-Fargo shotgun messenger had laid two of the bandits out with a couple of volleys of his sawed-off shotgun. They had figured they would make a rich haul but they had been one

minute too slow. The two bandits were strangers in
the district where we were.

We got into Empire, a telegraph station, and we
wired to Earp that there had been some excitement and
there were two unknown hombres dead—killed by
parties unknown, but they were the same highwaymen who had held up the Butterfield stage earlier and
there was nothing to tell who the two were.

Then we went on to Tucson and we notified the
sheriff of Pima County, Arizona Territory, and also
Ranger headquarters, that the Wells-Fargo shotgun
messenger had saved the day for those two dead highwaymen were neatly riddled with buckshot. And we
all felt so pleased at the way this messenger had gotten
rid of two badmen that we chipped in five bucks
apiece and congratulated him on his courage and told
him we'd like to have him in the Arizona Rangers.
He kind of grinned and said that was his first job as
messenger and didn't know how long he'd last. He'd
been on the police force in New York City and had
tuberculosis and had come west to be cured. A plucky
kid!

I told one of the boys that when we came back we
ought to get a piece of board and word an epitaph like
this:

These two gents died with a disease called "Cold
Lead." TAKE WARNING! Don't try the same as
they did.

So we set up that sign and the way of the wording
of the message and the business-like way these highwaymen had been killed did strike some terror to the
hearts of badmen and there were plenty who infested

that part of the West while the State of Arizona was in the making. The Arizona Rangers in their method of enforcing the law and order, were patterned after the famous Texas Rangers and the Canadian Royal Mounted Police. They always got their men.

In all those tough towns there was always plenty of money, gold and silver easy won and easy lost, changing hands so fast it made the tenderfoot's head swim to see it. Wherever there is money, there is bound to be women and without them, in spite of all the gold and the shootings, life in the Wild West would have been pretty dull.

Most of those women were as tough as the men they preyed upon, but others were nervy and noble. There was Calamity Jane, a woman who was one of Custer's scouts and a darn good one. She was in town when Wild Bill Hickok was killed by McCall, and while the men were gaping and getting ready to commence to think about going after McCall she did it singlehanded. She had come out without her shooting irons but that didn't stop her. Finding the murderer in the meat shop, she picked up a cleaver and with the back of it beat McCall into submission and sat on him until the slow-witted men arrived.

CHAPTER V　　　　　　　More Bad Men

"**K**INDA FUSSY, AINT yer?" said the lady
who ran the restaurant, usually called the
hash-house, when a tenderfoot from the East told her
she forgot to soak the beans and they weren't fit to
eat.

"Eat 'em stranger; eat 'em all," came a calm voice,
and I looked up and saw a lanky cowboy with his six-
shooter covering the Easterner, who couldn't do anything but obey.

I was sorry for the tenderfoot, not because the beans
were as bad as he said, but they had been cooked and
dished out by a woman, and women on the Western
frontier were too scarce and precious to be criticized.

They might be bad women, bad cooks, and even bad-lookers, but only another woman was allowed to tell them so. So the tenderfoot had to eat his words and, what was worse, every last one of the beans.

Some of these women were not so bad, some were good cooks and good shots, like Faro Nell, who could shoot a glass of whisky out of a man's hand or the heels off a man's boots and did it many a time.

Faro Nell would have rated as a pretty girl any place, any time, but beauty isn't everything. She had other good qualities.

Men used to do exactly what women told them. I remember in Wichita, Kansas, in the seventies, the most brazen hussy was Ida May, who ran a joint aiming specially to please Texans. Among her admirers was a gunman named Clay Allison, who turned up one day with a toothache. Ida May told him about a good dentist at Las Anima. She said he would pull the tooth all right. but when Clay got back from the trip the toothache was still with him and they found that the wrong tooth had been pulled.

"Go back to that fool," said Ida May, "pull out half a dozen of his teeth and see how he likes it."

Clay did as was ordered. Going back to the dentist, instead of laughing gas, he hit him over the head with his revolver butt, and drew six of his teeth with the dentist's own forceps. Everyone who heard about it agreed that Clay did just right, especially since a woman had told him to do it.

A well-to-do young cattleman gave this same Ida May $2,000 to buy a new piano for her honky-tonk. It was ordered, delivered, and Ida paid $250 down.

By the time the seller called for the next installment, the madam had spent the rest of the two thousand and waved the collector away with a gun.

The merchant got a court order to take back the piano which would not have meant much but it happened that the great and only Wyatt Earp was employed by the City Attorney just then. He called with four piano movers who each grabbed a piano leg with one hand, and flourishing a six-shooter with the other carried the piano out. Earp followed up the rear with a gun and the piano stool. A few days later the same admirer and some others chipped in $1,750 more and the piano was back, "full-paid and non-assessable."

Yes, women stood ace-high in the frontier towns of those days. They were scarce in the cow towns and mining camps and held in great value. Some of the cowboys had hardly ever seen one and many of them who would ride after a band of murderous Apaches or shoot it out with badmen or cattle rustlers would tremble and their knees shake if a pretty girl glanced at them. I know; I was that way myself.

The greatest and most famous of all these women was Calamity Jane, the Joan of Arc of the Golden West. When I was one of General Custer's scouts I had heard that one of the scouts he used at times was a woman but never believed it possible until later when I got acquainted with her. Then I knew that Calamity Jane could do anything but settle down. The only reason that Sitting Bull's Indians did not get one woman's scalp among the others when they wiped out Custer's command at Little Big Horn was because she was sick in bed with pneumonia, the only illness she ever knew till her last one.

Calamity Jane was promiscuous. It would be a lie to say she was not a loose woman and she lost most of her looks early with her teeth, but that face and man-like figure looked mighty good to folks in time of trouble, which was when she most often turned up, a sort of hard-riding, hard-boiled, straight-shooting angel.

"Don't paint that gal with an upward look," I heard an old-timer advising an artist who was making pictures for a book on the Romantic West. Calamity Jane was always looking down at the trail or straight ahead for ambush. "And don't give her no halo. She'd look like hell in a halo. Most of the time she'd be wearing it over one ear and some of the time it would be rollin' around the saloon floors."

In 1872 when she was scouting for a small band of army officers, they were surprised by Nez Perce Indians. One of the officers, Captain Egan, was shot off his horse and would have been scalped if the girl scout hadn't shot the Indian, lifted the wounded man onto her horse and gotten him out of danger.

"Well, Jane," said Egan gratefully, "you're a good girl to have around in calamities."

The name "Calamity Jane" was fastened on her right then and she made good on it lots of times. Jane, whose real name was Martha Canary, had learned to be a frontierswoman at the age of 13 which was none too early. Most of the men and women I have met who made names for themselves, were thrown on their own as kids, instead of waiting until they were old enough to vote before they learned anything harder than to play on a saxophone.

Calamity's parents got the gold fever and came out from Missouri but in Montana the mother died, the father got discouraged and headed back home. Then he died, leaving Jane at the age of 13 with five younger brothers and sisters to bring up. On the way out she had learned to ride and shoot like a cowpuncher and had one of the sharpest pairs of eyes in the West. She got her first job as scout with the cavalry under false pretenses that she was a young man of 18. Before they found her out she had taken pains to show them how good she was with horse and rifle and on the trail.

I got acquainted with Jane when I was helping the United States Marshal in Dodge City as Deputy Marshal. Dodge City was some wild town! Jane welcomed me by saying:

"You did a good job in Deadwood. I hope you will make good here."

I was sent with a posse to catch a New Yorker who had robbed the Dodge City Bank of $100,000. I found him in a gambling house in Deadwood and when I showed him my deputy's badge he agreed to come along quietly. In Dodge City the crowd was hot for hanging and burning him on the spot. I felt sorry for the fellow and we managed to sneak him out of town and landed him in Leavenworth Prison. This man had gotten away with all the hard and dangerous part, escaping as far as New York where there was small danger of his ever being caught. But to be absolutely safe he decided to skip to Canada where nobody could bother him in those days.

He was one of those fellows I can't understand, born without any "bump of locality" and kept getting lost and turned around until he found himself broke, pretty well out West again and thought he might as well go the rest of the way. At Deadwood he had just won $250 in a gambling joint when I grabbed him. The bank paid me $500 for my work on the case.

Folks first began to take notice of Calamity Jane around 1879 when she was the sweetheart of the Seventh Cavalry teamsters. The Colonel of the Seventh aimed to divorce her from the outfit and ordered her to keep away under threat of heavy penalties. For a while Jane was a waitress, which she hated because it was too peaceful, and as soon as possible deserted for an outdoor job with a gun.

Calamity Jane was born to ride a horse. She used one of the best saddles that the frontier has ever turned out. It was of Dodge City make and a plains model, a double-rig style that had a cinch in front and one behind and was good for any kind of riding done on the range.

Her shooting irons were a .45 caliber Colt six-gun, frontier model, and the good old Winchester carbine .45-70. Jane was a crack shot with that six-shooter, and cowpunchers and miners that knew her were always itching to back her against some hombre that thought he could shoot. I remember one morning at Dodge City when a bunch of buffalo hunters were wrangling about who was the best shot. Bets were made and the amount soon grew to $500. A stake-holder and umpire were chosen. The match was to be between Calamity and a buffalo hunter who had the reputation of being an extra crack shot.

Judges were chosen for each side and a stake was set up with a notch in its end. Into that notch was stuck a silver half-dollar, the slim shining end toward the shooters.

Somebody had been sent to find Calamity Jane and before long she rode up on a buckskin horse, slid out of her saddle and handed her six-shooter for the judges' inspection.

I had met Jane but didn't know her well at that time so I took a good look at the young woman, for I had heard considerable of her. She was then about twenty-four or twenty-five years old. She was rather tall, well built and in later years she showed how much endurance there was in that slim wiry body. Her skin was well tanned by wind, sun and storm and sprinkled with freckles. She had a lot of dark brown hair that was covered up by a large tan sombrero. She wore chaps and she was at home on some of the worst bucking-horses that had ever come into Dodge. I'd say she was about 130 pounds weight and she carried her body well.

The judges inspected Calamity Jane's Colts, said it was in first-class condition, and then her rival was called and submitted his gun and it was approved. Calamity's friends were there and so were the buffalo hunter's crowd. A quarter was tossed. Heads was to shoot first. The lucky cast was Calamity's. The umpire loaded her six-shooter, then that of the buffalo hunter.

The two lined up at 150 paces, leveled and took aim, waiting for the word, "Fire!" The Colts in Calamity's hand barked and then the gun of her opponent. A cheer went up from the young woman's side for Calamity's bullet had struck the silver half-dollar's slim edge and buried the coin in the ground ahead. The bullet of her opponent had snapped the stake in two parts. The judges declared Calamity Jane winner over White-face Jackson, the buffalo killer, whose friends had been so sure of his aim.

I saw quite a lot of Calamity Jane around Dodge City, and some time later I ran across her again. She came into an Army Post where I was doing scout duty and asked for a job mule-skinning (freighting with mule teams). She was up against it and needed a job badly, for with her she had a small boy four years old who she said was her own kid. She called him Charlie Canary and I never knew him to go by any other name during the years I knew both him and his mother, Calamity Jane.

When asked how many mules she could skin, Calamity answered with a strong word and added:

"I can skin ten, twelve, fourteen, sixteen, eighteen!" Skinning meant driving—she could handle an eighteen-mule team like the best of them.

Well, she got her job and she proved her claim. We took up a collection among the scouts and got her and the boy settled in camp. They soon grew into army life. I have seen her drive a string of mules, sixteen of them, and turn around in a small space, sweating and swearing like the toughest old mule-skinner in the army. And I've seen Calamity throw the government diamond hitch with lightning speed. I've watched her turn an eighteen-mule team of the jerk-line variety in such a small space you'd swear it never could be done.

But there was something else to remember about that young female mule-skinner in those days, for clinging to her waist, on the seat beside her, was a little freckled kid, little Charley Canary, who sat beside his mother as she did the hard work that meant food for herself and boy. And little Charley pretty soon became as much a part of the army camp as his mother. For there wasn't a buffalo hunter or scout who would forget the kid when he came to spend his pay. Candy and playthings fell into the kid's hands. A small hand-carved wooden gun tickled him most of all. It was whittled out by an admiring scout.

Calamity Jane signed up in the army as a mule-skinner at Fort Zarrah, Kansas Territory. But she followed her career in the army for some time, first as a mule-skinner, and then later to have a settled place to take care of her boy, she ran a little eating-room for the soldiers and scouts. I remember Calamity well as I ran across her from time to time at Fort Dodge, Fort Niobrara, Fort Robinson, Nebraska Territory and in Deadwood. And I can most always see her now with a small, chubby, red-faced boy, his short, little, booted legs and feet sticking out from the seat beside his mother as she swung around a curve, then squaring himself once more and looking up into her face with his brave little grin.

Calamity Jane had a lot of nerve and she was a good judge of human nature, both of which stood her well in the life she was forced to follow. Her voice was nice and soft when things were going well but could grow harsh in an instant when she was mad, and I have seen her eyes snap and flash with hatred when she was treated wrong.

After the boy came, she lived for him alone. He turned out well too, but his death broke Calamity Jane. She said she had nothing to live for after he was gone.

She was happy as assistant to "Wild Bill" Hickok in Dodge City, helping him in making raids on robber hideouts and the toughest gambling dens where too many customers had been murdered. When on a raid she carried two .45-caliber Colts besides a Winchester rifle and only a very high-class gunman could get away from her alive. But Jane had a womanly side to her nature. When a family of six came into town with no money and not enough clothing she went into a saloon and collected $250 and a lot of clothes for them.

A mean gambler struck a girl in the Silver Dollar Cafe at Dodge City and Jane rushed to her help. Bat Masterson and Wild Bill Hickok came in, but before they could do anything, Jane hustled the man off to jail with her six-shooter sticking in his ribs. After a dip in the horse trough the bad-mannered gent was fined $50 for disturbing the peace.

At another time a gambler's hand was raised to shoot when Jane put a bullet through his hand before he could pull the trigger.

Calamity Jane tried her luck at hunting for gold
but never struck a dollar's worth of pay dirt. One day
a tough-looking stranger wandered into the camp and
finding that one of the prospectors was a woman,
figured it would be safe to jump her claim. He was
digging away in it early the next morning when a
shadow darkened the hole and a soft voice asked:

"Are you comin' up or do you reckon you want to
be buried down there?"

The stranger took a look at Jane's gun and the face
behind it and came right up. Calamity took his gun
away, made him dance while she fired his own bullets
near his feet and then marched him down to the jail at
Central City, Colorado. It was disappointment at
failing in the gold hunt that made her take to drinking so hard.

Jane tried everything at least once in her life, including matrimony, with Clinton Burke of El Paso,
Texas, for about a year. But family life, like waiting
on table, was too quiet to last, so she divorced Burke.
I don't know what she charged him with, but the real
offense was that he was too peaceful to be the mate of
a wildcat.

As Jane grew old, many easy jobs and good homes
were found for her, but always she ran away back to
the mining town saloons. Quite a lot of money had
passed through this woman's hands, some of it going
for drink, though mostly she was treated, more went
for gambling but most of all to grub-stake down-and-
out miners. If any of them struck it rich they forgot
to come back and give her half.

Calamity Jane and the famous Wild Bill Hickok

were in love for many years. She died in a Terry hotel of too much raw liquor and pneumonia.

Calamity Jane's funeral was the biggest ever held in Deadwood. At her request her tired body was put in the ground in Mount Moriah Cemetery on the mountain outside of Deadwood alongside the body of Wild Bill Hickok—I reckon the only man Jane ever really loved. Wild Bill has a life-sized statue over his grave but Jane has only a stone flower urn over hers. On a stone is carved her name, birth and death. Nearby are Preacher Smith and Deadwood Dick's graves—those two that the old dime novels had so much about.

Of course, there were some that said Calamity Jane was the lady-in-waiting of the devil himself. I don't want to make out she was an angel. But I knew a lot of good free-handed, kind-hearted things she did, and she had plenty of friends that figured her the same as I do.

These mining towns were not all gamblers, gunmen, cowboys, miners and painted women. It was true that gambling houses and saloons never closed. Night and day the customers crowded the long bars and drank and the gamblers sat and played at the tables by the walls. When a man lost all his money he went off to the mines and dug out some more and came back and lost it all again. Many had six-shooters in their belts ready to their hands, and especially experienced fighters usually had an extra gun in some peculiar hide-out that would surprise everyone.

Professional gamblers could most always be recognized by their headlight diamonds and shiny silk hats. The click of the roulette ball was occasionally interrupted by the louder noise of six-shooters. After the bartenders had removed the casualties, play went on as before.

But there were also the religious people and the gay but highly respectable society circle who usually went to church too. The towns sprang up so fast that these different kinds of people were all mixed in together.

A church was likely as not to be built between a gambling joint and a dance hall, each of course with a bar attached. The sermon was often interrupted by shots which would make the congregation run out to see how many got plugged. But they soon came back and since the sermons were usually on the wickedness of these places, such outbursts were really helpful, better than the old-time stereopticon that went with the lectures. Some of the gunmen, after cutting a new notch on their gun, were quite likely to drop into the service for a while and "get right with God" by emptying a big poke of gold dust in the collection plate.

Men weren't supposed to criticize women and that rule went even for wives when they were untrue to them. The idea was that it must be the husband's own fault if his wife took up with someone else. It was allowable for the husband to talk to the other man in the case, but likely to be risky.

Mrs. Michael Galeen was one of the most attractive women I knew in Tombstone. Her husband tended the bar at the popular Crystal Palace Cafe and was jealous about her. Frank Leslie, "Buckskin Frank," that I served with as a scout in the army, and one of the most dangerous gunmen I ever knew, met Mrs. Galeen at a dance at the Palace and was very much taken with her. After a dance or two her husband interrupted and notified Mr. Leslie that if he danced again with his wife he would kill him. With his usual daring Buckskin paid no attention to this warning knowing that he was much quicker on the draw than Galeen and proud of the dozen notches on his gun. No bartender could be considered in his class for a moment.

Buckskin actually had the nerve to escort Mrs. Galeen home about 3 o'clock in the morning. As they got near the Cosmopolitan Hotel, where the Galeens lived, the husband opened fire at the couple from an upstairs room. His bullet didn't hit either of them for he was not trained to shoot at such a distance with a pistol. Buckskin, who could hit a mark with a pistol at 300 feet, replied with one shot and killed the bartender.

Three weeks later Buckskin married the widow and she became a sort of social leader in Tombstone. Life with Buckskin was exciting even for a wife who had been hanging out at the Crystal Palace Cafe. He had to keep up his shooting practice, but did not want to stay away from his beloved and he liked to show her how good he was with a gun. So he used to look into the kitchen and shoot an egg out of Mrs. Leslie's hand or into the bedroom when she was fixing her hair and shoot the curling iron out of her fingers. But she didn't like these attentions, so she ran away and married a bricklayer, about the only man in town who did not carry a gun.

It almost broke Buckskin's heart, but he recovered and turned his affections to Diamond Annie, a pretty girl who was so popular at Tombstone's red-light district that she was able to plaster herself all over with diamonds. Diamond Annie fell sick, feared she had tuberculosis, and Buckskin persuaded her to go away and live with him on his ranch in the mountains. They were giving a party there one day to a few friends when the whisky gave out and Buckskin had to ride into town to get some more. When he came back he found his sweetheart and Jim Hughes, another well-known gunman, acting in a way that didn't suit him.

Buckskin killed Annie with one shot and put another in Hughes' chest. Hughes lay as if dead and Leslie, believing he had killed him, sat down to his liquor. In time Leslie was convicted of killing Diamond Annie and sentenced to a long term in the Yuma Penitentiary, but was pardoned after he had served four years, as it was felt that he had had provocation and women were no longer so scarce.

Tombstone society liked to gather of an evening at the "refined" vaudeville house, known as the Bird Cage Theatre. Its plush-draped boxes were filled every night with a crowd of richly dressed men and women drinking champagne. There was a bar at the front and a horseshoe of curtained upper boxes around the walls; painted women in scanty costumes sang touching ballads of home and mother on the stage and then hurried to the boxes where they used their charms to swell the receipts of the bar and receive a rake-off on every bottle of champagne they could make their admirers buy.

One thing those women of the Wild West should get credit for is that the worst of them were more modest than ones that call themselves decent today.

A person has to know this to understand what a lot of excitement was kicked up by Prairie Rose in Ellsworth City, Kansas, one of the liveliest cow towns of the seventies. One night in a saloon Prairie Rose made a bet of $50 with a cowboy that she would walk down Main Street the next day without a stitch of clothing on. She made good and won her bet, but the street was deserted at the appointed hour and it is doubtful if many saw her except the referee and stakeholder.

Rose was known as a dead shot and carried a Colt in each hand on that walk. Any "Peeping Tom" would probably have gotten drilled between the eyes and no sympathy would have been wasted on his remains. The town always was proud of Rose, calling her the "Lady Godiva of the Plains." Even today a few old fellows like myself remember her with admiration. Her deed has been recorded by Professor F. B. Streeter of the Kansas State Teachers College. He didn't know Rose but he got his facts from a lot of us old-timers that did know her.

Many of these women had more influence than a modern politician and could be powerful as a friend or enemy. But, as I look back on those wonderful old days I am surprised at how restrained the women were about making trouble unless they had good reason to meddle.

Once in Salt Lake City to buy some supplies, the first thing I did was to go into a bar that was connected with a dance hall. It wasn't that I needed refreshment but because I had to see a man. Of course you might accidentally find a man at his place of business or residence, but whether you wished to do ordinary business or shoot him, you looked in the saloon first. As I stepped in I saw the famous Faro Nell sitting there, pretty as a picture, between two cowboys. Like everybody else I looked at her with admiration but her indifferent eyes hardly saw me at all.

At the bar somebody asked me if I had had any trouble with the Indians and I told briefly about finding one of the Express messengers scalped and of rescuing his sister. Just before I finished the story I stopped because I saw somebody coming at me from behind. Some men today don't know why they put mirrors behind bars. The mirror is so the drinker can see who is behind him and what he is doing. A bar without a mirror wouldn't have had many customers out West.

In the mirror I saw Faro Nell, pop-eyed, leave those two cowmen and come straight for me hot-foot. She didn't know me but, as I have said, a scout always suspects everybody. Nell stuck her pretty face close to mine and said, real low:

"Stranger, tell that all over again. Start at the beginnin' and don't leave out nothin'."

I did and she asked plenty of questions. It turned out I had saved her sister and it was their only brother I had buried. Women are funny. Sometimes the more you do for them, the less they think of you. Then again if something hits them right, they'll die for you. I could see by Nell's actions that my standing with her had risen considerably, and so could those two cowboys that Nell didn't even bother to talk to any more.

I watched them in the back-bar mirror, scowling

and growling, getting drunker and more jealous all the time. At last one of them couldn't stand it any longer. He knew better than to criticize a woman, but it might be all right to work on me. He lurched over, pulled my hat off and yanked my hair which I always wore uncut and plaited. And he called me things.

He didn't seem to have any gun on him so with one hand I ripped the shirt off his back and with the other punched him hard on the chin. He went down hard and got up slowly and Nell laughed. At that he pulled a knife and I was in a fix. If I shot a man without a gun, in a brawl of this sort, I would lose my job according to the strict rules of the company. If I didn't he probably would throw the knife and kill me. I hesitated a fatal second while he steadied himself to take aim.

Just then a gun barked twice beside me, as Faro Nell put two bullets into the cowboy's chest. I can remember they made two blue spots in the skin but he only staggered up, and up went the hand with the knife. Nell put two more into his stomach and down he went to stay.

Nell had a face as cool and peaceful as Pike's Peak, but what a temper when she got mad! That girl shot a whisky glass out of the hand of the dead man's friend, splintered the mirror with a couple of bullets, ran the bartender out from behind the bar, made him dance and finally shot the heels off his boots. I didn't see why she punished the bartender and asked her afterward. Nell said:

"I allus knew I'd have trouble with that coyote. Look at the shape of his head."

It was a small head over a thick neck and the skull rose almost to a point. Still it wasn't much reason for shooting his heels off. But what followed showed that she was right. He needed to be softened up.

I thanked Nell for saving my life. She smiled prettily as she said she hoped to do lots more than that for me. By this time there was nobody in the place except the dead man, Nell and me and the barkeep who was trying to put his heels on. As usual everybody else had faded away and Nell started cleaning her two guns. Just then in walked "Primrose" Johnson who was some sort of a peace officer and he asked Nell if she had killed the man.

"Sure," said Nell, "this man insulted my friend here and that stuff don't go here."

"Do you know who I am?" Johnson asked sternly.

"No," Nell answered, "and I don't care. This is our little party. Stay out or be carried out."

While she was talking, in walked "Blue Nose" Williams, a deputy marshall with a reputation for being harsh and bad. He used to brag that he didn't care for man, God, or even woman. Pointing at the dead cowboy, the marshal said:

"How did this corpse come here? Who is responsible for this?"

"I think it is a lady's place to defend a friend when he is in danger," said Nell.

"That doesn't answer my question," said the marshal.

I spoke up and said the lady had saved me from being killed.

"Look here," said the marshal, "if there is any ex-

plaining to do, you can do it in jail, for that's where
you are going."

"No," said Nell, "you won't take me nor this kid to
jail for acting in self-defense."

She spun around and nudged him sharply in the
side with the end of her gun and said:

"And if you're not satisfied, you can take the same
route as the man on the floor."

Then turning to me she said, "Quick! Cover him
with your gun." I did so in a hurry because I knew
her guns were empty.

"Now," said Nell, "we'll sit down and talk this
over and settle if anybody should go to jail," as she
loaded her Colts. "That bartender saw the whole thing
just as it happened, grab him and he can do a lot of
explaining."

The barkeep was a fat fellow called Dutch Johnson
and I brought him over and forced him into a chair
with my gun as a persuader. He was scared and gun-
shy and said at first, "I know noddings." I prodded
him with my gun and said, "Yes, you do you coyote.
You know plenty. Start talking before I drill you
with my gun. Tell what you know and don't lie or
I'll see if I can thoot through you and hit the deputy
over there."

With this encouragement Dutch told what he knew
had happened and the marshal said he was satisfied
that the proceedings had been legal and proper. Really
he didn't much like the idea of trying to arrest a mountain lioness like Faro Nell.

Nell invited me to have something to eat and we
went to the well-known establishment, "Mother

Grimes Hash House.'' On the way over, Nell told me she had a good friend who ram-rodded with the Bar G outfit. "He happens to be one of the Gardner clan from Kaintuck or Tennessee. Aren't you from the same family?" When I told her that I was, she was more than pleased to meet me.

Mother Grimes was a buxom frontier woman who always kept her gun handy in the bosom of her dress. She met us with her arms covered with flour, her sleeves rolled up to the elbows and explained that she was mixing bread.

"Excuse me, I can't offer you my paw to shake just now," she said. "Nell, get some supper for your-self and this young gentleman."

They arrested Nell for murder before I got out of town. Blue Nose Williams, the deputy marshal, em-ploying a braver man to do the job. But Nell was willing to be tried by this time. I stayed to tell my story, and of course, she was acquitted. Then Johnson Gardner, who was a distant kin of myself, offered us a chance on the Bar G Ranch. He said, "Stay with me and help trap some 'bar' and panther and ride the range." '

"I looked at Nell and said, "You bundle up your little calico belongings and come along."

We were ten days traveling to the ranch. It was surprising to see how nice and refined Nell was be-coming. She had taught school back East in better days and you could hardly believe that she had changed into Faro Nell, the quick-shooting wild-cat. Out of her dance-hall clothes and in refined costume she looked like a lady. I stayed up there on the ranch for over a year, punching cows and range-riding. Then I took my little stake and, as Nell was growing too fond of home life, I started out again and left her. We wrote letters to each other for a time and the last I knew of Nell she was in Paradise, California.

Poker Alice was another woman card player of the old pioneer days. She wasn't a professional but she played a better game than lots of the tin-horn professional gamblers. When a girl of only 12 years, her career as a gambler commenced. She took to dealing cards and at forty-eight she was still going strong the last time I saw her.

She was wonderful in faro bank, as well as playing a strong hand of poker and that's how she got the name, Poker Alice, which she carried well. This love for cards became a habit in her life which she couldn't throw off. She always played and loved an exciting game of poker. But it had to be square.

Faro bank was a part of her life and she was the winner of many a big pot. If she lost after playing all night she would laugh and say, "All right, boys, to-morrow night I'll have better luck." If she won she was always ready to stake a loser.

The largest jack-pot Poker Alice ever won that I remember hearing about was one of $10,000, but it didn't shake Alice one bit. The game was in Deadwood and this story was only told to me. Alice was heavily in debt and at the close of the game she went right around and paid up everybody she owed. It took all she had won and when everything was cleared up she had just enough left to buy her breakfast.

Alice never broke a promise and that dependability

.made everyone like her. Even the warriors of Sitting Bull going through Deadwood stopped at her place, knowing that here they would find a friend they could trust, and she fed them when they were hungry. She grub-staked many an old desert rat prospector and helped them in all kinds of ways.

Alice was quite a business woman. She ran a dance hall and her dance-hall girls had the best she could provide and they would lay down their lives for her if needs be. She was known the length and breadth of the West and nobody had a word to say against her.

In addition to her card ability Alice was a wonderful entertainer. She could throw any kind of entertainment from horse-racing to the riding of wild range-cattle. She was a fine horse-woman and could handle a cayuse better than many cowboys.

Connected with her dance hall were gambling rooms where everything ran smoothly. The game had to be on the square; no trick cards or cheating were tolerated by Alice. She paid a visit to Dodge City one time and told Bat Masterson and Wyatt Earp what she thought of crooked gambling that was going on there. Even the chief gambler came in for a piece of her mind. She said:

"In my neck of the woods everything must be run on the square. You would do well to come up to Deadwood and learn how to play an honest game."

To me the strangest thing about her was her streak of religion in spite of her public life. She closed down on Sunday her dance hall and gambling rooms and everyone who worked for her was expected to go to church. Every other place was wide open on Sunday and it was a good day to do business but she had her

own notions of right and wrong and she lived up to
them. Poker Alice herself taught a Sunday School
class and she was well posted on what was in the
Bible, I can tell you. Sometimes she held religious
services in her gambling rooms.

"I believe in resting on Sunday and working like
hell for the devil the rest of the week," she told me
once. I believe those were honest words for she lived
them.

Poker Alice drifted out to Colorado with her husband, who was killed in a mine explosion, and the
widow turned to gambling to make a living. Men
didn't like to see a woman around the gambling tables
and wouldn't play with her. But one night she rigged
up with rough khaki clothes like a miner, stuck a long,
thin cigar in her mouth, and puffing clouds of smoke,
sat down at a table and bought some chips. That suited
the rough crowd and they made no objection to her.
Afterwards she was never without her cigar.

There was always a Colt hanging at her belt, but
she used it only three times that I ever heard. Once
was to save her husband, Tubbs, that she married
after the death of her first husband, when he was attacked by a knife wielded by a man who hated him.
The next time was when she suspected a faro dealer
of cheating. She had lost a thousand dollars and watching him closely, found he was tampering with the
box. She got her money back.

Alice had a place at Sturgis, and a good many soldiers used to come in from the nearby military post,
Fort Meade. Her gun kept order most of the time, but
one night when she tried to collect from a soldier some

money he owed her, a row started. When the smoke from the battle cleared away one soldier lay dead at her feet and two others were wounded. Alice was tried and acquitted of justifiable homicide.

In her old age she took sick and the doctors told her that she would die unless she had an operation, and there was a slim chance even at that. "I've faced bigger odds than that," said Alice, and she went to the hospital—and lost.

There was one crime so bad that it was reckoned to be wrong even when a woman did it—horse stealing. When Marshal Heck Thomas was trying to round up the Doolin gang, he sent me from Fort Sill to capture alive a couple of lady cattle and horse thieves, known as "Cattle Annie" and "Little Breeches," who were working for the gang. Heck said that he had almost, but not quite, caught Annie. When somebody asked if he didn't feel disappointed that he couldn't get any closer, he replied:

"Oh, I dunno, look at these."

These were three bullet holes Annie had made in his ten-gallon hat. That lady had five notches on her gun and Little Breeches was just as dangerous. An Indian can never believe that any sort of squaw would be hard to kill and even old Geronimo, famous Apache chief, a prisoner at Fort Sill, offered to get them and scalp them, too. But there was some notion that Geronimo might forget to come back.

I took a couple of his sons, who were so serious about scalping the girls, that when we began to get near them I had to explain that the commander at the fort was aiming to have that honor himself. Steve

Burke, U. S. Marshal and fighting parson, joined us with a man named Tilghman, at the last minute.

It is always easy to trail women because their feet are smaller and shaped different. But when we found we had surrounded them in a little cabin we weren't so gay about how we were going to get them out alive and stay alive too. At last we tried a little trick on them. Lying low beside the window and door, we had the Indians go a long way off and then return making plenty of noise. The girls wakened in the middle of the night from a sound sleep and scrambled out thinking a pursuit party was a long ways off.

Parson Burke threw his arms around Annie and though he got his face pretty badly scratched, he managed to get hold of her gun and capture her. Tilghman and I did the same for Little Breeches who clawed us quite a bit too. And weren't they mad to be captured that easily! They were sent to a Massachusetts reformatory for a few years. Little Breeches died soon after she came out, but Annie lived long and respectably in Oklahoma. It was one case where a reformatory really reformed a very tough lady.

Yes, life would have been pretty dull on the old frontier without the always interesting and occasionally refining influence of women.

CHAPTER VI   Wild Bill Hickok

I N THE WILD, WIDE-OPEN days there were
quite a lot of tough men in the cow towns and
mining camps in the West. I knew most of the worst
of them. And to kind of balance these quick-shooting
badmen there were some sheriffs and marshals and
their deputies who never were scared of man, beast or
devil, and they were very quick with their Colts too.

I believe that Wild Bill Hickok was the quickest on
the draw and the surest shot of them all. I knew Wild
Bill very well indeed. He was a hunter, miner, adven-
turer and a terror of the cattle rustlers, crooked gamblers and bad men. I often met him at Tombstone,
Deadwood and other places where hot lead flew free

and easy, and also at Abilene, Kansas, when he was
making his big record as City Marshal.

Wild Bill was a wonder. In some of his fights it
seemed as if the more men that jumped at him at once
the easier and quicker he wound up the fight. Wild
Bill was different from all the other fighters I knew.
When odds were pretty near even, he was just a cool
and quick shooter, a good deal like Wyatt Earp, Doc
Holliday or Billy the Kid. When Wild Bill had all the
time he needed, say a whole second, to draw, aim and
shoot, he could do a neat job and always put the bullet just where he figured he wanted to put it.

When two gunmen are drawing on each other at
the same moment, the hardest shot is the head shot. It
takes time to get the gun up past broad targets such as
the stomach and chest, with the heart as the bulls-eye,
to the highest part of the body. The head is not only
a high and small target but also it's the easiest for a
quick dodger to yank out of the way. Just the same a
bullet through the brain, if you can manage it, is the
best shot because even if the man is not killed instantly,
at least he is paralyzed and doesn't shoot back as Bill
proved by his own death. If Bill had been shot through
the heart when his time came, instead of the brain, he
would have managed to get the man that shot him.

Bill used to plant his bullet in the center of the
forehead, just over the nose, but once when he made
that perfect shot, it proved to be a bad blunder that
almost cost him his life. His enemy that time was a
bear that had a slanting forehead made of bone, hard
as rock and maybe an inch thick. All it did was to
make that bear almighty mad. In the next few minutes

when he had it out with the bear, Bill learned a few things about rough-and-tumble fighting.

It was when Bill Hickok, single-handed, fought ten of the McCandles gang and killed the leader and all but two of the others, that they first started calling him "Wild Bill."

"When the six of them had me down across the table I thought my last moment had come. So I just got wild and slashed about, like a bear with a death wound and I reckon that's how I came to get through with the job," Bill explained when he got on his feet again.

It was when the man went wild like that, that he was different from any other fighters I have ever seen. At those times he took on a speed that is more than natural for any man to have and Bill never had it at other times. But he didn't know how fast he really was.

To hear Bill you'd think that everybody else was so slow that they gave him plenty of time to dodge a knife from one man, duck a pistol bullet from another while going around the room shooting and cutting them down. I asked him how he could move so fast and Bill answered:

"Well, that's the way it looked to me. Those d . . . n coyotes all acted like they moved slower than cold molasses."

James Butler Hickok was the name his mother gave him and why they changed it to Bill, he never knew. He said they first called him Shanghai Bill because he was more than six feet high. They forgot the Shanghai after the McCandles fight. Names came to people on the frontier for all kinds of reasons. My name was Raymond Gardner but everybody called me Arizona Bill.

Like all the other crack fighters I knew about, Bill started in as a kid, swapping all his toys for an old, single-barrel flint-lock pistol that he learned to shoot on his father's Illinois farm. He was in the Civil War and in the little border wars between Kansas and Missouri; always was hungry for a fight. About 1860. Bill got a job running a stagecoach station on the road to Topeka, Kansas. He and a helper had to look after some 25 horses, feeding and cleaning—that was easy, but keeping horse thieves from stealing them was dangerous.

Nearby was the McCandles ranch, run by two no-good brothers who started in rustling horses to sell to Southern rebels. It wasn't long before they had their eyes on the coach company's cayuses. The McCandles boys told Bill one morning they were going to run the horses off anyway, but if he wouldn't make any trouble they would slip him a dollar or two. Of course if he put up a fight it would mean that the stagecoach company, besides losing their horses, would have to bury their caretaker.

"That so?" drawled Wild Bill. "Anytime you're honing to rustle them cayuses you come right along. Only you've made a mistake about who's goin' to get buried."

Next day Jack and Jim McCandles, with eight other rustlers, rode up to the stagecoach station. The horses were locked tight in a strong stable made of logs. Bill had shut himself in a dugout, also of logs where it

stuck out of the hillside. Its one room had no window
or other opening except the heavy log door.

When Bill refused to come out and be shot in the
open, the gang picked up a log and using it as a batter-
ing ram, soon broke in the door of the dugout. Jim
McCandles, with a Colt in each hand, jumped through
the opening. It was no time for fancy head-shooting
so Bill drilled him through the heart with a rifle. A
rifle is a clumsy weapon at close range, so Bill had
thoughtfully used it for that first shot and then
dropped it for his six-shooters.

With these he killed the next three that came
through the door in the first rush. Four were gone but
the other six got in and tackled Bill. Bill emptied one
revolver and grabbed up his Bowie knife, shooting
with one hand and stabbing with the other but he was
now taking as well as giving wounds. At last one of
the gang hit Bill such a thump on the head with a
pistol butt that it fractured his skull and knocked him
flat on his back across the table. At that very minute
Jack McCandles threw himself on the fallen man and
raising his knife high started to drive it through Bill's
heart.

I know it is hard to believe that anyone could be
thoughtful and saving at such a time. But Bill had
been saving one last cartridge for a tight pinch, which
this moment certainly was, and now he let McCandles
have it through the heart. Bill told me this himself.

With dying hand Jack struck heavily, but death
prevented him from changing his aim when Bill wrig-
gled out from under it and the knife stuck in the table
top. But Bill was just beginning to fight. He snatched

the knife with the hand that now dropped the second empty revolver, up he jumped with a knife in each hand and about this time became like a wild bear with a death wound, like he told me.

A minute later and the dead on the floor had grown to six, and Bill, spurting blood in a dozen places and with a flap of bloody scalp hanging down almost over his eyes, seemed to be getting stronger every minute. Of the four that were left, two were badly wounded, and they started to run with Bill after them.

The two unwounded men reached their horses and got away. One of the wounded managed also to get away, but died of his wounds the next day. The other ran down a hill to a tree where he started to reload his gun. Just at this moment Bill's helper returned from a day's hunting trip and was so startled by what he saw that he could only stand and gasp. Bill snatched the helper's gun, ran down the hill, killed the wounded rustler who was reloading his gun, and collapsed.

The stagecoach arriving soon after brought first aid to Bill. He needed it, with a fractured skull, his scalp hanging over his eyes, his cheek laid open with a jagged wound, three knife-thrusts in his chest, and one in his left forearm, a bullet in his left hip and two through his right leg. A year later he was as well as ever. One of the two men who got away from him alive used to say:

"If we had that fight to do over again I'd know how to manage better. The trouble with Bill is that just as you pull the trigger on him, he ain't there no more. The way to plug Bill is to aim where you know he ain't, and then maybe he'll run into the bullet."

When he wiped out the McCandles gang Bill had hardly recovered from the wounds the bear had given him. Bill was driving a wagon load of freight from Independence, Missouri, to Santa Fé, New Mexico, and behind him, a mile or so, was Jim Farley with another load. Just where the road passed through a narrow gulch he met a big cinnamon bear with two cubs. A cinnamon usually gets out of a man's way when a grizzly will look for trouble, but some hunters say that a cinnamon is worse in a fight because it is quicker.

This bear was ugly on account of her cubs, coming forward growling and full of fight. Bill saw that he would have to kill the animal, which he reckoned would be easy to do. His main thought was to kill her far enough away from the team so the horses would not be frightened and maybe upset his freight. Jumping down from the seat, he ran on ahead with two single-shot pistols, one more than he expected to need, and also a knife. It was funny to see how foolish Bill used to look when he told what happened next.

Knowing the bear couldn't pull a gun on him, Bill walked up within a few feet, took his time and made one of those neat forehead shots of his. The bullet bounced right off the bear's thick, slanting forehead— all it did was to make the bear start right after him. Bill had just time enough to fire his second pistol, sending a bullet into the bear's left shoulder. It didn't break the shoulder, but it weakened it so that Bill got hardly more than a one-arm hug, as they clinched.

A two-arm hug would probably have broken Bill's back and cracked his ribs. A one-arm bear's squeeze is bad enough, but Bill was able to stand it. With his left hand at the bear's throat he interfered with her attempts to chew the top of his head off, at the same time stabbing her in the belly with his knife. When the bear let go of him with her good right arm, in order to do some clawing, he had a chance to draw a full breath and bringing his right hand up, slashed at her throat. All this time the bear was standing on first one hind foot and then the other, using the free foot to claw Bill's legs which had to hold almost the entire weight of both fighters.

Farley, coming up about a half hour later, saw the team standing idly and, in the road ahead, a disemboweled bear, with a man's left arm in her mouth. Underneath the bear was the rest of Bill, one seeming as dead as the other. Bill's head, shoulders and legs had been so thoroughly ripped up that Farley had no doubt that the flesh would never heal, even if Bill lived out the day. The scars remained all his life, but they were soon criss-crossed with knife and bullet marks from the McCandles gang and others.

Bill's fame brought him the honorable but dangerous job of City Marshal of Hays City. The chief business of that town at that time was gambling. Since most gamblers are crooked because that is the only way they can make a steady living at it, a lot of shooting went with the business. If a customer had been skinned and he kicked too much, the gambler was liable to get nervous and shoot him for fear that the kicker was going to pull a gun. So sometimes the customers would shoot first and then call everybody in the place to come and examine the cards and see if there

were some extras in the gambler's sleeves or pockets.
When, as sometimes happened, the dead gambler was
found to have been playing straight, the customer was
criticized and might even be tried for manslaughter,
but was pretty sure to be acquitted.

It was the marshal's business to look into all shootings and, if they did not appear to be proper, he would
arrest the shooters. Also he had to quiet the badmen
who once in a while went on a spree and shot up the
town. At this time, General Phil Sheridan was in command of about 2,000 soldiers, at nearby Fort Hays,
stationed there to keep the Indians peaceful. The soldiers always came to Hays City to get rid of their
month's pay, a thing they can do almost as quick as
sailors.

One day Bill decided he had to arrest a fire-eating
army sergeant who had been smashing up a saloon. On
stepping in he found that the brawling sergeant was
surrounded by a dozen of his own privates, all armed
with pistols, as was customary in Indian fighting. Bill
told the sergeant that he would have to arrest him.
The sergeant told Bill that this probably wouldn't be
an easy or healthy job.

This Bill admitted, but said he would try just the
same and such was Bill's reputation, even at that time,
that these 13 armed men hesitated at facing the marshal's two guns. Finally the sergeant had a right smart
idea that satisfied everyone. Seeing that Bill, though
taller and longer-armed, was about 30 pounds lighter,
he proposed that they fight it out with their bare fists
in front of the saloon. If Bill could lick him, the sergeant would be his prisoner without any more argu-

ment. If he licked Bill, the marshal was to be the sergeant's prisoner for the rest of the day, and be led
around by a lariat, like a trained bear, anywhere the
winner wanted to drag him.

The sergeant was the heavyweight bare-fisted champion of the fort and didn't see how he could lose.

"Shore," said Bill, "yore idea is accepted and we'll
start pronto."

Both handed their hardware to the bartender,
stepped outside and squared off. The marshal hadn't
studied boxing but he knew all about knife fighting
which means feinting, dodging and striking quick and
hard. The thing was over in less than a minute. Bill
ducked a couple of punches and then thumped the
champion on the chin. As the sergeant was falling he
hit him again over the heart so hard that he lay there
unable to get into the real battle which followed.

Most soldiers I knew were pretty good sports, but
this bunch wasn't. They pushed Bill around and started to beat him with the butts of their revolvers.
Against these the marshal had nothing but his fists
until the bartender broke through the circle and handed
him back his guns—and then Bill went into action
quick. In the next few minutes he killed six of the
soldiers and managed to get away with seven bullet
wounds.

After hiding all night in a buffalo wallow, Bill
crawled more than a mile to the ranch of a friend.
There he heard that General Sheridan had turned most
of his 2,000 men out on a hunt for him. For three
weeks the marshal lay at death's door, secretly visited
by a doctor. In all that time no soldiers searched the

ranch because it was so close to the scene of the shooting.

The general had been told by one of the soldiers
that the man who had killed six of his soldiers had
gotten away unwounded, and figured that he would
keep going all night, so he ordered the search to begin
at a distance of 20 miles. In a few months Bill was as
well as ever. The number of wounds that man collected astonished me. His body came to look like an old
battlefield that had been fought over so many times
that the scars ran into each other. He couldn't be sure
who gave him half of them.

Bill tried his hand at prospecting for gold and silver,
but, like Calamity Jane, never had any luck. He visited
New York City once and when the cabman charged
him five dollars for a fifty-cent ride, paid it, then
knocked the cabman cold with one punch on the nose.
As soon as he was settled at the hotel, Wild Bill went
in search of the nearest gambling joint where, in one
night, he lost every cent he had brought with him.

A theatre manager saw a chance to make some
money out of Wild Bill's reputation which was bigger
in the East than the West and he made him a proposition. Bill had to accept or go hungry and as he was
broke, he signed up. They played to good business
wherever they went, but Bill was not a good actor and
he wouldn't take advice. He was willing enough to
shoot down whole tribes of Indians (stage Indians)
with blank cartridges, but he wanted to do it in his
own way which a tenderfoot audience often did not
understand. The manager soon saw that all he needed
to keep the crowds coming was to keep Bill's name up

on the billboards. So one night, just before the show moved to the next town, he paid Bill off and said he could not afford to hire him any more.

Bill shook hands, got on the train and went West. He didn't know that an actor made up to look like him, was to take his part at a third of Bill's salary and was going to be advertised everywhere as the great and only Wild Bill Hickok. Eastern audiences liked the fake Bill better than the real one and everyone was satisfied until someone brought the news West to the genuine Mr. Hickok.

Wild Bill packed his bag and said he would have to see how correct the fellow was. He caught up with the show at Binghamton, N. Y., bought a ticket and sat quietly through the show until the man who had slaughtered a whole band of howling Comanche Indians single-handed and rescued the manager who was tied to a stake, acknowledged the name, Wild Bill Hickok.

While the audience delightedly cheered, Bill, who didn't think the Indians had been killed right, jumped on the stage. He threw the manager down into the orchestra pit, and then with one punch knocked out the fake Wild Bill.

At this point all the Indians lying around the stage forgot they were dead and started to get up. As fast as they got up Bill knocked them down again until the last of them crawled off the stage. Bill then blew on his knuckles to cool them, made a short speech of explanation and returned to his seat with the request to get on with the rest of the show.

This wish was not granted, the actors refusing to

go on while this critic was in the house. There was an intermission until a policeman arrived. Bill advised him to bring at least six more. When eight arrived Bill thought it a large enough posse, so he could go peaceably without losing respect for himself.

Next day he was fined three dollars, paying it willingly in the belief that the story of what had happened would kill the show. For good measure he informed the company that he would kill them himself if it didn't. They decided to play Shakespeare.

Just twice before he became famous did Bill make the mistake of sitting with his back to an unlocked door; the first time in Ellsworth, Kansas, he came within a hair of being shot down from behind and the second time it really did happen. Bill had been messing around in a small love affair in which a local charmer threw over a local badman, Big Bill Thompson. Big Bill had promised to kill Wild Bill for cutting him out but Hickok was always hearing threats like that.

The next day he went into a restaurant, carelessly seating himself with his back to the door and ordered a bowl of stew. It would not have been so bad if there had been a mirror that Bill could look into to watch the door. But there wasn't and pretty soon the waiter, a colored man, set the stew down in front of him.

Bill did not hear the door open, but glancing up, he looked into the Negro's face and saw reflected there all he needed to know about what was going on behind his back. The waiter's face was gray with terror, his eyes and mouth were wide open. Bill wasted no time looking around. He threw himself under the table, just in time for a bullet from Big Bill's gun to pass through the air where his back had been, sending bowl and stew in all directions.

While Wild Bill's body was on its way to the floor one of his hands was reaching into a pocket and drawing a derringer and before he hit the floor, and before Big Bill could fire again, he put a derringer slug between Big Bill's eyes, killing him instantly.

In the course of his work as City Marshal, Bill had to kill or be killed by a crooked gambler named Phil Coe. The undertaker got Phil but the deceased had a lot of friends and relatives who foolishly tried to avenge him. One of these was his brother, Jim Coe, who came looking for Bill at Cheyenne. Bill was sitting in a saloon where he could watch the door and also by looking in the mirror see the faces and fronts of those standing with their backs to him at the bar.

In came two strangers who merely looked at Bill, then went to the bar, turned their backs to him and ordered drinks. Bill did not quite like the way they looked at him and when one of them spoke he remembered that the voice sounded like that of Phil Coe and guessed that it was his brother Jim.

Wild Bill was armed only with a derringer and only one of its barrels was loaded, but what was more important, he was ready for anything that might happen. Without warning the two men whirled around and drew their pistols. Before Jim Coe could get his gun high enough to fire, Bill had shot him just over the eyes. At the same time he jumped from his chair and threw the empty derringer in the other man's face. That man's bullet missed and before he could fire again

Bill picked him up and threw him down on his head
so hard that it broke his neck.

Yet it was possible to get the drop on Bill and even
shoot him if he did not suspect you. Bill was standing
at the bar of a saloon in Wichita, when a young
stranger came in and with a friendly smile asked if he
wasn't Wild Bill. Hickok replied that folks did call
him that.

"Well, I shore am lucky," the stranger said hap-
pily, "because I got something for you that my cousin
wanted you to have."

So saying, he reached into his pocket, whipped out
a pistol, put it against Bill's head and fired. Down
went Bill like a log, half his head covered with blood.
Sure that Bill was plenty dead, the young man ran
out, jumped onto his horse and dashed out of town

But Bill, fooled though he was, had yanked his
head aside enough so the bullet instead of going
through his brain, had cut a gash in his scalp and
stunned him. The moment Bill opened his eyes, he
made for his horse, waving all aid except to know
which road the man had taken. Late that afternoon the
stranger heard the sound of hoofs behind and looking
around saw a dreadful sight.

There was the man he thought he had killed and
who still seemed to be a corpse because the setting sun
shone on his head, wet and red with blood. I reckon
Bill must have been crazy with pain because when his
bullet toppled the stranger out of his saddle with a
broken back, he took out his knife and cut from the
man's scalp a ribbon of skin about as large as the one
the bullet had taken from Bill's. The man was a cousin

of that same Phil Coe and he died a slow and painful
death.

One day Bill Mulvey, a badman, went on a rampage
in Hays City. Wild Bill as marshal had to try to arrest
him. Why Hickok did not get the drop on him first
and arrest him afterward, he never could explain. The
result was that Mulvey put the muzzles of two Colts
in Bill's face and said:

"No, I arrest you."

The marshal agreed that Mulvey had him right and
then the badman began to tell him what he was going
to do with Bill. In the midst of it Bill looked over
Mulvey's shoulder and shouted:

"Don't hit him. He is only fooling."

Mulvey turned his head, saw nobody was behind
him and pulled both triggers even before he turned his
head back. But Bill had jumped aside, and pulled his
own gun, put a bullet through Mulvey's head while it
was still turning.

Wild Bill used to pick his own battlefields when he
could and sometimes he chose queer ones. Hearing that
a dozen killers had been sent to Abilene to shoot him
and were liquoring up in a saloon to nerve themselves
for the job, Bill had a friend go to the saloon and men-
tion, where the crowd would hear it, that he was
taking the next train out of town. The gang hurried to
the railroad station and sure enough, there was Bill
sitting in the very first seat in the first car facing them.

They all took the train and were planning how to
get him onto the platform when he suddenly appeared
to them, with a gun in each hand. He gave them the
choice of being shot where they were or of jumping off

the train which was moving at about 30 miles an hour. A moment later the brakeman on the last car was surprised to see a dozen men tumbling over each other in their rush to jump off the rear platform. One was killed and two badly injured.

Wild Bill got off the next stop and took the first train home. I asked him why he had picked a train for the fight. His answer was:

"I had often wondered what one man could do against a gang on a train and reckoned it would be a good chance to find out."

It was the way Wild Bill did things while he was City Marshal in Abilene, Kansas, that first gave him the fame that spread all over the cow towns and mining camps. Abilene was at the north end of a 1,000-mile cow-puncher's waste—a trail from Texas. The cowboys were weeks on the trail with mighty little rest night and day. And when the herd was at last driven into the big railroad pens to be loaded into the cattle cars, the cowboys were paid off and rode break-neck for the saloons, dance halls and gambling joints.

An extra fine bunch of crooked gamblers, badmen, bandits and painted women had collected in Abilene to trim these roistering cowmen of their money. For the first two years there was no law nor order in Abilene; nobody to interfere with anything. And then the decent people of the town commenced to put the brakes on. One after another of a long string of city marshals tried to quiet things down but didn't get anywhere. A calaboose was built but the cowboys tore it down as soon as it was roofed in. One of the city marshals was a former chief of police of St. Louis,

who promised to tame the wild cow town inside of a
week. Before he finished his first day he took off his
badge and went back to St. Louis.

Tom Smith was brought in from a tough mining
town in Wyoming to handle Abilene's badmen. It
was not long before he was shot to death and chopped
to pieces by two cattle rustlers.

At last the job of marshal was offered to Wild Bill
Hickok at $150 a month and half of all fines. He was
known by the good work he had done in Ellsworth
and Hays City as marshal in those wild towns. Bill
rode into town and after pinning on his badge went
into the liveliest saloons such as the Alamo, the Bull's
Head and the Elkhorn. He had a talk with the bartenders, gave some advice to the tin-horn gamblers,
and looked the dance hall women over. Bill wore his
hair long as most plainsmen did at that time, and his
curls hung down over his shoulders. He was a neat
dresser, and besides the two Colts at his belt, he carried
a knife and a sawed-off shotgun.

Everybody knew Wild Bill was no bluff. So when
he gave notice that there was not going to be any more
wild shooting by the cowboys, the shooting up of the
town stopped. After a few barroom shootings Wild
Bill gave another order—every cowpuncher coming to
town must check his guns and they would be given
back when he left. They didn't like this; they felt
lonesome with their empty holsters. But nobody was
itching to have a gun argument with Wild Bill.

After Bill had made his round of the saloons and
dives that ran wide open day and night, the badmen
talked over what he had told them. There wasn't much

doubt that he meant what he said and before many
hours they had a chance to see the new marshal in
action.

He got word that the town council wanted to see
him—it was the town council that had given him the
job as peace officer. He found the council had a piece
of important business on hand but couldn't vote because it lacked one of having a quorum. A member refused to attend the meeting and tied things up on purpose. Would Bill go and talk to him and try to get him
to come to the meeting?

The new marshal hunted up the member but no
amount of talk budged him an inch.

"Reckon there ain't no use sittin' 'round waitin'
for me. I ain't comin' to the meetin'," said the councilman.

"Maybe you aint aimin' to, but you're comin' just
the same," said Wild Bill calmly and he grabbed the
man, threw him over his shoulder like a sack of meal
and trudged down the main street to the council room.
The new marshal dumped him in a chair and leaned
against the door to guard the room until the meeting
was over.

If there had been any doubts that the new marshal
was on the job and meant what he said or would do
what he set out to do, that handling of the town
councilman settled them.

Bill was a careful man and cleaned his guns every
morning. He was as faithful in practicing his draw and
keeping up his target shooting as a singer or a piano
thumper. He could fire six shots from a Colts through
a small knot-hole, standing a hundred feet away and

fired them so fast you couldn't count the shots. Bill would set up two rows of tin cans and ride between shooting from both sides and never miss one.

Wild Bill was something to look at, standing six feet two inches tall, and dressed in a costume like a grand opera star as he did his daily revolver practice. I have seen him put six bullets into a 25-cents piece in six seconds at 100 feet. Lots of others watched him too and it was interesting to see the funny look on the faces of crooks. He could kill at that same rate. Once he shot six men dead in what couldn't have been more than six seconds, the cowpunchers who saw the fight told me.

Yet Bill was killed by a mean, little drunken rat named Jack McCall. Richard Stephens, whom I met in Deadwood, and who is now living in Seattle, almost as old as I am, was in the saloon when Bill was removed from a mighty useful life. Stephens still owns the hand full of cards that were in Wild Bill's fingers. They became famous ever after as "the Dead Man's Hand."

The hand consisted of the ace of clubs, the ace of diamonds, the eight of spades, the eight of hearts, and the queen of hearts. It will be seen that all four suits are represented. Wild Bill's cards would seem strange today, for they are the kind used in playing Mexican monte in his time. There are no index figures in the corners and the queen of hearts has only one face and that does not have the wooden expression of the queen in a modern pack.

Mr. Stephens was part owner of a dairy herd which browsed on the wild grass at Crook City, near Dead-

wood, and was delivering buttermilk to the Mann &
Lewis Saloon in Deadwood when Wild Bill played his
last game.

"I stopped to watch the game and rest, for I remember now that it was a hot afternoon in August
with no breeze in the gulch," said Mr. Stephens. "I
was just thinking that I must get back to my ranch
before nightfall and hoping there would be no Indians
lurking in the jack-pines. I was glad to know that we
had a man like Wild Bill Hickok around to protect us.

"The proprietors of the Mann & Lewis Saloon invited Bill to make their place his headquarters, feeling
that his presence would be good for business and a
valuable protection against crooked gamblers. In the
poker game on this particular day were Charley Rich,
Carl Mann, one of the saloon proprietors, and Captain
Massey, a former Mississippi River pilot. They were
all joking together.

Although Bill joked with the others he was not
happy because for the first time in years he was sitting
with his back to the door. His instinct as a gun-fighter
rebelled against this. Scattered through the West were
many men who would have liked for one reason or
another to have the fame of ending Wild Bill's career,
and he didn't like to be tempting fate. Often he glanced
over his shoulder as men entered the saloon.

"I didn't crowd close to the players because that was
not considered good manners on the frontier and might
lead to a funeral, but from a respectable distance I
heard Wild Bill say:

" 'I would reckon it a favor, Charley, if you would
change places with me.'

" 'I am not having any too much luck today myself,' said Rich, 'and I ain't aimin' to give up an advantage for a fool superstition.'

" 'It ain't superstition,' said Wild Bill. 'I am comfortable when I am in yore chair and I feel like a fish out of water sittin' here.'

" 'Why don't you try raisin' me out of this seat?' asked Rich.

" 'That's a right pious idea,' said Bill. 'Somethin' tells me this hand won't be beaten. I'll h'ist you a red stack.'

"While this talk was going on I was leaning on the bar with my back to the door. I didn't see Jack McCall sneak in and only noticed him when I heard the roar of a heavy revolver. The bullet struck Wild Bill in the head, came out his cheek and entered Captain Massey's arm. Bill had been smiling as he pushed the stack of red chips into the center of the table and he was still smiling when he fell face downward onto the table and slid to the floor.

"McCall swung swiftly about and threatened the bartender, Harry Young, with the revolver. Then he ran out and tried to mount his horse, but the saddle slipped and he fell to the ground. Seeing he would not have time to tighten the saddle girth he ran into a nearby butcher shop and hid."

Mr. Stephens turned his attention to Wild Bill, but he soon saw that he was dead. With the others he helped to lay out the body and while they were doing so he took the fatal cards, the "Dead Man's Hand," from the stiffening fingers. In the excitement nobody thought much of a hand of cards. When Stephens returned to his ranch he had them in his pocket and a little later when he showed them to some of the admirers of the great gunfighter they offered to buy them. But he would not sell.

There was some talk of lynching McCall, but strong men were in control in Deadwood and kept the hotheads in check. In the evening a mass-meeting of citizens was held to try McCall for his crime. The court was not a real lawful court, but it was considered the best possible kind of court in Deadwood. They chose a "miners' jury" to render the verdict.

Because miners made their living by working in the mines, they were reckoned about the most unprejudiced jury that could be picked to try murder among the townspeople because there was small chance that they would have any interests or tie-ups with the gamblers, saloon or dance-hall keepers.

McCall got a tricky lawyer who told him to tell the jury that Wild Bill had murdered his brother in Dodge City, Kansas, and that he was taking a natural revenge. The hard-handed but soft-hearted miners' jury believed it and voted a verdict of not guilty.

The rat had gotten away with murder, but he was so proud that he had killed the quickest deadshot in the West that pretty soon he began bragging that his story about the murdered brother was a fake. At Laramie, Wyoming, they decided to do something about it.

McCall was arrested and charged with murder in the Federal Court at Yankton, Dakota Territory. The court decided that the miners' jury at Deadwood had no lawful standing and, therefore, there was no double jeopardy. McCall was found guilty and hanged.

Wild Bill was buried in Boot Hill Cemetery on the side of a mountain just outside of Deadwood and later on was taken up and moved to Mount Moriah Cemetery, higher upon the mountain. A traveling artist, named Riordan, happened along and made a life-sized statue of Hickok. He carved it from red sandstone and it was set up on Bill's grave. Visitors have chipped off souvenirs and one hand and arm of the statue have been nicked away, the last I heard.

Right next to Bill's grave and in the shadow of that stone statue, Calamity Jane is buried. Her grave hasn't any monument but in the stone urn placed to hold flowers there are are fresh blossoms and a small grave-stone marks her name.

CHAPTER VII   Billy The Kid

A LOT HAS BEEN said and written about a very
capable and fast working badman, Billy the
Kid. I knew Billy the Kid and once had drinks with
him, together with General Lew Wallace, the writer,
and Billy listened while we swapped yarns about old
frontier days. Billy hadn't killed more than half a
dozen at that time and nobody knew what a bad
hombre that youngster was. Later on I met him again
with General Wallace and that time we all knew he
was the toughest proposition in the whole wide Wild
West.

Billy the Kid was a natural born gunman, and he

had the nerve and courage of a grizzly bear. In the few years that he lived, Billy made more trouble and killed more men than anybody in the West in such a short career. He had a lot of friends, and so did most all badmen. Billy was a great pet of the women. He had a nice smile, treated them like they were real ladies and was a neat dresser and a good dancer. Well, that's about all the women needed to know to like him.

But that boy had killed twenty-one men before he was twenty-one years old, not counting Indians. Nobody but a cold-blooded murderer had any reason to kill that many men in that short time. That's why I believe Billy the Kid was the worst of all the badmen I knew. Sheriff Pat Garrett ended Billy's future prospects when Billy was twenty-one years old, and I have often wondered, if the Kid had lived another ten years, how many notches he would have added to the twenty-one on his Colts.

Billy's real name was William F. Bonney, and, like thousands of other youngsters, he was playing around the streets of New York with wooden guns, imagining he was shooting Indians. One day his father and mother moved West and the very things he had been dreaming came true.

I wouldn't say that Billy was a quicker or straighter shooter than some of the others, like Wild Bill Hickok, but he had perfected himself in all the various lines of gun-fighting further than any other man of his age. It was his ambition to be the most dangerous man in the West, and nobody can deny that that is just what he was.

He was one of the very few men that I ever knew

who could stand at a bar and by looking in the back-bar mirror aim backward over his shoulder and hit his man. I know people have done it in the circus and on the stage, with a mirror attached to the butt of a rifle or shotgun. It is one thing to take your time and aim at a target that won't shoot back, but it's something different to risk your life by firing over your shoulder instead of turning around and making sure.

The Kid did this, not to be smart, but because sometimes he had to, and it gave him the advantage of surprise. A man who was stalking him and who stepped in the saloon door and, seeing Billy at the bar back-to, thought he had plenty of time to come close, take aim and get him right. Billy's two Colts were in plain sight in their two hip holsters, and Billy's hands were nowhere near them.

Unseen by the man who was stalking him, one of Billy's hands would travel up the front of his coat and into a breast pocket, known as the "quick pocket," where a third gun, a derringer, was carried for such emergencies. A half second later the muzzle of this third gun would peep over Billy's shoulder and spit straight-shooting lead into the man who thought he had the Kid where he wanted him.

Another almost impossible hard trick that the Kid did was to shoot with a gun in each hand at two different targets at the sametime and shoot straight. I often practiced two-handed shooting, but I never could do that. Most cowpunchers were pretty quick and accurate, but no marvels. The miner usually wasn't quite as good as the cowboy, but better than the bartender. There wasn't much reason for bartenders to be good with a gun because while they were pulling a cork or starting the bung in a beer barrel, anybody could get the drop on them. The barkeep's real protection came from the other customers, who wouldn't let anybody shoot him because it would mean a needless delay between drinks.

The tin-horn gamblers carried a derringer in a shoulder holster up under their arms. Sitting around a table playing cards, the cowboys and miners had their guns on their belts down below the table. By the time one of them would drop his cards and reach down and bring up his Colts the tin-horn had his derringer out from under his arm and had shot him.

From what I read and hear, the gangsters nowadays, though they live by killing, are not as handy with a gun even as the old-time bartenders. They don't practice enough and they don't have to because the whole scheme of man-killing has changed from duels that were usually pretty fair fights to just plain murders. The idea now is to trick the man into ambush, called "putting him on the spot." The spot is surrounded by enough men with shot guns and machine-guns to throw so much lead that they could hardly miss him with their eyes shut.

There was no machine-gun in Billy's day but when things seemed to call for it, experts like Billy the Kid knew how to turn their six-shooters into a pretty fair imitation of a gangster's sub-machine gun, by a trick that was called "fanning." This wasn't done often because in most fights when the odds were even or anything like even it was not good tactics to fan guns.

But when a gun-fighter found himself in the same

room with a dozen men who wanted to get him and
though he might have the drop on them, might be in-
though he might have the drop on them, they might be
inclined to rush him. That was not fast enough—
nothing would be fast enough except fanning. You
couldn't fan a modern revolver or even one of the old
ones without filing and readjusting the firing mech-
anism so that if the hammer was pulled back even a
short distance and released, it would explode the shell.

The gun-fighter who thought it a good time to
fan a dozen men who were almost on top of him,
held the gun in whichever was his better shooting hand
and swung the muzzle across the crowd as he would
today with a machine-gun, pressing the trigger all the
way back and at the same time, knocking the hammer
back with the palm of the other hand, in a series of
quick blows, that had a sort of fanning motion.

Fanning empties a gun in less than a third of the
time required by ordinary thumb-cocking and firing.
As soon as one gun was empty it would be dropped
and another being fanned in no time. The knowledge
that some of the most famous quick-shooting badmen
could pump a dozen bullets into a posse before they
could cross a room was something to freeze a man
right in his chair.

There were lots of other things to be learned before
a man could call himself really educated in the use of a
gun. It wasn't enough to be able to shoot as well with
one hand as the other. He also had to be able to do
the "border shift" with lightning speed and no fumbling. This was nothing but shifting the gun to the
other hand when the gun hand was wounded.

It was a life-saver in many cases, but not always successful, as was shown in the case of Long-Haired Jim Courtright, who was famous for being quick on the draw. He met Luke Short, who was short in paying a gambling debt to Jim, outside the White Elephant Cafe, at Fort Worth. A bullet from Short's gun shot off Courtright's hammer thumb. Courtright tried the border shift, but before his gun could pass from his right to his left hand he was drilled full of holes. Some that were there and saw it told me that Jim's trouble was that he didn't miss his thumb soon enough, not until he had wiggled the stump a couple of times without getting any action. That may be so. I have been wounded enough times to know that often in the excitement of a fight a man doesn't feel a wound or even know he has been hit until the excitement is over. Sometimes another person has to tell him that he has been plugged.

To tell what Billy the Kid knew about gun-play would be like telling what a college professor knows about his business. Billy's father died early without knowing that his promising son was to become one of the country's most talked about badmen. His widowed mother settled down in Silver City, New Mexico, a right lively mining town where an ambitious boy could learn all about the things that are bad and dangerous to know. And Billy worked hard on getting an education on just two subjects, gunplay and card playing.

By the time he was fourteen years old Billy had practiced so much with his gun that he was itching for an excuse to work on a human target and one day he

found one when a blacksmith bothered his mother.
The blacksmith had been a useful citizen and it was
more than suspected that the botheration hadn't been
very serious, all of which roused popular feeling on
the dead man's side. Billy ran away to Arizona. With
another boy they shot down a couple of unsuspecting
Chiricahua Apache Indians, stole their ponies and their
season's catch of furs, which they sold for enough to
set themselves up in the gambling business.

That blacksmith was No. 1 of the Kid's killings
and he was only fourteen at that time. His first job
was as monte dealer. When a drunken soldier kicked
because he thought Billy was giving him a crooked
deal, the boy shot the trooper. As the dead man was
a United States soldier, this killing was taken seriously
and Billy lit out for Mexico where he cheated, robbed
and killed until that country grew too hot for him and
he found it safer to go back to his native land.

But he always kept up close relations with Mexico.
To help his friend, Segura, the Mexican gambler, out
of jail, Billy swam the Rio Grande on horseback, held
up the jailer and carried his friend back across the
river. Billy was a cattle thief for a while and then decided to do a little honest work as cowpuncher.

In old Lincoln County, New Mexico, where they
had the most bloody of all cattle wars, Billy got a job
with John Tunstall, a rich young Englishman who
had come out to enjoy free life in the big open spaces,
but not no mix up in gun battles. Billy always liked
Tunstall, because he treated him liberally.

The ranch Tunstall leased was claimed by one of
the warring cattlemen and a big posse of expert gun-

men and cattle thieves came to seize it. Tunstall told
his employees with dignity that he had done nothing
unlawful, that they could not touch the cattle and that
he would see a lawyer about it.

"But they are comin' to kill you, you darn fool,"
said Billy.

"Be civil, my man. Remember you are speaking to
your employer," replied Mr. Tunstall, severely.

Tunstall's men persuaded him to move into town,
but he refused to move quickly. A shot through his hat
warned him to get going, but it was too late, his
pursuers surrounded and killed him.

Billy and his friends organized another posse with
the help of a sheriff who saw eye to eye with him, and
they came back and killed all the men who had killed
Tunsall. Billy was known as the most desperate and
successful cattle rustler in the West, and for this reason
was hired to fight in the war in Lincoln County between the McSween-Chisum party and the Murphy
party, each side having a sheriff of its own. Billy
fought for the McSween side, with fifty men, which
included forty Mexicans who were not worth counting
as gun fighters, against a Murphy army of sixty first-
class gunmen. After a few killings Governor Axtell
ordered the Mexican aliens with the McSween outfit
to quit the country, leaving Billy with only ten men
against Murphy's sixty.

Billy held out in McSween's adobe house. Under
cover of darkness the Murphy men threw bombs and
set the roof on fire. There was nothing to do but
rush out in the daylight. Old Mr. McSween, a religious
man, walked out, Bible in hand and a prayer on his

lips, but neither did him any good. He and six of his outfit were pumped full of bullets.

Billy's policy was different. He came out swearing and shooting with both hands. He dropped Murphy men all around and, finally, as if by a miracle, fought his way through to safety without a scratch. Only one other, a Mexican named Salazar, who shammed death, escaped. It was not really a miracle so much as it was that it is hard to hit a smart gun-fighter, because you don't dare to take time to aim at him for fear he will plug you first.

Like many another thief and murderer, the Kid was generous with other people's money and property, kind to dumb animals, and would weep tears over sentimental songs.

My friend, General Lew Wallace, was appointed Governor of New Mexico to replace Axtell, the no-good Murphy partisan. The new Governor called on all warring cattlemen to lay down their arms. The Kid left for a distant part of New Mexico and the Governor sent word for him to come and see him. The General invited me and another scout to come in and act as witnesses while the Kid was talking. The old General called out pleasantly:

"You need not be afraid of me, Billy. Come in."

"And what's more important, you needn't be afraid of me, General," blustered the badman as he swaggered in.

Billy had been hired by the cattlemen of Lincoln County to kill off the "snoozers," as the sheep men were called. The cattlemen didn't like the sheep men, who came West later, because they believed what has been recently proved true, that sheep crop the grass so close that in no time they turn the grazing lands to deserts.

They had sent Billy to argue with them in the only effective way they knew, with bullets. Billy had been doing his work too quickly and thoroughly, so the General, as Governor, had sent for the outlaw to ask him to stop. Before they got down to business Billy mentioned that he was broke and hoped the General wouldn't be annoyed if he held up a few people that evening. General Wallace promptly "lent" him $40.

Billy said he couldn't go back on his friends, the cattlemen, and said he could see the Governor's predicament, because the law-abiding citizens were prodding Wallace to do something. Billy agreed to let himself be arrested for the killing of "Buckshot Roberts." By the time of the trial he figured some other excitement would be filling the public mind. If by any accident he happened to be convicted, which wasn't likely, the Governor was to pardon him. It has been said that Governor Wallace did not keep his promise to Billy, but there had been so many complications and aggravations that he can hardly be blamed.

The Kid went to jail, but soon got tired of the confinement and he resented their distrust in refusing to let him have a gun for his usual daily practice. As the jailors understood that it was a friendly sort of murder trial and didn't really mean anything, he does not seem to have been carefully guarded. One day he just walked out and started robbing and killing again.

During the 80's, the leading citizens of Lincoln County, that is the honest ones and there was a considerable number by this time, thought they had seen about enough of the Kid's killing, robbing and terrorizing. Constable Longworth, a nervy fighter, was outfitted with a posse of forty men and finally surrounded the lone bandit in a house at White Oaks. The constable told Billy that the odds against him were 41 to 1, and since resistance was hopeless, he might as well give himself up peacefully. The Kid's reply was to dash out at them with guns blazing. Once more he shot his way through to freedom, unhurt and killing six men of the posse. This setback made the forces of law and order all the more keen to get Billy.

All the fighting cowboys along the Canadian River were enlisted for the duration of this war to wipe out Billy the Kid. With a bunch of these fighters Sheriff Pat Garrett laid an ambush near Fort Sumner, where he expected Billy to visit a Mexican woman. After dark they saw a shadowy form sneaking up to the Mexican woman's house and they pumped the shadow full of lead. But it was only a small-time murderer, one of Billy's pals. At the last minute Billy had gone back for his tobacco.

In my scouting days, I noticed how often lack of tobacco will make men turn back when nothing else will. I have been in expeditions where our coffee, sugar, salt, liquor, flour and most all other necessities and comforts were lost in some river but as long as we had tobacco we would go on. Whenever an expedition lost its tobacco, it usually stopped right there until some one rode all the way back for a new supply. In those days most people smoked a pipe or chewed, which was considered respectable and even good enough manners. Wealthy and toney people prided themselves on a handsome, big, brass cuspidor or "goboon" in the parlor. People who were not so fancy used to spit tidily in the corners of the room. In barrooms they would aim at knotholes in the floor with great accuracy.

Garrett, one of the most persistent law officers the West ever produced, now dogged the bandit without let-up. At last the Kid saw that he was certain to be caught and with three others gave himself up. Taken to the jail at Las Vegas the citizens insisted that the only practical way to get rid of this mad dog was to lynch him. It would certainly have saved a lot of trouble, but the sheriff and his posse were against a necktie party and got him safely to Santa Fé. He was later tried for the murder of Sheriff William Brady, convicted and sentenced to be hanged. The Kid had it in for Brady and hid behind a wall and as the sheriff walked by had shot him and helped himself to the murdered man's pistols and rifle.

The sentence didn't bother Billy at first because the original "gentleman's agreement" between Governor Wallace and the badman had been that if he was to be tried and if convicted, to be pardoned. But now when the date for execution drew near and no sign of a pardon, he complained bitterly. Billy forgot that the deal was over another murder, and that he had broken his part of the agreement by escaping from jail and building up a new record of murders against himself. Public opinion was so strong that General Wallace would hardly have dared to let this killer free, if he had wanted to.

Billy didn't really believe that they were so mean as to intend to hang him in cold blood until one day Sheriff Garrett rode away to White Oaks to order the lumber for the gallows. The Kid decided to free himself and no time could be better than that very day, with the sheriff absent.

The little jail had not been safe enough to hold Billy so they had him locked up in a big room on the second floor of the courthouse at Lincoln since the trial. Here two deputies, J. W. Bell and Robert Ollinger, were appointed to watch him day and night. Also his hands were handcuffed and a heavy pair of leg irons made walking slow and clumsy and running was impossible.

Bell and the prisoner were friendly enough but Ollinger and the Kid hated each other like poison. This was because Billy had murdered a couple of Ollinger's best friends and the deputy kept telling the condemned man that he was going to swing for it.

At noon Ollinger went across the street for a bite of lunch, leaving Bell playing cards with the murderer. The Kid accidentally on purpose, dropped a card from one of his manacled hands and Bell, in a fatal moment of carelessness, stooped to pick it up. The outlaw leaned over the table and snatched the gun from Bell's holster, shoved it in his face and forced him to march ahead of him to the armory, a room near the one he was confined in. He liked Bell and had no special yearning to kill him for he had been kind to him but when Bell made a break for the rear stairs, Billy shot him dead with the deputy's own revolver.

Ollinger, hearing the shot from across the street, ran

around to the back of the courthouse with a cocked six-shooter in each hand. He heard a voice from an upper window call sweetly:

"Hey! Ollinger."

Ollinger looked up to see his own double-barreled shotgun, loaded with buckshot, pointed straight at him with the outlaw's finger on the trigger. Billy had slipped his small hands from the handcuffs and held the shotgun in both hands.

The gun roared, and Ollinger slumped to the ground, a charge of buckshot in his breast. As he lay there the Kid stepped out on the balcony and fired the other barrel into the deputy's already lifeless body.

He then forced the jail cook to catch and saddle the black horse of Billy Burt, the county clerk, for him, then galloped away to the west. The nervy young killer of twenty-one years and twenty-one notches on his gun had cheated the gallows—but his end was not far off.

The sheriff grimly finished his gallows and said it would stand until Billy danced from it at the end of a rope. When Billy clanked down the courthouse stairs and clattered out of town riding side-saddle like a society lady, he wore leg irons that had been riveted on over the top of his boots without any key. The sheriff had explained to the blacksmith:

"I don't figure to take them off 'till after the hangin' so we don't need no key."

Billy the Kid galloped out of town and across country until he reached the ranch of Octaviano Salas, who knew him well enough not to be surprised at seeing him out of jail. His son, Ladislao Salas, of Lincoln, who recently traded Billy's leg-irons for a 48-pound sack of flour, tells what happened:

"I remember it so plainly because the Kid was riding with both legs on the same side of the horse. When he came close we could see that around each ankle was an iron band and that a chain connected the bands.

"I was only a boy of seven years then, but I had heard a lot of talk about the famous outlaw, and my father knew him well, as did most of the people who lived in the village of Lincoln and on the ranches and little farms here in the valley of Rio Bonito.

"Of course we didn't know that Billy had just shot his two guards to death at Lincoln. In those days news traveled more slowly than now with the radio and the telephone. But we did know that Billy had been convicted of murder and was being held in the courthouse until the day of his execution, which was near.

"We could see that Billy was in a big hurry as he rode across the wheat field, his horse's hoofs trampling the tender growth. My father was working out in the field and Billy rode up to him. They came to the house together, my father walking by the side of the black horse.

"Billy asked father to help him take off the leg-irons, and father did so. The irons were made large to go around the entire bootleg so that it would be impossible without the aid of a knife to remove the boots.

"But with the boot tops cut away it was easy to take off the boots, then slip Billy's feet out of the irons. And he still had a pair of boots to wear, without much top, to be sure, but still better than nothing.

"Billy told my father he was very hungry, so father gave him some frijoles and tortillas and coffee. When Billy had gulped down his fill he mounted the black horse and rode rapidly away to the west toward Capitan Mountain."

The sheriff had his job to do all over again. He raised another army of cowboys and started out after him. One of the clues he found was the following, written with the lead of a bullet on the wall of a shack he slept in one night:

"There are twenty-one men I
have put bullets through
And Sheriff Pat Garrett shall
make twenty-two."

But a woman betrayed Billy's last hide-out and the sheriff was soon on his trail.

A cocked revolver in one hand and a knife in the other, and in his stocking feet, Billy sneaked at night into a house where Sheriff Garrett happened to be watching. The sheriff had an idea that the bandit would do that very thing, and as the shadow crept toward the only lighted room, Garrett's gun roared from the darkness and Billy the Kid's career was over. Strangely enough, he had not died with his boots on, as everybody figured he would.

Pat Garrett told me how he got Billy. He had a tip that the Kid was hiding somewhere in a town called Fort Sumner—used to be a fort. Billy should have lit out across the border into Mexico, but there was a girl living at Fort Sumner he was sweet on.

"On the night of July 12, 1881, I got to Pete Maxwell's ranch at Fort Sumner," Garrett said: "I left my two deputies outside the ranch-house and went in to see Maxwell, whom I knew well. Peter was lying in bed in a corner. I put my Winchester against the wall and sat down on the bed to talk with him. I told him I had heard that Bill had been seen around there. He swore he hadn't seen him. I knew by his manner that he wasn't telling the truth, and while we were sitting there, Billy came in.

"He had gone across the road, I learned afterward, and ordered a Mexican woman there to get up and make him some coffee. Billy had lots of friends there; thought he was quite a hero. When he came back to the ranch-house he saw my two men and spoke to them in Spanish. They made no answer and he darted into the house and upstairs in his stocking feet. My face was in the shadow when he appeared in the doorway, and he darted over to me with his knife in one hand and his gun in the other. He had his gun within a foot of me when he laid his hand on my knee and demanded, 'Who are you?'

"He sprang back instantly and fired. But I had fired first and the ball went through his heart. I fired a second time but the bullet went over him. He had fallen—dead."

Billy the Kid had a right to his reputation as a quick shooter and all-around badmen. But some frontiersmen of the old days got famous for things they never did at all. Probably the queerest case of this kind was Deadwood Dick. When the old dime novels were being read by everybody they fastened on Deadwood Dick for a hero, and had him doing things he never heard of.

I knew Deadwood Dick mighty well for years. We were army scouts trailing together, rounding up Indians who were on the warpath. He was as brave a man as ever lived and he sure had all kinds of experiences on the frontier. He was a Pony Express Rider, he had fought Indians, was a scout and a guide, and had been sworn in by United States Marshals on many a posse that tackled badmen and stage robbers. He rode as guard on stagecoaches that carried gold bullion out of the Black Hills—and this was just about the riskiest job a man could have. He sat up on the seat with the driver, a fine target. And he never knew whether he was going to face robbers or redskins around the next curve in the road.

In those paper-cover novels Deadwood Dick was always a hero, fighting off road-agents, upsetting avengers, interfering with cutthroat badmen and rescuing the pretty girl just at the right moment. Well, I'll tell you about a real case where Deadwood Dick and I went out to trail a stagecoach robber and did save a pretty girl from the outlaw's clutches.

But Deadwood Dick never had anything like those wild experiences the dime novel writers pinned to his name. He and I laughed about those hero stories lot of times. Deadwood Dick's name was Richard W. Clarke, and after many years of rough frontier life he settled down in Deadwood, South Dakota, and died of cancer a few years ago.

Dick and I were together on the last scouting job he ever did. We were in Fort Dodge, Kansas Territory, and the Kiowas and Comanches under Chief Santana and Lone Wolf had been raiding, murdering and scalping at Summit Springs. While we were at dinner one day a couple of scouts rode in with a wounded companion. They had had a brush with a party of redskins who were on the warpath, and General Miles, with with General Carr was in command, ordered out the troops. The cavalry and a pack-train took the field at once and we scouts set out in advance. Bat Masterson was in my scout party.

At Sycamore Springs, on the Kansas line, we met up with Billy Dixon. He said that the situation was pretty bad and wanted to know if there were troops following us. We camped at Sycamore that night. Here our little advance party of scouts was joined by ten more scouts. General Miles had hurried forward. With these scouts were four of the Ross boys who had lost horses and cattle in the Indian raid, so that by the time we left Sycamore our party numbered about fifty men, all well armed. At the Texas line we met a company of Texas Rangers.

We reached Adobe Walls, which at that time was on the Texas-Indian Territory line. About a hundred Kiowa and Comanche Indians tried to surround us and that afternoon a stiff battle was on. Deadwood Dick was badly wounded by a shot through the hip early in the fight. He was carried to the shade of the Walls and looked after while the rest of us fixed up to hold off the attack until the troops reached us.

The inside of Adobe Walls was loop-holed and this gave us pretty good defense, but in spite of that the battle lasted nearly two hours of steady shooting.

One of the Ross boys was badly wounded but no other casualties. And Billy Dixon said he thought we had the Indians on the run. Rifle fire stopped about an hour before sundown. We went outside the Walls and counted the dead. Our accurate shooting stood us well for we counted thirty-five Indians stretched out on the sod dead and we knew that for the time being at least we had gained a victory over Santana and Lone Wolf.

The troops arrived next day under Generals Miles and Carr and a detachment was sent out to pursue the Indians. General Miles congratulated us on our success in standing off the redskins.

Deadwood Dick was taken in an ambulance to the field hospital and cared for. The next morning I rode over to see my friend, and in spite of his wound he lay there smiling cheerfully. But he said he was done fighting Indians and was going back to Deadwood and settle down. He kept his word and settled down to more peaceful work.

And after a while a queer thing happened. Reports began to come in that Deadwood Dick was robbing stagecoaches—instead of guard of the stages, he had turned robber. These rumors annoyed Dick and made his old friends sore. I was stationed over at Fort Meade and used to ride in on horseback every day to get the mail for the post.

One day as I was getting the mail bag, Deadwood Dick rode by with his fishing tackle and told me he was going to a little settlement called Spearfish, about eighteen miles above Deadwood. I said I would join him if I could get a couple of days off, so after delivering the mail at the army post, I rode over to Spearfish and stopped at a house run by a woman who called herself Missouri Nellie, a friend of Deadwood Dick.

News came in unexpectedly while I was at dinner, brought by a lone Indian from the Sioux Reservation, by the name of Whistling Elk, that the Cheyenne-Deadwood stagecoach had been held up and the driver had been killed. Whistling Elk did not say much that would give added information, as he was in a hurry, but he did say that he heard the robber was Deadwood Dick.

I fed and watered the Indian's horse and gave him some tobacco and coffee. I wanted to have him help me trail the bogus Deadwood Dick. Whistling Elk said he could get another Sioux scout, Running Eagle, to help me. He sent word through that mysterious grapevine telegraph and Running Eagle came in with the report he had met a tough hombre who was awful drunk and who had talked bad. Running Eagle said he had left the man on the high lope with the paleface shooting many bullets after him. Running Eagle's wife arrived later with the camp outfit, and they made camp back of Nellie's place on the creek.

About eight that night in popped Deadwood Dick and I told him it was said that he had held up the coach and got away with a pile of money. I waved him down with a gesture to keep quiet and to let me do the talking. But my talk was interrupted by the arrival of the sheriff and his posse. He said he was trailing a very suspicious character and he would like to get some information concerning a bandit. He asked if Deadwood Dick was there. Dick smiled and stood up with his pockets turned inside out. The contents he had dumped on the table, tobacco, pipe and matches with a lone silver dollar. This Deadwood Dick did not seem at all uneasy when the sheriff interviewed him concerning the stagecoach robbery. After the sheriff and his men had gone Dick laid plans to capture his namesake.

Dick said he thought he could capture him alone but he'd not take any chances. He had a confab with Running Eagle and Whistling Elk and they worked out the plans to round up the bandit.

Dick said that very likely we would have to bring him back dead. He asked if I would ride over and see my commanding officer at the post and try to get leave of absence until this renegade was caught or killed. This I did and joined Deadwood Dick and the Indian scouts fully equipped for anything we might have to tackle. I also dug up a pair of handcuffs and leg-irons that might prove handy if we decided to bring the outlaw back alive.

We were finishing an early breakfast when another Indian scout came in from up at the head of the Hot Springs country with word that the outlaw was there in camp and that he had kidnaped a white woman and was holding her captive. That news started us off pronto.

We were in the neighborhood of the springs about noon. Suddenly I smelled the smoke from a campfire and I knew we were nearing the place where we would find what we were after. We halted. Dick and I got off our horses and turned over the saddle-horses and the pack animals to the Indians to be taken care of. We separated, each going in a different direction in order to move in on the outlaw and surprise him.

I was the first to drop into the creek. As I did I saw a fine-looking young girl with a bucket dipping up water from the stream. I knew from Running Eagle's description who she was.

I walked up to her with my six-shooter drawn and told her not to make a sound. She set the bucket down and raised both hands while I bent over and whispered to her, asking her where the outlaw was. She pointed cautiously ahead of me and pulled her hands down and I put my finger to my lips for silence. Then she threw her arms around me and grasped me tight as she whispered I had saved her life.

She opened the back of her dress and showed me the bruises across her shoulders—cruel cuts and welts that had been made by a whip. I pulled her dress close across her back and told her to keep quiet and we'd take care of the outlaw.

As I rounded the bend in the creek, I heard loud voices. Deadwood Dick in a firm command was telling someone to surrender. And an ugly voice yelled back, "Never!" And then I heard a shot and saw the gun smoking in the outlaw's hand. His bullet missed. Deadwood Dick made a move for his gun but before he could raise it, two shots rang out quickly from Running Eagle's rifle and those bullets put an end to the question of surrender and to the career of the bogus Deadwood Dick.

I brought the girl around to Dick and told him about her ill-treatment. He looked at the outlaw and as he lay dying, he asked him if he had anything to say. Before the man could speak, he died. And as he breathed his last, the girl reeled and fainted. We examined her for injuries and removed some of her clothes, bathed and dressed her wounds to ease up her pain. She told us the money from the stagecoach robbery was safe in the saddlebags of the outlaw, and so it was.

We searched for identification of the dead outlaw, but found nothing to prove who he really was. There was a reward notice in his vest pocket that had a photograph—a close likeness to this man—but the paper was so badly wrinkled and bloodstained that we could not make it all out, but we saved the paper for further study.

After the young woman had been somewhat restored from her experience, she told me who she was. She was a Miss Ruth McDaniel, of Farransdale, Connecticut, her home. She had come out into the West from Pennsylvania, where she had been teaching school, and had been on her way to Oregon when she was taken from the stagecoach by the outlaw. She was on her way to meet her brother in Oregon where they planned to homestead.

I sent Running Eagle back to Spearfish for extra horses and some fresh clothing for the girl. Also sent word to Missouri Nellie to come back with the scout with some food that could be fixed up hot for the girl.

The relief party arrived in camp about five o'clock that evening and we soon had a cheerful fire blazing and Nellie was busy making some hot soup for the girl. She was resting quietly and we were counting the money from the robbery. We found it was all there. We buried the outlaw where he fell and put up a wooden cross, saying that Person Unknown died and was buried on that spot by unknown parties.

Then we built up a rousing big fire, which Running Eagle said would drive the evil spirits from the Hot Springs. Deadwood Dick felt well satisfied at the result of our trailing this bandit, who had been doing him and his name harm, for it was the same man who had been passing as Deadwood Dick and who had held up the stagecoach the day before.

Dick did a good deal of prospecting but never struck anything very rich. For a while he carried letters at $1 each from Pierre to Deadwood. Letters addressed to persons who had stopped a bullet and had been buried in Boot Hill before the letters arrived, were sold to the highest bidder at an auction.

Dick was a picture with his long curls, his boots, buckskin clothes and his .45 Colts hanging at his right hand. But that gun had no notches in it. Dick always said he had never killed a white man and an Indian didn't amount to enough to bother to cut a notch for.

Deadwood Dick is buried in a grave cut out of the rock on Sunrise Mountain, across the valley from Mount Moriah where so many famous pioneers rest. His friends put up a little monument over his grave.

From many of the stories written about the Western badmen you get the notion that they lived romantic, almost heroic lives. The truth is that in spite of their daring and skill they lived mostly short, worried and wretched ones. Those that escaped the bullet and the gallows usually became miserable drink-beggars in the same saloons where they once were terrors.

I remember one of these poor old wrecks who used

to win quite a few drinks by writing with chalk on
the floor or the bar these very lines:

"A beggar'd be bandit, if only he dared.
And bandit turns beggar as soon as he's scared."

CHAPTER VIII

Horse Thieves and Cattle Rustlers

AT THE TIME I remember it, Alder Gulch was just as wild as Tombstone or Deadwood ever was. It was one of the toughest towns in the West. Alder Gulch was in Montana and at the top of its mining boom 21,000 men lived and loved and fought and killed one another there. The many dance halls, barrooms and wicked resorts were never closed night or day or Sunday and were always full. Miners came in, got roaring drunk and played with sacks of gold dust which the tin-horn crooked gamblers got away from them pronto, and then staggered back to their camp to dig out more.

The town of Bannack was the nearest real town,
75 miles away from Alder Creek, and Bannack had
a sheriff. But he didn't stay in office long, because a
tough hombre of a very different stripe soon arrived—
smiling, popular, highly thought of at first, and he
got himself elected sheriff. But he was a killer at heart
and a desperate gambler. This was Henry Plummer, a
peace officer in daytime and a bandit, thief and murderer at night.

Nobody knows where Henry Plummer came from,
nor his real name, but handwriting sharps who have
studied his neat signatures after he became sheriff, agree
that it was a new name he had just taken on. Nobody asked strangers about their past, or if they did,
it was taken as a sign that they were so drunk that their
friends usually dragged them with their darned fool
questions away to sleep it off before the shooting had
time to start.

Everybody took to Plummer right away. He was
an educated man who could not only read and write
but used long words which most of us didn't understand. Even the ministers used to be knocked out and
have to agree with him when he threw a word of Greek
or Latin at them.

In those rough, tough days most everyone but a
blanket Indian thought that what the West needed
most was something we called "culture" and they
looked up to any man or woman who seemed to have
a little of it. As soon as the man got rich, he bought
a grand piano, that nobody in the family could play
and a lot of books that perhaps nobody could read.
Most of the sheriffs in those days couldn't read the

"Reward Offered" posters tacked up in their offices.

As quick as a little mushroom, the mining camp had set up saloons, gambling joints and dance halls. There was talk of an "opery house," where some day they hoped to hear grand opera singers sing opera in a grand foreign language that nobody could understand.

Now this newcomer Plummer seemed to be just full of what we were all looking for. He had fine clothes and smooth manners that made honest, rough men kind of ashamed of themselves and the women thought he was wonderful. Women were scarce but they were powerful friends. Bannack was proud that this culture hombre had honored them by coming there.

Plummer was a gambler, but that was nothing against him because gambling was a respected profession in those days, like being a doctor, or lawyer or real estate man, that is, if people believed he was an honest gambler. They used to say that some of those gamblers were straight and maybe they were. The crazy way those fool miners used to bet their gold dust, a gambler didn't have to cheat to win. But Plummer's gambling was only a blind to cover his real business of being a bandit.

The only people who were worried about this new leader who talked about "suppressing the ruffians" were the gangsters, but they soon found out that he was one himself. Before long, Plummer formed a gang of his own called the "Innocents" because so many of them were hardly more than boys. Of course he kept his bandit connections in the background as long as he could.

Bannack already had one sheriff, its first, named

Crawford, honest enough but not too active, probably because he knew that active sheriffs soon landed in Boot Hill Cemetery. But little as he did, it was too much to suit Plummer. At first, Crawford couldn't figure out why this smooth stranger was always going around finding fault with him among the honest citizens, but one day he suspected the reason and accused Plummer of being a crook on the side.

The answer was a bullet. When the two had emptied their guns, each had a slight wound but the feeling was all against the sheriff. He might have killed their culture man. So Crawford gave up his job and Plummer was elected sheriff in his place. Just as he was elected, Henry married the prettiest woman in town and went on a honeymoon. Before leaving, he appointed four deputies, and one of them was G. H. Dillingham, an honest supporter of law and order. But the other three appointments kind of surprised everyone because they were three well-known badmen.

It was a long honeymoon, and good people prayed for the new sheriff's return to put down the worst outbreak of crime they had ever known. When he did come back things became worse. Dillingham, the honest deputy, overheard the others planning to rob a storekeeper named Dodge and warned the man. For doing this, Dillingham was shot down by Hayes Lyons, one of Plummer's "Innocents."

Henry made a great show of arresting his own gangster but let the jury know that if they didn't turn him loose there would be new graves up on Boot Hill. They took the hint.

In the day-time Plummer was mostly on the job,

as sheriff and good citizen of Bannack, but it was noticed that he yawned a lot and was often taking a nap when people called. He explained this truthfully by saying that he was doing considerable secret work but he didn't say that he worked nights as head of the "Innocents." This band grew to be one of the biggest and best organized of all the robber outfits in the West. Besides the bunch of gunmen who did the robbing, he had spies at Alder Gulch and other mining camps and even drivers of some of the stagecoaches were in his pay.

As soon as anyone struck it rich the news was rushed to Plummer. He ordered other spies to inform the outfit when the next big shipment of gold dust and nuggets would be sent to town. A dozen coaches would rattle to Bannack or Virginia City safely as long as no gold was on board, but as sure as there was a fair-sized shipment, it would be robbed on the way. The miners and the express people tried secrecy and every trick they could think of. They would let everybody know that they were shipping a lot of dust and then not do it but nothing would happen. Maybe next day at the last minute, they would shove the treasure onto the coach, only to have the bandits know somehow and hold up the stage.

It was found later on that the driver or his "shotgun" (assistant who rode along as guard) would tip the bandits off that he was carrying gold by giving signals, such as removing his hat and mopping his forehead at the top of a certain hill. It was noticed that one driver had a habit of singing when he got to one particular gulch and the next time he was ordered not to do it. This was unfortunate because the bandits had just changed their system and had told him to keep quiet if he was carrying anything worth robbing.

Misunderstanding his silence, the bandits stuck up the coach and finding nothing worth having, they were sore and they beat up everybody, including the driver who had no chance to explain. Things finally got so bad that miners were trying to find some other way to ship gold out of the mining camps.

People began to think that Plummer was too refined a man to make a good sheriff, but it took some time for them to find out that he was in cahoots with the outlaws. In the meanwhile he got away with at least three murders, the first was his pretty wife that he beat to death, either from jealousy or because she knew too much. Right after that he killed his old friend George Cleveland, but was not questioned on either case. A little later the sheriff and three of his gang shot up a Bannack Indian camp, killing half a dozen people.

For this he was questioned but explained that he had left town on account of hard feelings over the Cleveland killing and happened to ride along with the other three men without knowing what they had been up to. The explanation was accepted and he saw to it that his three gangsters were set free after their trial.

About this time honest people began to suspect what was going on and whisper it to each other, but to openly accuse Plummer of being a bandit leader was about the same as suicide. The "Innocents" got so bold that they worked in what was really a sort of uniform. Besides a special kind of mask, Plummer's men always wore a handkerchief tied at their throat in a sailor's knot, with the ends at an angle, that became famous as the "road agents' knot."

Charley Reeves, Bill Moore, Bill Mitchell, George Ives and Frank Parrish were among the older men of the gang. Most of them had heavy beards, but Plummer himself wore only a mustache and some of the others were just boys. Everyone, young or old, carried a double-barreled shot gun, two Colts and a long-bladed Bowie knife, named after Col. James Bowie, who died at the Alamo with one of them in his hand. The shotguns and revolvers used the old cup-shaped percussion caps. Many of the men had a derringer tucked away in pockets or under armpits.

Sheriff Plummer's spies warned him that everybody was onto him but he didn't see much to worry about. The gunmen, with all the other crooks and gamblers, were with him while the honest folks were so scared that nobody dared to talk about electing another sheriff. Folks got used to having the coaches robbed right along and if Henry and his "Innocents" had stuck to that line they might have lasted a lot longer than they did. It was some of their other doings like the Lloyd Magruder murder that at last stirred up the people.

Magruder was a store-keeper of Bannack who decided to retire, not because he was so old or sick, but because he was tired of trying to do business where a robber and murderer was running the law. Selling his store he set out with quite a bunch of money, a herd of cattle and other belongings for his home town of

Lewiston, Idaho. Four friends went along with him as a sort of guard to protect him on the journey.

In Sheriff Plummer's outfit were four men who also had been figuring on retiring and this gave them an idea. Toward noon of the first day out, four armed men overtook the Magruder party, telling that Sheriff Plummer had sent them as a guard because he had just heard that some badmen were aiming to make a stick-up. Magruder should have turned back, even if he had to shoot it out with the sheriff's men. But he went on to his death.

At Lolo Pass in the Bitter Root country, Plummer's men murdered the others in their sleep and threw their bodies in a ravine, with such of the livestock and other property as they didn't want. With the rest they headed for the Pacific Coast and meant to take a steamer for the East where nobody would know how they got their money.

But Hill Bachey, Deputy Marshal of Lewiston, was an old friend of Magruder and the murder made him boil over. He began to call on every honest man, prosperous enough to feel he had a stake in the country and ask whether he wanted to be murdered or do something about it.

Quietly they enlisted a bunch of Vigilantes. These gained in numbers and Plummer must have known something about them, but, since they didn't do anything at first, he went on, bolder than ever, actually being recognized in a badly-planned attempt to rob a man named Hauser. Nothing happened because the Vigilantes were not quite ready.

A German boy, named Nicolas Thiebaut, driving

a pack of mules between Alder Gulch and Bannack, was asked to deliver $200 in money, because the coach wasn't safe. When his body, without the mules or cash, was found, it was the last straw. The Vigilantes made their first move, trying what could be done lawfully. William Saunders, a young lawyer from the East, turned up in town, some say accidentally, and some say he was brought in by the Vigilantes who were soon also to be known as the "Stranglers." At the trial he ran the prosecution with a snap in the courts of Montana that had never been seen before.

Plummer and his bunch did some extra fancy work in the way of frightening witnesses and muddling up the testimony, so that one after another of the band got away but at last the guilt for the murder of the German boy was fastened on George Ives. Lawyer Saunders' life was in danger every minute, but in the courtroom and out he was surrounded by a body of stern-faced men, with guns eased in their holsters and eyes fastened on any badman in sight. The jury got the usual threats but it had heard from the Vigilantes, too, and some were members. So Ives was convicted.

Plummer likely would have fixed things so his man would break jail, that night or the next, but the "Stranglers" gave him no chance. They took Ives out of jail and hanged him, then and there.

Everyone could see that such long and expensive trials would never wipe out the gangs so the idea was given up. Instead of bothering with courts and lawyers the Vigilantes visited the various hiding places of the gang members and hanged them to the nearest tree. Most generally they would stand them on a box, pull

the noose tight and then kick the box out from under
their feet. The first few whose necks were stretched
had nothing to say, but Red Yaeger, speaking through
his hemp necktie, surprised them by saying that his
chief was Sheriff Henry Plummer.

This was so interesting to the Vigilantes that the
noose was removed and Red was invited to sit down
comfortable-like and talk some more. He did, naming
everybody in the "Innocents," giving their pass-word
and all sorts of other inside information. When he
couldn't think of any more to tell them they stood him
up on the box and finished the hanging. But he had
delayed things long enough to have the pleasure of seeing them bring in one of the men he had named, "Bald-
headed Brown," to swing with him.

By this time Plummer was good and scared and
made his plans to leave town, but he was greedy to take
along with him as much of his plunder as possible. So
he put off leaving just one day too long. He had got
most all of his gangsters together into a sort of camp
ready to shoot it out with the Vigilantes, but since he
still pretended to be an honest sheriff, he could not
very well be with them.

There was something of a rebellion in the camp because he had just built a scaffold, where for appearance's sake he was aiming to hang an unimportant
member of the gang. Some thought that wasn't right.

It was a peaceful Sunday afternoon in December,
when the Vigilantes came for Sheriff Plummer. You
would hardly expect a man with so much on his mind
to be taking a nap, in his sister-in-law's home. But
there he was and without his guns when he was waken-

ed by the tramp of many feet in the hall. The Sheriff
jumped up and was feeling for his Colts when masked
men burst into the room.

With scarcely a word, they marched Plummer down
to the gallows he had built for a less important murderer. At sight of the noose swaying in the cold wind,
he dropped on his knees in the snow, whimpering and
begging for mercy and a fair trial. Knowing that a
small army of bandits was in camp only a few miles
away, the Vigilantes wasted no time. Reading the
sentence they had privately imposed on him, they
rushed Henry onto the platform and in three minutes
he had given his last kick.

At the same time that Plummer was getting attention his two most daring and cruel lieutenants, Ned
Ray and Bill Stinson, had been surprised and caught
by the Vigilantes. But they were no cowards. They
fought and cursed to the last. They were still cursing
when their bodies were yanked dangling into the air.

Dutch John Wagner, the slickest member of the
gang, was not easy to take, but the Vigilantes got him
in time, and he was hanged with a little extra speed.
Joe Pizanthis, a Mexican, was still harder to catch
and he shot one Vigilante and wounded another during the pursuit, but he soon danced on the air.

Jack Gallagher, Hayes Lyons, Frank Parrish, Club-
foot Lane, Boone Helm, all tough members of the
outfit, were run down and hanged. The Plummer gang
was at last wiped out. Other gangs beat it out of the
state and the Vigilantes were glad to get back to their
regular work, leaving the protection of life and property to a new and honest set of law officers.

So that was the end of Henry Plummer and **his** nervy scheme to get himself made sheriff so he **could** run his outfit of robbers, hold-up men and murderers without any worry of being caught by law officers.

Many of these things I have told of Henry Plummer are told in a whole lot more detail by Hoffman Birney in his book, "Vigilantes," printed by the Penn Publishing Co., Philadelphia. It makes interesting reading.

There was another man who was just about as lawless who worked a different scheme. He set himself up as a Judge and he did his hold-ups and robbery tricks right there while he was holding court.

This man was a friend of mine, Judge Roy Bean, of Langtry, Texas. He hung a sign out over his saloon marked, "The Law West of the Pecos." This was an area of land about the size of England and though he was really only a Justice of the Peace he took on all the duties and powers of a judge, jury, governor, sheriff, coroner and everything else. Judge Bean did so so many funny things that nobody knows all his doings, but Everett Lloyd wrote a book about them and the State of Texas is keeping his old saloon as a museum relic.

Roy Bean is supposed to have come from Kentucky, and after wandering around the West, turned up in San Antonio, Texas. He left San Antonio about the time the Southern Pacific Railroad track crews began laying rails West. He had a sort of traveling saloon and commissary, and moved from point to point wherever the crew camped. One camp was at Vinegaroon, just west of the Pecos River. Then he moved his saloon to Miles Canyon, and after that he set himself up in the town called Langtry, and that's where he became famous.

Bean was chosen by the ranchmen who figured he had all the necessary qualifications for a judge. He owned a saloon which made a good courtroom; he was a squatter on railroad property and he owned one law book. Judge Bean could read if nobody hurried him, but he was such a poor hand at writing that he had to have someone make out his legal documents for him. He didn't need that old law book because he made up his law out of his head, to suit any case that came before him.

But Judge Bean had one advantage over all other judges, high or low, that I ever knew or heard of. When he sentenced a man to be hanged, he knew just how the poor devil was going to feel, because he himself had once been hanged, in California, and cut down, just in time, by his Mexican sweetheart. A poet of the Wild West wrote this jingle about the Hon. Roy Bean:

> "Judge Roy Bean of Vinegaroon
> Held high court in his own saloon,
> Fer killin' or thievin' or other sech fracas,
> Bean was the law out West of the Pecos,
> Set on a keg and 'lowin' no foolin'
> Closed ev'ry case with, 'that's my rulin'!'"

That's pretty good poetry; words everybody can understand and hit the nail right on the head. Nothing fancy, but true, every word of it.

A vinegaroon is a small scorpion and its poison has

a sour smell like vinegar. Some people thought lots of
Judge Bean's decisions were pretty sour, but they suited
the ranchers because he was death on the horse thieves
and rustlers. His election was confirmed by appointment from the right Texas authorities of the other
side of the Pecos, but it was only as Justice of the
Peace, and that job has mighty little authority. But
Mr. Justice Roy Bean never hesitated to try any sort
of case. When he sentenced a man to be hanged, the
job was done right then and there. He never allowed
any appeal to a higher court because he did not admit
that there was such a thing. "And, anyway, what do
those city fellers know about it?" he asked. "They
might reverse me."

Judge Bean heard that judges are not supposed to
make laws, only to interpret them. He was the most
famous interpreter the West ever knew.

According to the law it was just as much murder to
kill a Mexican or Chinaman as an American-born
white, so the Judge's only law book, *The Revised
Statutes of Texas*, said nothing about race or color.
Soon after Bean got his appointment, a white man
killed one of the Chinese cooks, working for the railroad construction gangs. Chinese were plentiful and
considered heathens of less value than a good burro.
This case hardly seemed worth the trouble, but Judge
Bean would always try any case brought before him.

When the prisoner was brought into the saloon,
Judge Bean opened court in his usual manner by
pounding on the bar with the bung starter and shout-
ing:

"Hear ye, hear ye. This Honorable Court is now in

session, and if anybody wants a snort before we start, step up to the bar and name yore poison."

This always meant a spurt of business. While Bean was hustling, pouring out the drinks for the prisoner at the bar and everyone else, he picked out a jury from among the customers. When everyone had been satisfied, he removed his beer-stained apron and put on his "judicial robes" as he called them, which were an old black alpaca coat.

The white man, not thinking that anybody would be mean enough to make a fuss about it, had been pretty careless and the evidence against him was so strong that nobody could pretend he hadn't killed the Chinaman. Late in the afternoon, in spite of many adjournments for refreshments at the bar, both sides were finished and the judge adjourned court until the next day.

In the morning he opened court with a yawn and this speech:

"Gentlemen, I have read this book from cover to cover all through the night and nowhere do I find it is against the statutes of the State of Texas for anybody to kill a Chinaman. Therefore, I find the defendant not guilty."

The jury, all ranchers, sitting on kegs and whisky cases, probably would free the prisoner anyway, but he didn't give them a chance. The Judge got scolded more often for his leniency than the capital punishments which he imposed.

Usually he was hard on Mexicans but always would marry them for a small fee. One pair he had married came back after a few months and told him they were sick of one another, so he divorced them. Somehow word of this got to Judge Brown of El Paso, who wrote Judge Bean that he ought to know that a Justice of the Peace has no right to grant divorces, although it was all right to marry people. Bean wrote back that if he could tie people up he reckoned he could untie them.

Horse thieves were usually strung up when and where they were caught, but for some reason or other one of them was tried before Judge Bean, who found him guilty. Again, for some reason that I never heard, instead of ordering him hanged by the neck, he sentenced the thief to a term in the State penitentiary. The prison authorities couldn't accept a committment from a Justice of the Peace, so there was nothing to do but to let the man go. The Governor wrote Bean a sharp letter, telling him he had no power to send anyone to a penitentiary. The Judge wrote back:

"I am the law this side of the Pecos. You take care of your side and I'll manage mine."

The arguments of lawyers and the rules of evidence usually gave no trouble because most anything went, but Judge Bean knew all about contempt of court and had his own idea of how to use it. A young lawyer from El Paso used to insist on juries and knew how to work on their sympathies so well that most always his clients were found not guilty. This made Bean sore, so the next time the lawyer appeared in court the Judge asked sternly:

"Have you got yore credentials to practice law?"

"Why of course," answered the lawyer who had

not expected such a question in this free and easy court, "but they are in El Paso."

"If you haven't yore credentials, you can't practice in my court," ruled Judge Bean. When the lawyer argued, he was fined for contempt of court and when he refused to pay, Judge Bean ordered him chained to a tree outside the saloon where all day he sweated in the hot sun, while Judge Bean drank cool beer on the porch. Nobody brought the lawyer anything to drink because the Judge made a ruling that anyone who did would also be in contempt and receive the same sentence. Late in the afternoon a friend of the lawyer came along and persuaded Bean to let the prisoner go. He never tried to practice in that court again.

One day the body of a man, killed by a railroad train, was found and the matter brought before Judge Bean, who also took on the powers of a coroner. The men who found him said that they found on the body a revolver and $44.20 which they laid on the bar before the Judge. Judge Bean placed the money in his pocket and said:

"I find the deceased guilty of carrying concealed weapons and fine him $44.20."

All fines went into Bean's pocket and they most always came to exactly what a search of the prisoner showed he had on him. Judge Bean told me that this was to repay him for the use of his courthouse which bore the name of "The Jersey Lilly" in honor of Lillie Langtry, the famous old-time actress the town was supposed to be named after. Also he had to have the money, he said, to make up for the loss of business while he was holding court. Since adjournments for refreshments came about every twenty minutes and the trials brought crowds of extra customers, I couldn't see that his losses in trade at the bar were very much.

Once Judge Bean sentenced a young stranger to be hanged for breaking into a railroad car, but first let him write a letter to his mother. The Judge, looking over the stranger's shoulder, was just about able to spell out the words. When he read that the doomed man had $400, the Judge let out a yell and told his assistant, W. H. Dodd:

"Gosh! We made a mistake! This man don't deserve to hang. The court reverses itself."

But reading a little further he saw that the money was in a New York savings bank and told them to go ahead with the hanging. There was a large crowd at the scene chosen for the execution and Dodd found an opportunity to let the man escape.

What the Judge ruled one day was no precedent for the next day. Once he freed a friend on this interpretation of the pistol-toting law:

"If a man is standing still, he isn't carrying a gun, but, if he is walking, he is traveling and the law says a traveler has the right to carry one for his own protection."

A man who owed Bean money had the nerve to start competition, selling drinks and meals in an abandoned box car. Bean walked in at his rival's busiest hour, covered him with a gun and demanded his money. When the man said he couldn't pay, Bean said he was a receiver, seated himself at the door and told the customers to pay him on the way out. After about an hour of this the debtor decided he might as well pay the rest, and he did.

If a customer hadn't the exact price to pay for his drinks, Judge Bean found nothing in the statutes requiring that the seller must give change for a large bill until convenient, which might be the next day or the next week. This decision was a very profitable one for the judge. While trains were filling at the big water tank, their passengers had just time for one drink at the Jersey Lilly bar across the road from the station. They usually didn't pay until the warning whistle blew. Those who laid down just the right amount were all right. But for those who handed the bartending judge a large bill or a $10 or $20 gold piece it was too bad because this was never convenient for the judge to make change.

A traveling man, putting down a $10 bill for a glass of beer was handed one dollar in change. He was lucky to get even that, but he put up a howl that he had been robbed. The judge snatched it away saying:

"I find you one dollar for contempt of court."

"You can't do that," protested the drummer, "court ain't in session."

"This court is always in session," said the judge and that settled it because the man had to run to catch his train. The Judge never played those tricks on his regular customers or his friends, like me, only strangers. But one of his short-change victims took a cruel revenge. He happened to come back to Langtry for several days on business while Judge Bean was in San Antonio.

The Judge had a pet bear he thought a lot of and he

kept it chained to his bed post at night for protection. The visitor found out Judge Bean's address, went to the railroad station and sent this telegram, signed with the name of the Judge's Mexican cook.

"Bear dead. What shall I do?"

Next day the Mexican was surprised to get this order from his boss:

"Skin bear and send me the hide."

When he got back the Judge's first question was to ask, what was the matter with the bear?

"Nothing was the matter with him," answered the Mexican, "until you ordered me to skin him."

By that time the wicked stranger was far away beyond the Pecos.

Bean once caused a short panic in Wall Street when, with his red bandanna handkerchief, he flagged the special train carrying Jay Gould and his family and got them to visit him for a couple of hours in his saloon across the road. The report reached New York that Gould's train had been wrecked in the desert. Gould had heard all the antics of Roy Bean and he got out of his private car and had a nice talk with Roy.

The Judge invited Lillie Langtry to visit the town that, he wrote her, had been named for her. The actress could not manage it at the time but offered to give the town a drinking fountain. Bean wired back the following in just ten words:

"Gift not appropriate. Langtry citizens do not drink the stuff."

Whatever his superiors thought of Judge Bean's decisions they were popular enough in Langtry. He hanged only people that most everyone agreed ought to be hanged and his fines were softened by a funny speech and usually a few compliments for the prisoner in other lines than the particular offense he was being fined for.

One day a tough cowboy rode his pony into the saloon and rapping on the bar with his gun yelled for a drink of "pizen." Going behind the bar, Judge Bean took out a jar containing centipedes and vinegaroons, poured the preserving alcohol in a glass and handed it to the vicious customer. The cowboy shouted: "I can't drink that stuff. It will kill me." Bean leveled his own gun over the bar and said:

"Ye ordered pizen. Now drink it."

Then he laughed and made his customer stand treat for a delighted crowd.

Bean came to Texas as the result of being hanged in California. When only 24 he fell in love with a young Mexican señorita who had been kidnaped by a Mexican army officer and forced into marriage. Bean challenged the Mexican to a duel and killed him. The slain Mexican's friends proposed to administer "miner's justice" by hanging Bean to a nearby tree, leaving his feet dangling a few inches above the ground. The devoted señorita who had been watching the proceedings from a nearby hiding place came out when the lynchers had gone and cut Bean down. He gave her a kiss as a reward and married another Mexican girl.

Judge Bean was an occasional, but not steady drunkard. Sometimes he would not drink for months. After his last spree he was found unconscious from what seemed to be a stroke of apoplexy at 10 o'clock in the morning and never regained consciousness. He was buried in the Del Rio Cemetery where he rests under a big tombstone inscribed:

"JUDGE ROY BEAN

Justice of the Peace

Law West of the Pecos."

CHAPTER IX   The James Boys

FASHIONS IN CRIME seem to change and I've
noticed many changes in my lifetime. There have
always been gangs of killers, but their ways have been
different. Nowadays gangsters are just plain murderers
and seem to kill for the fun they get out of it, and I
notice they have foreign names mostly.

But in the earlier days these bands of desperadoes
were different. Probably very few of my readers knew
much about Jesse James and his outfit, but when I
was a young man the "James Boys" had the country
considerably excited. But this gang, like many tough
outlaws of that period had a streak of decency about
them. This little case of a barroom acquaintance of

mine, Black Jack Ketchum, gives an idea of what I mean.

Black Jack found a miner had played a dirty trick on him and he started out to kill him.

"Draw your gun," said Jack. "This will be your last chance to use it."

"I haven't got no gun," said the wretch, "and I haven't no money to buy one with."

"Well take this and get one," said Jack, handing him a twenty-dollar bill, "and get yourself a bottle of whisky and you better look in at the undertaker's and pick out your coffin."

The miner looked gloomily at the money and answered:

"Say, Jack, can't we put off this shooting party until some other time? I want to go to my little daughter's christening in the morning."

"Oh dammit, I can't kill a man who wants to go to his little daughter's christening," growled Jack. "Get out of here." And he let the man go, money and all.

A modern gangster would figure Jack was crazy to give anyone a break like that. More likely, if he knew about the christening, he'd turn a machine gun on him right at the church steps and if some of the bullets hit the daughter, that would be all right too.

Most of the old-time highwaymen, like the James boys, had been all right until the Civil War gave them a bad idea about settling things with a gun. It was always a poor idea to call on bandits unless one had been invited. Well, I had not been invited to call, but I was out of grub, things you can't bring down with a rifle,

such as salt, sugar, coffee and tobacco, and there I was
right in the middle of the Ozark Mountains, one of
the wildest bits of country in the United States. So I
took a chance and walked right up to the front door
of a log cabin which I knew was the James hideout.

I made plenty of noise because unless a stranger
want to get bitten or shot he better not surprise a dog
or bandit. When I knocked, the door was opened by a
good looking, husky, middle-aged woman. She had a
six-shooter on her hip and a rifle handy but she had
made up her mind that I was harmless, let me in and
wanted to know who I was. I told her that my name
was Raymond E. Hatfield Gardner, that my parents
came from Kentucky and that my mother was a Hatfield.

I had hoped that this relationship might be a good
thing to tell the James boys about, but I hardly expected that the woman would cry out:

"I am your cousin. My mother was a Hatfield."

As she was older than me, she told me I could call
her Aunt Belle and that I could have anything I
wanted. We had been talking along about family matters for some time when a hard-looking face showed up
in the doorway. It was Jesse James who had listened
to us from behind a wood pile and then watched me
through a window before showing himself.

"What's all this about?" said Jesse. He didn't look
friendly and his hand was close to his pistol holster.
Aunt Belle introduced us and started to tell him about
me but Jesse interrupted:

"That's what he says, but how do you know?"

"I know because he has Hatfield written all over

his face," Aunt Belle answered, "and he's hungry. You go on and kill some chickens for us."

Jesse's face showed that he had no intention of doing anything of the kind, just then. But to my surprise, Belle had her gun out quicker than greased lightning. She didn't hold it on him the way a man does. She sort of shook it at him, as she talked, the way a woman shakes her finger at a man when she lays down the law.

"Go right out and get them chickens this minute if you know what's good for you. You know who runs this house."

Jesse's face got red all around his whiskers. I suppose he was ashamed to have a stranger see a woman get the drop on the famous bandit and order him around. He followed orders. It was a good thing that I managed to keep my face straight because he was the boss outside the house. I stayed there quite a while during which time both Jesse and Frank James became real friendly.

It was a risky thing to be friends with such celebrated bandits just at that time. I was young and not only broke, but wondering where I could find something to take the place of my scout work for which there was less call all the time. My Indian and scout training had fitted me to become an outlaw, my Hatfield blood gave me the right temper and there I was, good friends with the two best-known men in the game.

One side of me was tempted, but the other was disgusted. It was great to be famous, but, kind of cheap to have to hide behind a wood pile and let a woman face strangers. The bunch never enjoyed a good night's sleep and many a time we all had to grab guns and crouch by the windows till daylight because one of them had heard a twig snap during the night. The only times they were free from care were when they were good and drunk.

One day the thing they were always dreading happened. Officers rode up to the house from about the same direction I had come. Jesse and Frank crept out the back door, one taking a position behind the wood pile and the other behind a rock. Aunt Belle, with a .45 Colt in each hand, stood behind the door and ordered me to talk to them. I told them that the men who had been living in the cabin had moved away about two weeks before. Maybe my words convinced them that they might as well move along and maybe they had a feeling that something would happen if they didn't.

If those men had started to enter the house they would have been mowed down by bullets from front and both sides. None of the lead would have been from my gun, but I would have been too mixed up in the killing to explain and would probably have had to join the gang. Aunt Belle was proud of the way her young relative had talked the officers away from the door, and the James boys were so pleased that I could see they were going to make me an offer. Lucky for me Aunt Belle saw it too and headed it off by some strong whispering to the boys.

If I had been invited to join the band and refused, they would have thought me some sort of spy and fixed me so I would not tell on anybody in this world.

Such things are bound to happen to anyone foolish
enough to be friends with outlaws and they usually
end up by making him an outlaw too.

Once Aunt Belle took her rifle and rode off telling
me she was going to get some deer meat. When I asked
to go along she ordered me to stay in the house where
it was safe. It was funny, a woman saying that to me,
who had been brought up in the saddle and hunted
ever since I could remember. She came back with a
good-sized deer and while I was helping dress the carcass and hang it up to cool out, I said,

"You're handy with a knife."

"I can cut up a man, just as well," my aunt replied.

When the venison was dressed, Aunt Belle told me
they were going away for a few days on business and
to make myself at home. This was a surprise but
visitors don't ask bandits about their business. After
they had ridden off I took my fishing tackle and with
my dog, walked down to a creek. There I took off my
shoes and cooled my feet while I fished.

I had pulled out a fine catch of trout when I heard
a splash and my dog growled. I got my rifle handy and
sat watching the other side where the sound came from.
The dog knew better than to bark, but low, muttering
sounds warned me that he thought something important was still over there.

After a few minutes a magnificent-looking man in
gray, on a fine gray horse pushed through the bushes.
He had a silver-mounted saddle and expensive boots
with silver initials C. Y.. The stranger asked me if I
knew where he could find Belle Starr. My answer was
to ask who he was.

He placed his finger on his lips and slowly forded
the creek to our side where he dismounted, worrying
the dog as well as me. With a smile he told me not to
be afraid because he was not an officer. Again I asked
who he was and this time he whispered:

"I am Cole Younger."

Aunt Belle had told me a lot about this handsome
bandit who always dazzled the women and I now
recognized the man. He wanted to know how to get to
camp and I was just going to show him when we heard
a woman singing along the trail. It was my aunt, who
cried out:

"Hello Cole Younger. Welcome to our camp."

When we reached camp we found Frank and Jesse
there. You'd have thought it was a family reunion,
they were so glad to see each other and asked so
anxiously about how the boys in various gangs were
getting along. Many of them were getting along fine,
keeping well ahead of the sheriff's posse and making
profitable hauls, but there was also some grief because
some of the others had stopped bullets or danced at the
end of ropes.

I had to help Aunt Belle in the kitchen because she
was as fussy about that dinner as if the President of
the United States had dropped in. She baked a cake,
cooked corn pone, served my fish, trimmed with fried
potatoes and broiled venison steaks over coals in the
big fireplace. Belle made me broil the fish, and while
I was at it, Jesse asked if I knew Cole and, of course, I
said I'd heard a lot about him. Cole smiled and asked
if it was good or bad.

I told him, "pretty darn good."

Cole with his fine horse, his beautiful saddle and his swell suit was quite a hero in my eyes. He looked me over for a few moments and seeing how I felt asked me how I would like to work with him.

Aunt Belle came into the room just as he was making the proposition. She said sharply:

"No, that boy is goin' straight. I want you fellows to keep your noses out of my business. He's a cousin of mine. That goes for all of you."

Belle was as quick on the draw as any man and everybody knew what she meant. Then she cleared the boys out of the dining room and told me to change my clothes and set the table. When we sat down she asked Cole Younger to return thanks for the food.

It did not surprise me when Cole spoke a reverent, and to my mind, a first-class benediction, because either Frank or Jesse had been doing the same thing pretty well at every dinner I had eaten under their roof. The reason was that Younger, like the James boys, was the son of a Baptist minister. They stuck to their religion to their deaths and it was a great consolation to them in their worried and dangerous lives. Somehow their religion and their man-killing never seemed to interfere with each other. They were as pious a lot of murderers and robbers as I ever knew.

Cole Younger bragged that he could have made a good minister or actor if he had wanted to. I believe it. Anyway, he made good on one of those claims later on.

I met Cole Younger in Butte, Montana, after his long stretch in jail. He was then known as the Reverend Dr. Younger and was preaching the Gospel with great success, telling rough miners how he had committed lots of crimes, how his life had been spared by the Lord's mercy, how he had been sent to prison and finally repented all the sins he had committed. He was a fine godly-looking man.

"My friends, allus remember that crime does not pay," he warned me. Preaching must have paid because when he heard I was broke, he gave me ten dollars, for old times' sake.

After dinner that day at the James camp I lay down on my bed where later Younger came in and talked to me as he sipped his whisky and, by the way, he had the good sense to sip instead of tossing it down as was the frontier style. After he had asked a lot about me, he gave me two ten-dollar bills, just twice as much as he handed me 40 years later, but that doesn't mean that robbers only make twice as much as parsons. They make many times more but they can't keep it.

As the weeks passed I got more troubled about how I was going to get away from that nest of bandits. When I spoke of going, Aunt Belle wouldn't hear of it. She had a motherly fondness for her relative but, as far as she was concerned, it would have been safe enough to disobey. The trouble was that the James boys wouldn't hear of it either and I had a good idea why. Bandits take no needless chances and they feared that I might let slip something about where they were hiding. If I had insisted on going they probably would have sent somebody down the trail a piece to shoot me "by mistake."

My release came unexpectedly. One of the members of the gang that were always coming and going, rode

up with his horse all in a lather to report that a sheriff
and a big bunch of deputies were on their way to the
cabin. An hour later Aunt Belle and all were bidding
me farewell, on their way to the Cherokee Country
where they made things lively for a while. I was free
and took good care not to run into those officers.

Poor Aunt Belle! She was born Belle Shirley, only
daughter of a judge in Carthage, Missouri, well-
educated, a good musician and a bang-up horse-
woman. She and her twin brother Ed were only 15
when the Civil War broke out. Being of a family with
strong Confederate sympathies, Ed joined the Missouri
Bushwhackers, becoming a Captain in Quantrell's
bloody band of guerrillas. In this sort of outlaw warfare the twin sister was used to run messages through
the Union lines. Her brother's death strengthened her
hatred against the Federals.

She grew friendly with the James and Younger
boys, became the sweetheart of one of the gang, Jim
Reed. After the war they took time to get married,
but the judge did not care for his bandit son-in-law
and refused to recognize the marriage. He sent her to a
boarding school, but Jim thrilled the girls' dormitory
by bursting in at night and carrying away his wife in
her night dress. The judge then sent her out to an
uncle in Colorado and again Jim took her away.

After the birth of their first child, a girl, the parents
decided to recognize the marriage and life might have
been peaceful if Jim hadn't killed the man who had
killed his brother. A price was set on his head and after
that the little family was always on the move, until
Jim was killed by his supposed friend John Morris

for the reward. John never collected because by some mistake the body of another man who happened to get shot at the same time was brought to the authorities. After this, Belle returned to the James outfit and was arrested several times, but released because of the charm she had over the jailers.

Belle was a dead shot and if real mad could outswear a mule-skinner. But she didn't often forget her early breeding and demanded the treatment due a lady. She always rode side-saddle and thought a man's saddle immodest for a woman. After a while she married Sam Starr, brother of a Cherokee Indian who had sheltered Jim Reed. They settled in a camp on the Canadian River, at a spot known as Younger's Bend. There in a comfortable cabin they lived in style with some of the luxuries of her girlhood. She dressed well and sometimes visited high-toned watering places. But in spite of Belle's ladylike ways, her home became known as the center of the outlaw gangs that were operating then over a big stretch of country. She sympathized with them and sheltered them. In a large cave not far away from her home she hid some of the worst outlaws from the authorities.

Aunt Belle wasn't too ladylike to be guilty of a few crimes and she and Sam Starr both served a year in the House of Correction in Detroit. Sam was often in trouble and was finally killed in a dance-hall row. Later Belle's only son, Ed, was shot in a saloon fight.

Following Sam Starr's death Belle Starr went straight for a time and it was even suspected that she was working with the law officers. A neighbor named Watson, a fugitive from justice, knew that Belle Starr had heard of his crime and fearing she would betray him, he shot and killed her from behind as she rode past his place on February 3, 1889. Nothing was done to Watson and Aunt Belle's death went unavenged.

The James boys got their education in courage, daring and violence under that dreadful, able but evil teacher Quantrell. With forty men Quantrell fought against 300 until he fell riddled with bullets, but not until they had killed about a hundred of the enemy. Most all of Quantrell's band were hunted down and killed, except the James boys who happened to be away at the moment.

Frank James swore he would have revenge for Quantrell. A posse of four men tried to arrest him. He shot three of them dead, but the fourth as he fled gave Frank a terrible wound in the hip, from which he never really recovered. In spite of this injury he went on robbing and fighting. Sometime later he pulled off his first bank robbery when he looted the Commercial Bank of Liberty of $70,000. A party of six well-armed militiamen were sent to surround the James boys, who had been found in a house. Jesse was suffering from a bad fever then, but sick and dizzy as he was, Jesse came to the door and shot four of the militiamen dead, while the other two ran away.

At Russellville, with Cole Younger and several new recruits, they looted the local bank of several thousand dollars. There was a hot chase after this, and one of the outlaws, Oll Shepherd, was trapped and surrounded by twenty men. He stood with his back to a tree and refused to surrender. Using two revolvers he

shot until he had killed six men, when he fell dead
with seven bullets in his body.

Jesse James' strength and endurance were wonderful. Once he fought and rode with two big bullet
wounds in his lungs.

At Battle Mountain, Nevada, a gambler tried to
cheat Jesse at cards thinking he was a simple country
boy. Jesse showed up his trick and shot him when the
gambler moved his hand toward his gun. A large
number of gamblers, gunmen and crooks threatened
the youth. Jesse and his three friends fought their way
out and killed eight gamblers without losing a man.
After this they were reckoned as heroes by other victims of gamblers.

After robbing the bank at Gallatin, Missouri, they
fought off a whole company of militia sent to catch
them. They raided the Kansas City Exposition while
a crowd was looking on. Before going away with the
$10,000 they had stolen, Jesse James risked capture
by stopping to save a little girl who was in danger of
being run over by the horses.

It has been figured that the James boys robbed fifty
banks and killed 100 people but nobody knows exactly. After a while the James and Younger boys found
how helpless and easy to plunder the stagecoaches and
railroad trains were and did nothing else. This line of
crime paid big for some time but in the end it ruined
them, because it made all honest people so mad that
they forced the authorities to get after the bandits and
kept after them.

It was a tough job. Anyway you went at catching
the James boys was like putting salt on a bird's tail. If

a few officers went after the bandits, they usually found them, in an ambush, and got their heads blown off. If a big posse or even the militia were sent after them, it cost lots of money. The bandits just skipped from one hiding place to another until the pursuers ran out of supplies and money.

Even the law-abiding people protected them by lying to the officers who followed. It was safe to lie to them but almost certain death to tell them the truth about Jesse James. The James and the Youngers did showy things too that won the sympathy of people who did not know them. Once when they were raiding and killing in Mexico, they won a battle with the local Mexican bandits who had kidnaped Alice Gordon, a pretty girl from the American side. They gallantly rescued and returned pretty Alice to her family, which made lots of folks forget the 100 murders they had committed.

Among other forces sent against the bandits was the Pinkerton Detective Agency. The James boys and their gang won a pitched battle with a strong force of the Pinkertons. But now there was no let-up in the pursuit and it began to tell.

The Youngers became separated from the James boys for a time and John Younger was killed by Captain Lull. A brave Pinkerton detective, John W. Wicker, discovered the James' hide-out in Missouri and planned to trap them by telling them he was an honest farmhand looking for work. Jesse James saw through the trick and tortured the detective by slashing him with knives to make him tell the plans of his employers. But he died without telling anything.

Before Jim and Cole Younger were caught and sent to the penitentiary at Stillwater, Minn., Jim's jaw was broken by a bullet but he fought on for 20 minutes with his mouth wide open in a sort of bloody yawn.

Well, being an outlaw and holding up banks, railroad trains and stagecoaches was exciting but being hunted all the time and jumping from one hideout to another wasn't much fun. Those boys got good and tired of keeping out of sight off in the woods somewhere and they go hungry for the life of a town where they could buy a few things, fill up their cartridge belts and eat a hotel meal. But before it was safe to come into a town, some kind of a deal had to be fixed up by their friends with the sheriff or city marshal. This wasn't so hard to arrange because mostly always the town officers would rather look the other way and let them come in for a day or two in a peaceful way rather than have them come shooting.

A deal of this kind was made once in Abilene, Kansas, while Wild Bill Hickok was marshal in that lively cow town. A man named Gross was clerk of a hotel there and slept in a cottage outside the hotel. One day a circus came to town and a lot of people rode in from out of town to see the show. Among the visitors was a man the clerk knew who had three cowboys, all strangers to Gross, with him. He asked to have them all put in one room, even if some had to sleep on the floor.

They stayed four or five days, went to the circus, did some shopping, drank some at the saloons and did quite a lot of gambling. Hotel clerks have pretty sharp eyes and one day Gross said to his friend that the men in the room with him were not cowboys.

"Who are they?" Gross asked.

"Well, if you'll promise to keep it under your hat, I'll tell you. Come up to our room after twelve o'clock tonight and I'll introduce you."

And that night in that room Gross had a pleasant visit with Jesse and Frank James and Cole Younger. Frank James, the first to speak said to the hotel clerk:

"Our friend has told us all about you and we are not afraid to have you know. In fact, it's best."

"How does it come that Wild Bill does not know you?" Gross asked.

"He does know us," said Cole Younger. "He has seen us often in Missouri in war times, but he has been promised by our friend here that we will make no bad breaks in town, and will not in any way make trouble for him. All we want is a rest for our horses and ourselves and a fresh supply of ammunition and clothes."

Gross, still puzzled that these three notorious bandits of the frontier should be resting peacefully in a hotel room within the knowledge of the law, particularly Will Bill, said:

"I can't understand Wild Bill doing such a thing."

"Well," Younger replied, "it's the smart thing for him to do. Of course he would like to round us up, but our friends are watching every move he makes day or night. If he tries to get us by himself, it's three to one, if he tries to get help, we'll get him if we die for it—and he knows it." At that time there was a ten-thousand-dollar reward on the heads of the James outfit, but Bill, in spite of his bravery, did not knowingly go beyond his depth.

So the outlaws had a few pleasant days in wide-open Abilene, saw the circus, got some new clothes and ammunition and were ready for the next train robbery. Not even Wild Bill Hickok was hungry to tackle the outfit in the hotel room.

Jesse James was finally killed at St. Joseph, Missouri, while he was unarmed and hanging up a picture. He was living under the name of Howard and his killer was known as Charles Johnson, who was aided by his brother. At the inquest Howard's wife admitted that the dead man was Jesse James, much to the surprise of the public. The so-called Johnsons were really Robert and Charles Ford, two alleged detectives who had been engaged in the hunt for the Jameses for several months on account of the large reward offered for their capture. According to some people they were former members of the James gang.

Jesse James' funeral was attended by crowds of people from all around and he was treated as if he had been a national hero. Two or three months later Frank James gave himself up at Jefferson city and that ended the strange history of the James boys.

The Dalton gang committed more crimes, stole more money and murdered more people than did the James boys and the Youngers combined. But the Daltons and their allies, the Doolin gang, started a little later and never caught up with the reputation of the James boys.

There were eleven children in the Dalton family, three sons and four daughters of them becoming a credit to their respectable parents, while the other four sons turned into bandits. Bob Dalton, the youngest,

took command of the gang when he was only twenty-
two. His brother Gratton, who was more cautious
than reckless Bob, followed him humbly and so did
the other brothers, Emmett and Bill Dalton. The Dalton brothers robbed and killed over a surprising area
of territory. They rode all over Kansas and Texas, one
robbery following another at places many miles apart
Their followers were young cowboys, who learned to
shoot straight from the saddle as they rode at full
speed.

Like the James boys, the Daltons settled down to
robbing trains and stages, with an occasional bank
that looked extra good to them. But in the end Bob
Dalton got too ambitious and thought he could put
the record of the Jameses and all other robbers in the
shade by robbing two banks in the same town at the
same time.

The town picked for this honor was Coffeyville,
Kansas, with its two banks close together on the same
street. It was the most carefully-planned raid the
Daltons ever attempted. With their guns hidden and
their faces disguised with false whiskers, the band
rode into town unnoticed. They rounded up in a side
street, tied their horses and strolled on to the main
street, still unnoticed.

But nobody can foresee everything and one little
accident spoiled everything. In crossing the street one
of the town's merchants saw that some of the whiskers
were false, which started him thinking and watching.
When three of the strangers walked into the Condon
Bank, the merchant peeped in just in time to see Gratt
Dalton point a gun at the cashier.

The merchant started running down the street yelling that the Condon Bank was being robbed, which brought out every citizen with courage and a gun. To their astonishment they found that the First National was also being robbed by Bob and Emmett Dalton. The citizens formed in two groups and began firing into the doors of the two banks. I have often heard men who were in that gun battle speak of the calm of those bandits, who in a hail of bullets made the officers of the banks turn over their bags of gold and packages of money.

Not until the two divisions of the gang had signaled each other that both banks had been completely looted did they start shooting their way out. Out in the street they were faced by a body of determined, straight-shooting men. Four of the outlaws went to their deaths, their bodies full of lead. Bob and Gratt were among the killed and Emmett Dalton was severely wounded. The bullets fell like rain as the citizens and officers of Coffeyville surrounded the desperate bandits. Dick Broadwell got the farthest on his attempted escape, for he reached his horse, but as he tried to swing into the saddle a bullet caught him and fatally wounded him. His faithful horse carried him out of town, where he was picked up in the road, dead.

Emmett Dalton might have saved himself, but as he ran towards his horse he stopped to rescue his dying brother Gratt. Emmett was put in jail and the bodies of the other boys was claimed by their mother. Four citizens of Coffeyville were killed in the gun battle. This ended the Dalton gang, although one of its toughest members, Bill Doolin, through no fault of his own, survived to form a new gang and do about as much harm for quite a while. Bill escaped the Coffeyville misfortune because his horse went lame on the way to the robbery.

In Doolin's gang was Little Dick, one of the best scouts in the Indian Territory, a mighty useful man when the gang was trying to shake off a posse in the wilderness. Another was a famous killer known as Bitter Creek who had for a sweetheart one of the prettiest girls in the Southwest, called Rose of the Cimarron.

Once when Bill Doolin, with Bitter Creek and several others was staying at a hotel in Ingalls, Kansas, to have a bullet wound in the leader's foot treated, they were surrounded by a large posse. The gun battle began in the hotel, from which the bandits moved over to the hotel's barn, built as stoutly as a blockhouse.

Bitter Root was caught without his gun. In the storm of bullets Rose of the Cimarron carried her lover's gun to him. It was hanging in a second story room of the hotel and Rose got it, descended from the window by a rope made of torn strips of sheet, because the stairway was full of deputy sheriffs. She had yet to cross the yard where the bullets were flying, but with the gun concealed in her skirt she won through. When she reached Bitter Creek he was seriously wounded, but she handed him his gun and he was able to use it.

At the end of an hour dead men were strewn all over the street—three marshals among them—and the hotel was already full of bullets, when the scene of the battle shifted to the barn. Bitter Creek escaped, but so weak was he from loss of blood that he fell from his horse.

Bill Doolin took careful aim at Marshal Speed, but weakness made his hand shake and he missed him. Doolin and Bill Dalton were the last to leave the barn. Dalton stopped to aid Bitter Creek as he lay bleeding by the wayside. Overtaken by officers, Dalton shot Marshal Shadley from his horse before the officer could draw. Red Buck and Dynamite Dick, after escaping from the posse, returned and rescued Bitter Creek. They fled through the timber and reached an outlaw cave with Bitter Creek alive, but suffering greatly with his wounds. Three others were wounded. Rose of the Cimarron carried medicine and bandages to the wounded men and told them about the officers' moves.

These bandits in many cases won the love and devotion of attractive and romantic girls. Bill Doolin, the chief villain, fascinated the pretty daughter of a minister. It is to the credit of Doolin that he thought more of his sweetheart, who later became his wife, than he did of his life, for he risked it again and again and finally lost it in order to pay her a visit, even for an hour or so. It cannot be said that she did much toward reforming him.

In time Bill Doolin came to be regarded as a greater bandit in some ways than even the James and Younger brothers. Three of the most determined peace officers, Heck Thomas, Bill Tilghman and Chris Madsen, known as the Three Guardsmen, hunted Doolin and never gave up. They rode after him into the forest and mountain hide-outs, across miles of desert country, carrying the heavy equipment needed to keep **them** provisioned for an indefinite journey.

During the later years when Bill Doolin's **band** was being cut to pieces, he married his **minister's** daughter and she bore him a child. This wild, **reckless** man longed to put the old outlaw life behind him **and** start over. Although he was closely watched **and** hunted he gathered together household goods **and** provisions, loaded them in a wagon and with **his** wife and child started out for a quiet and lonely **part** of the West. When they reached Burden, Kansas, **his** wife wrote a letter to the owner of the hotel at **Ingalls,** where the famous gun battle had occurred when **Rose** of the Cimarron helped the gang to shoot their **way** through.

Deputy Sheriff Tilghman traced the letter **and** managed to catch Doolin in the tub, taking a **bath.** But the bandit was not quite naked, for under **one** armpit hung a holster holding a revolver. Tilghman had the drop on him and brought the bandit **into** Guthrie, Oklahoma jail, from which he **promptly** escaped to Arkansas where he had plenty of **friends.** But he could not resist sneaking back for another **visit** to his wife which was also to be his last.

Marshal Heck Thomas had an idea that he **would** do that very thing and was waiting for him with **a** shotgun full of buckshot. When Thomas stepped **out** of the bushes and ordered him to surrender his **answer** was a bullet that missed. The marshal's gun **roared** and Doolin died with his boots on.

Women shed tears over Doolin's death, **because**

love brought him to it. Men liked Bob Dalton's end better because he went out in a blaze of glory, although biting off two banks at once is more than any bandit can chew.

CHAPTER **X**   Necktie Parties

THE WILD WEST was full of thieves in the old days and they were a God-awful bunch. But there was one big and prosperous territory where there wasn't any gold or money to get hold of. This was the big cattle country with ranges of miles and miles of grazing herds. There was nothing worth stealing in the ranch-houses but there were millions of cows on the ranges that were worth around $25 each—sometimes more, sometimes a bit less.

So there was a lot of cattle stealing. We called cattle thieves rustlers and the law of the range was to shoot a rustler on sight if caught stealing cows or hang him to any handy tree if the cowboys took the time and trouble to hold a "trial." Cowpunchers ride the range in the saddle, just about live on horseback, and when they are on foot they are pretty near as helpless as a fish on the beach or in the bushes. To steal a rancher's horse was a crime that carried the death penalty pronto.

Cattle rustling was the bane of the ranchmen's life. On the vast, unfenced, unpoliced prairies, reckless scoundrels could easily sneak up in the night, pick out a batch of the finest and fattest beef animals and drive them miles away before sunrise.

When cowboys caught a rustler they knew just what to do and the rustlers knew what was coming to them. So, if surprised, the cattle thieves tried to shoot first. As a result of these cattle-stealing raids real wars, like the famous one in Lincoln County broke out and hundreds of men were killed. Sometimes the cattlemen would round up a bunch of rustlers without shooting them at the time and then would indulge in the luxury of a lynching. But the rustlers often had friends that would try to get even with the cowboys and that brought on the wars.

Back in the early days, two of the worst badmen, cattle rustlers and horse thieves that I ever met were George Britt and William Hilligoff. They had been guilty of many crimes, but no one ever caught up with them until Dave Cook was elected City Marshal of Denver and made it his job to track them down. He did this almost unaided and brought them to town a few days after their last crime.

When Cook was elected Marshal of Denver, he printed a notice saying that he would agree to find

stolen stock, when notified within 24 hours after its
disappearance and that if he did not find it he would
pay for it himself after such notification. That was
quite considerable of a bargain and lots of us watched
to see if he could make good.

The two rustlers were very slick thieves and they
had robbed many ranches before they were even suspected. They put on disguises, and after they were
caught, in their trunks were found false wigs, beards
and Indian war paint. They mostly worked at night,
creeping up on a sleeping herd of cattle and quietly
leading away a dozen or so of the finest. Usually the
cowboys were asleep at the time beside a crackling fire,
so that the noise of the cattle's hoofs was not heard.
The two rustlers would then change the brand on the
cattle's hide and sell the stock as soon as possible. But
when they began stealing horses they sure ran into
trouble.

One day in December, 1867, a well-known ranchman named McIntyre came to Denver with a drove of
horses and put up the herd at McNassar's Corral
which then stood on the site of The American House.
The next morning the horses had disappeared and Mc-
Intyre was good and sore. The animals were fine ones
and the loss would have cost him quite a bit of money.
He had little hope of recovering them, as up to that
time the thieves had been able to make their escape in
spite of the wide-spread alarm which their robberies
had caused.

But Cook reckoned he could find the stock and said
so. In looking about he discovered that Britt and Hilligoff, that he knew only as tough gamblers, had dis-

appeared from the town. He figured that if they were
not guilty of this they sure must have been up to some
mischief. He deputized a marshal named Rhodes and
together they started off to find out.

The weather was freezing cold but the officers rode
on, stopping only to make inquiries for the men they
were after and to get their meals. Any ranchhouse
would always feed a man traveling over the range.
The trail was struck at Platte Bridge and followed by
the officers to Boulder, Colorado, where they lost it.

Two days and nights were spent by the officers
trying to run their game down. On the third day City
Marshall Cook returned to Denver, but he left Rhodes
in Boulder. He had scarcely arrived when news from
Captain Barron of the Bijou Basin Detective Association came in, telling him that two men answering the
description of Britt and Hilligoff had passed there
acting kind of suspicious. Barron's message said that
the men had asked for something to eat and had paid
in gold. They had seemed nervous and were anxious
to get on to Denver and hit the trail northward. They
had with them quite a lot of luggage, including a
number of branding irons which stuck out from the
pack. Cook figured that these were his men and started
right after them.

At that time there were no railroads and all the
travel was done by stagecoach, not a very pleasant trip
in cold weather or when there were bands of half-
starving marauding Indians raiding around. It was
necessary to keep a constant guard on all sides of the
coach to protect passengers from the Sioux, Cheyennes

and warlike Arapahoes. At Cheyenne Wells, Cook got information that made him feel certain that he was on the right track. He changed his uniform for a stage-driver's outfit and sat up alongside of the coachman.

After they crossed the Kansas line he heard of the men more frequently, and just after passing Fort Wallace actually saw them. They had hired out as laborers and were carrying picks and shovels. They did not look like ordinary miners or workmen and the way they handled their tools looked wrong. Cook told the driver to stop the coach and get down and pretend that something had gone wrong with the gearing. The driver did as he was told.

Hilligoff and Britt did not suspect the shabby-looking stranger who was now standing with his back towards them only ten paces away until he turned upon them with cocked pistols and as usual presented an aim which they saw would be fatal. Cook shouted "Hands up!"

The thieves hesitated a minute and then saw that Cook meant business.

"It's no use," said Britt, "he's got us!" and up went their hands.

Cook disarmed them and handcuffed them. He spent the night at Fort Wallace waiting for the return stage and the marshal had to stay up with his prisoners all night to guard them. He had been up for four nights and was pretty well tired out. He sat on the floor of the narrow cell, his feet resting against the opposite side, while the two prisoners reversed his position, their feet resting against the same wall which the marshal had his back against.

Cook dropped off to sleep in a few minutes in spite of himself. Drowsily, Cook felt his pistol slowly being drawn out of its holster by his side. He shook himself, slapped his hand on his gun and found it half-way out, one of the rustlers having pulled it out with his feet. After that Cook asked for two of the soldiers at the fort who volunteered to help him keep watch.

It took five days for the marshal and his prisoners to reach Denver and I was told that Cook slept for 24 hours after he reached home. Britt and Hilligoff were afterwards tried and sentenced to three years' imprisonment, each, but both escaped after serving a year. Neither has ever been heard of since, although it was rumored that they were lynched by a Mexican mob for trying to rustle cattle over the Border.

After this capture Cook's reputation was made as one of the finest peace officers on the frontier. When asked how he managed to spot the two thieves in a group of laborers, Cook said that out of the entire bunch the boots of only two men showed that they had not been working long in the fine red sand of that country. In other words, they must have been the latest addition to that laboring gang. With such small clues as these Cook usually found his man and cattle rustlers didn't like him.

I knew another peace officer who was a terror to cattle rustlers and horse thieves. This was Steve Burke, one of the straightest deputy marshals I ever worked with on the old frontier. Back in the roaring 80's and the still roaring early 90's he was the kind of religious leader that was badly needed in the mining towns. He always carried a pair of nickel-plated guns in holsters hanging at his side, even when he was preaching the Gospel in the pulpit. At a very dangerous time Steve was appointed Deputy United States Marshal and was responsible for helping to line up such desperadoes as Bill Doolin, of the infamous Doolin gang; Crawford Crosby, better known as Cherokee Bill; Little Dick West, Jim Dy, Pink Lee, Andy Kuykendahl, Ollie Yantis, Buck Lucky, the Daltons and the Buck gang.

Steve was then living around Lawton, Oklahoma. He could use a six-shooter equally well with either hand and with a flexible twist of his body would keep up a shower of bullets with mighty good aim. There were three other extra good deputy marshals at this time—Billy Tilghman, Heck Thomas and Chris Masterson. Steve Burke, of course, could not work with them on Sundays when he was preaching the Gospel.

My acquaintance with this parson, who was quick on the trigger and long on prayer, dated from the time when Billy Tilghman told Steve one Sunday morning just before church that they needed his kind in law enforcing and that he was going to have him made Deputy United States Marshal. Steve said he would think it over, which he did, and early Monday morning he came to Billy's office to be sworn in. Steve Burke's combined Gospel and six-guns proved a strong argument against the cattle thieves who were then operating in Indian and Oklahoma territories.

On a dry branch of Cherry Creek, about fifteen

miles from Denver, a quiet man settled with a herd of sheep. He gave the name of S. K. Wall and now and then rode into Denver for supplies, but spent no money for whisky nor at gambling joints. He lived in a little dugout tent like a hermit, doing his own cooking and tending the sheep. He also set up a log hut in a bunch of willows near the bed of the creek and was prosperous. George Witherill and another badman, Jack Wight, figured that Wall must have quite a bunch of money hidden away because he never wasted any.

So Witherill and Wight loaded their rifles, straddled their horses and made a visit to Wall one Sunday afternoon. They found him lying quietly on a peaceful hillside watching the lazy sheep as they grazed on the tufted grass. Supposing they had come on a friendly visit Wall greeted them pleasantly and while they talked, one of the visitors, still wearing a friendly smile, leveled his rifle at the sheepherder's back and fired, the ball striking the rancher in the neck

In spite of his astonishment and the gush of blood, Wall sprang to his feet and rushed down the hillside, hoping to to get to his cabin in the willows where he had his rifle. The murderers ran after him, overtook him and finished the job with a few more shots.

They buried the body under a pile of rocks and took their time searching for the money they felt sure Wall had hidden somewhere in his shack. But they found nothing of value in the cabin and they ended their search with only the murdered man's watch and pocketbook and a certificate of deposit in a Denver bank. But they had the dead man's flock of sheep which they could drive off and sell.

To neighboring ranchmen the murderers explained that they had bought out Wall and that he had moved away. But when Witherill came into Denver one day and presented the dead man's certificate of deposit at the bank, the cashier refused to pay it because the signature of Wall was a clumsy forgery. This aroused suspicion and Witherill and Wight moved out of the district, driving Wall's flock of sheep to market.

The whole situation looked so suspicious that a party started off to Cherry Creek to investigate. Going up the dry creek towards the missing man's cabin, they were not long in making a discovery. As they walked along the bed of the creek their attention was attracted to a bunch of wolves standing around a pile of stones on the hillside, not far from the gulch. They seemed to be pawing at the stubborn rocks and sniffing the air as if they had found something to eat. The animals were frightened away by a pistol shot, fired into their midst, and walking up to the heap of stones the searchers found a fleshless arm of a human being sticking out of an opening. It showed traces of the teeth of the wolves and shreds of clothing were scattered about the place. Removing the heap of stones they came upon the decaying body of the unfortunate sheepherder, Wall.

There was no longer any doubt as to the fate of the sheep rancher and it was plain enough who had murdered him. A posse at once took up the trail and Witherill and Wight were overtaken. They would have been lynched but sheriffs' officers that were in the party wouldn't allow a "necktie party." In due time they were both put on trial, convicted and sentenced to long terms in prison. But after serving a few years behind the bars they were turned loose and so they found opportunity to continue their careers.

Witherill made the acquaintance of a man named Jansen at Ironton, Col., who owned a valuable four-horse team and a big ore wagon and outfit for hauling ore from the mines. Witherill lured Jansen over to Silverton, pretending that he had ore to be hauled from a mine he said he owned. That was the last ever seen or heard of poor Jansen, and his bones lie somewhere in some abandoned prospect hole on some mountainside. Witherill turned up in Pueblo with the Jansen team and wagon which he sold for $400.

After loafing around the town for a while and enjoying the money, Witherill worked the same game again on another victim. He hired Charles R. McCain, who had two teams, and they started out from Pueblo. Witherill told McCain he was the foreman of a mine that had a lot of ore to haul to the railroad. They camped that night at Beaver Creek, eighteen miles from Canyon City. Both laid down under their blankets in the wagons, but McCain didn't wake up again in this world. Witherill watched until he heard his victim snoring and then sent a rifle bullet crashing through his brain. To completely finish the job he picked up an ax and split the teamster's head open. The rifle was fired so close that the bullet passed entirely through McCain's head and the bottom of the wagon and still had enough force to flatten itself on a stone.

When found it had bits of bone and blanket sticking to it.

Following his usual way, Witherill buried the body under rocks and dirt, scrubbed the bloody spots from the bottom of the wagon and drove the two teams to Canyon City, where he sold them.

When her husband failed to return Mrs. McCain raised an alarm and a posse was soon on the trail of Witherill. He was caught at Goulding's stables in Canyon City and upon being searched, $250 was found in his pockets.

The news of the capture of Witherill spread rapidly throughout Canyon City. All night the streets were alive with men and the prospect of lynching was the only subject of discussion. Little knots of men assembled on street corners and in doorways, but all the time the real organized lynchers were secretly and silently making their plans and masks were provided for the "necktie party." Two of them knocked at the back door of the jail and when Sheriff Griffith opened the door, sprang upon him and throttled him without making a sound.

After the sheriff had been put out of the way, the crowd of masked men filed into the jail and took the keys to the cell from the sheriff's son.

The dim light burning in the jail showed Witherill in his cell, standing on the defensive. He was ordered to come out:

"Come in and take me out."

He had broken his wooden bedstead to pieces to get a weapon, and when some of the party stepped forward to take him at his word he used the club with

desperate energy. There is no telling how long Witherill might have held his own against the crowd had not
one of the "necktie party" drawn his Colts and shot
the murderer in the shoulder, knocking him down. He
was then quickly overpowered and led out of the cage,
with a noose around his neck and his hands tied behind
his back.

Surrounded by a solemn but earnest crowd, Witherill was marched down to Main Street to a telephone
pole, about one hundred yards from the jail. The
doomed man was halted at this pole and the rope
thrown over the cross-bar by a practiced hand, and
the end of the rope was grabbed by fifty strong and
willing hands. The triple murderer was given a moment to confess. This he refused to do, and he was
drawn up five or six feet from the ground. After some
seconds he was lowered until his feet touched the
ground, and he was asked to confess the murders of
Wall, Jansen and McCain. But when he still refused,
he was yanked up until his feet cleared the ground by
some twelve feet and the rope tied.

Witherill's helpless body, dangling against the pole
as he strangled to death, was watched by the assembled
crowd without any sign of pity. He deserved what he
got and everybody knew it. When satisfied that he was
dead, the crowd went quietly away leaving the ghastly
figure at the end of the rope. This ended the career of a
sheep thief who was also a murderer whenever a few
dollars were to be gained by a killing. I never heard
what became of Wight.

It was sometime after the last of the Apache Indian
wars that my brother Charlie and I had a ranch in the

Basin Country in Arizona. We were aiming at an early roundup and got word that a bunch of cattle rustlers had been raiding our herd and some others, including the old G Bar Ranch. This riled us up because we had worked hard and had a pretty good sized herd of cows. Charlie and I took along a cowboy whose name was Picketwire Johnson and we started to round up the cattle rustlers, instead of our herd.

Quite a number of cowboys from neighboring ranches over in the Granite Gap country joined us and we were a pretty strong party when we started to work our way into the Spotted Horse Creek territory where we figured we might find the rustlers and some of our cattle. It was a rough country, full of canyons and brush and rim-rock—just the place for rustlers and outlaws to work in.

I remember well our first night out. We camped at the foot of the Castle Dome Mountains where Beaver Creek came in about six miles from Montezuma's Wall. We knew this area had quite a lot of water and grass so we made this section our headquarters. We did not have wagon roads those days—just wild game haunts and cattle trails to guide us, for you see we were in a country that had not often seen a white man.

We camped for the night and had plenty of wild game. The water was fine. Pure, fresh, cold and sparkling came the water from the rocks so the outlaw and rustler as well as ourselves were well provided for, and we knew we'd have to run 'em out. While we discussed our plans the sheriff of Limestone Gap, Fred Hawkins, rode in and dismounted. He had a couple of deputies with him and four Navajo Indian trailers.

Now everyone knew the reputation of these trailers.
We knew for certain that when these Indians got on
the trail of anything it was all off for those they
trailed. They always got their man.

I told the sheriff I was glad he was there. I thought
we might need him and his men. So it was decided that
in the morning we would ride into the stronghold
country and if we didn't find our rustlers there we'd
likely find them over in Bullpen Canyon. Sheriff
Hawkins said he was dubious about the rustlers heading over into the Clear Creek country. He thought
they would go down Beaver Creek and to Verde where
they would have an outlet for the stolen cattle and
then into Old Mexico.

We called the confab off for the night and turned
in after our trip over rough country. As we were sitting down to breakfast a lone rider from the X W
Ranch rode in and said they were rustling cattle over
in the Palisades Mountain country right then. They
had killed the owner of the stock there and had made
off with the women.

We didn't stop to hear any more. We knew action
was called for. We must round up that band for we
couldn't stand to let a woman be kidnaped and ill-
treated by a bunch of rustlers—and let 'em get away
with it.

I took the lead as we headed out and after about an
hour's hard riding I came into the foot of the stronghold and found there fresh ashes from a campfire.
They were still warm. I circled around cautiously,
picked up horses' tracks and started out toward the
Verde River. There I picked up more tracks and saw

the party was headed across the Moggolon Rim country. I knew then there was a good chance to overtake
those rustlers.

I rode about and hour and suddenly came up to my
first rustler. The varmint had a cow down and was
branding her. He had butchered her calf for fresh meat.
Seeing red, I jumped from my horse, grabbed my rifle,
ordered him to throw up his hands. He knew the Law
was hard and fast upon him. As he started to raise his
arms, a rope whined and a noose fastened itself around
his throat. I turned to see where it came from and saw
it was from one of the Indian trailers who also had
ridden down on him.

The Indian dragged his man to the neaerst sycamore
tree and threw the rope over its branches. He jerked
him up and left him hanging. And there he hung for
about an hour struggling and kicking until a bullet
ended his worthless life. That ended the first rustler's
career. But we had four more to round up.

I told Picketwire Johnson we had one scalp to our
credit and from the opinion of Sheriff Hawkins and
Picketwire it looked as if we were on the trail of the
rest of the renegades. After hanging the lone rustler
someone suggested we cut him down and plant him.
The sheriff was against that plan. He argued to let
him hang as a warning to those who might come along.
We followed his suggestion and this event gave the
name to the canyon. From that time it was known as
"Hangman's Canyon."

Heading on into the head of Big Beaver, we found
a maze of tracks and from what our Indian trailers
told us we were on the trail of the rest of the rustlers.

Sheriff Hawkins and I decided to go on and reconnoiter —to search for the other rustlers and the women they had taken prisoners. We rode all day until about an hour of sundown. We reached the foot of the Palisades when dark overtook us. We went on until we found good grazing for our horses and wood for our fire. I left Sheriff Hawkins to make some rough kind of camp while I scouted the section trying to pick up a warm trail of the outlaws. I had ridden a mile or so from where I had left Hawkins when I scented the smell of smoke ahead.

Dismounting, I tied my horse "Baldy" in a thick copse of juniper. Then I took my rifle and scouted afoot. Nearing the smoke I crawled up to the top of a bluff, careful to avoid disturbing any rock or gravel.

Then I saw the outlines of four men and two women. It was plain enough to me these were our rustlers and I had them ambushed. I had only one good lariat and that would not hang four men. From my position I could see that the women, bound hand and foot, were tied to some cedar trees. That sight made my blood boil.

I waited from my lookout point for sometime. I heard horses' feet and then I saw Sheriff Hawkins and his posse with the Indian trailers hunting me out. I knew someone was coming up the trail afoot and I found it was one of our Apache trailers. Another one of the trailers made into the rustlers' camp—drew his rifle and ordered them to surrender.

We on the bluff saw it and we answered with a fusillade of rifle shots that assured the Indian we'd be there in short order. Two of the rustlers started to head out from the campfire and our lariat ropes swished over their heads and jerked the rustlers off their feet. The other two stood their ground. The women cowered there and screamed for us to spare them.

Picketwire Johnson got out his knife and cut the ropes of the two women and freed them. One of the girls said to give her a gun and she'd cover the two outlaws until we were ready to dispose of them. The girls were given the guns and we built a big fire and located a suitable place where we could hang four rustlers.

Dusk spread its shadows about us but soon our fire lit up the canyon. The rustlers pleaded and swore as we made our preparations.

The rest of the posse rode in about this time and we had plenty of lariat ropes to make up a nice necktie party. The youngest rustler was a boy about sixteen. He struggled to loosen the rope, but the more he jerked, the harder the Indian trailer pulled on the rope. Before the darkness of night set in on Palisades Mountain we had hung the rest of a gang of rustlers that had preyed on the ranch owners for some time.

Sheriff Hawkins decided to let the bodies hang until someone buried them, mostly for the example it might set for other outlaws. And it did. This hanging party ended cattle-rustling in the neighborhood.

The West has changed a whole lot since the old days. Stagecoach and train robberies have stopped. The tin-horn gamblers are gone and the two-gun badmen are asleep in Boot Hill cemetery. But there is still plenty of cattle stealing.

Eastern tenderfeet may be surprised to hear that

rustling is going on right now in places almost like in old times. Lots of people suppose it disappeared when the ranges were fenced in and the country better policed by Rangers and other officers, but they are wrong. The feeling nowadays against lynching has helped to encourage the rustlers and now they do their stealing with motor trucks.

Down in southern New Mexico the other day this sign was nailed to a tree beside the road:

$500 RE-WARD

FOR CATTLE THIEVES
JUST HELP US CATCH
THEM
WE WON'T HAVE NO
TRIAL

WILLS RANCH

Four or five bullet holes around the sign kind of made it look serious. It meant that the Wills Brothers, cattlemen, had stood all they were going to put up with in cattle rustling and proposed to do something about it next time without waiting for the law.

I don't want to try to justify lynching when there is law and order that can be depended on. Ranchmen don't get up necktie parties for the fun of it. I have been to quite a few myself and I have seen the vigilantes turn their backs when the rustlers swung into the air. Those lynching parties were made up of the best men in the country and they figured they were doing their

duty in the community just like they would help beat
out a prairie fire, or smoke out a wolf's den. Out on
the plains where they couldn't rely on the sheriffs to
stop the cattle stealing they decided the only way was
to attend to it themselves.

The National Cattlemen's Association, when they
talked it over in the convention in Phoenix, Arizona,
recently, rated rustling as one of the three or four most
serious things they had to face. It is going on in most
every state west of the Mississippi. States along the
edge of Canada and Mexico suffer most because the
thieves find an easy market for the stolen animals over
the international line.

The cattle rustler today is right up to date. He is a
streamlined model. In old pioneer days he would have
ridden around a herd at night with six or eight others
in his outfit, or he would have driven off a few animals
at a time and rebranded them with his own registered
brand. Here's what one of the cattlemen told at the
convention and it gives a good idea how rustlers work
nowadays.

A few weeks back four big-hatted Arizona cowboys
sat their horses very quietly behind a clump of iron-
wood and mesquite bushes which screened them from
a paved highway. Each man was armed with two
pistols and a rifle. After about two hours a big furni-
ture motor van rattled down the road. Across the road
on the other side from the hidden horsemen a dozen
fat steers were grazing. The big truck pulled over and
stopped. A man with tools got out and began to work
on a rear tire.

"That's a bluff," whispered one of the watching cowboys.

The four men unholstered their pistols. The driver of the van had also left his seat and was studying the landscape carefully. He appeared to be satisfied that there was no one watching him and he let down a heavy door that made a runway to the ground. Then he led a saddled horse out of the van and mounted it.

"By gosh, we've caught them this time," whispered one of the cowboys, but some of their excitement had been caught by their own horses. One of the animals whinnied good and loud. Quick as a flash the cattle rustler on horseback whirled about and jumped into the van. The second man slammed the door and before anyone could stop them the truck roared away. The cowboys fired a few useless shots, but all they had accomplished was to prevent the cattle being stolen.

Men with trucks are carting fat steers away every day and making a paying business of it. A truck can haul six to a dozen steers at once and there are several ways to dispose of them. If the steers can't be driven over the border they may be rushed to a secret spot, butchered quickly and sold in some market, the price being cut enough to stop any questions. Sometimes the rustler goes to a regular "fence." The stock is most likely to be in some butcher's refrigerator before the rancher knows they are gone.

In New Mexico, Montana and Arizona the law hasn't been able to stop these thieves. Those three States are boiling mad over the situation. Sheriffs' officers say that they are too few to catch the rustlers in States where distances are so great, the population so

scattered and unfenced ranges so extensive. The sign
posted by the Wills Ranch in New Mexico is said to
have done quite a lot of good in that neighborhood,
although the exact results are not given out. If the
outfits around the Wills Ranch made "coyote bait" of
some of the rustlers, honest ranchers won't shed many
tears.

In Arizona, near the mining town of Wickenburg,
this sign was posted recently:

"We are out after rustlers and will pay for same,
dead or on the hoof. Good money for information.
This offer is genuine."

Some of the cattlemen that are losing stock from the
thieves in the motor trucks are old-timers who have
not forgotten how rustlers used to be handled. In old
times it was quite a favorite way to deal with them by
what was called the "ride-away." When the cowboys
caught a rustler, they tied his hands and feet—his
hands behind his back—looped a noose good and firm
around his neck and threw it up over the limb of a tree.
Then releasing his feet they sat him up on his own
horse which wasn't hitched—and then they rode away
and left him. The cowboys knew that the horse wasn't
going to stand still forever and it gave the rustler a
little time to think over things and wonder how long it
would be before the horse started off to do some feeding.

In the old days when the sheriff or his deputies
rounded up horse thieves or cattle thieves, they took
them to jail until they could be tried. But if the thief
happened to be someone the ranchers had been trying
to catch for a long time, they were likely to handle the

case without judge or jury. A case like that happened in Wickenburg, where a cattle rustler had been locked up in jail until his case could be tried. After supper an outfit of cowboys rode into town and asked for him.

"You men can't have this prisoner," the jailer said. "He's guilty, but he'll hang legal. I have sworn to protect him."

"Who put you in office?" the leader of the cowboys asked.

"The people did, and I'll be true to them," said the jailer.

"Well, we're the people and we hereby remove you from office for the time bein'," the cowboys announced. In the same moment a lariat settled around the jailer and he was removed from his position then and there. Half an hour later the rustler was dancing at the end of a rope.

I have always thought women ought to stay around the house and look after the kitchen and their youngsters if they have any. But now and then women take to stealing cattle and when the cowboys run up against a lady with a bunch of cattle that have been stolen, they don't feel like treating her to a rifle bullet or a "necktie party."

Out near Durango, Colorado, a few years ago, cattle were missed from the ranches. It took quite some time and trouble before the cowboys rounded up three men—and a woman. They had got their hands on the right outfit, sure enough, because the three men admitted they had been stealing and butchering cattle along the La Plata Valley and Long Hollow District.

The cowboys decided to turn them over to the sheriff and the three men got State prison sentences.

But the woman, Mrs. Green Newton, said she didn't know anything about what the men were up to, although one of them was her own son. She was a big strong woman of the out-doors with a firm jaw and they said she was the brains of the outfit and called her the "Queen of the Cattle Rustlers." And here again the ranchmen had made no mistake. The lady cow thief was tried and convicted and sentenced to prison for three years.

There are quite some surprises now and then on the cattle ranges. Texas ranchmen around the towns of Menard and Rochelle were losing stock a few months ago and were puzzled to account for who was stealing them. There was a woman evangelist and her husband who were holding some rousing meetings in those towns and, of course, they were the last persons to suspect of cattle stealing. But the sheriff got information that, after holding her revival services, Mrs. Gatlin would change her white minister's robes for overalls and, with her husband's help go out and round up horses and cattle. Following this up, the sheriff found some stolen stock at a ranch the Gatlins admitted they had brought there. But they claimed they had bought the animals from a stranger. Gatlin was convicted, but his preacher-wife pleaded she was insane and she is locked up in the State insane asylum in San Antonio. Who would ever have guessed that a woman minister and her husband were mixed up in cattle rustling?

Way back in the old days, horse stealing was such a

nuisance that the Anti-Horse-Thief-Association was formed and covered the Midwestern area. The members were private citizens who had to take the law into their own hands and deal out rough and ready justice. There was nothing sneaking about it and none of them wore any masks. And they got no special joy in ending the useless lives of horse thieves. But they had to protect their property.

If a bunch of horses had been run off, a signal was given and well-armed ranchers with long ropes coiled and hanging from the horns of their saddles gathered at the agreed meeting place. When the members of the outfit had overtaken the thieves and captured them alive they looked about for a suitable tree. When this was found the silent party came to a halt and "court" was opened. One of the mounted men was chosen as judge and others made up the jury. Just as soon as the rustlers were proved guilty, sentence of death was passed and execution was prompt.

Nowadays in many sections of the Middle West horse stealing has gone out of fashion and it is automobile stealing and "stripping" that occupies the present members of the Anti-Horse-Thief-Association. The members, many of them deputies, go over the roads in fast motor cars and they give attention to the automobile thieves and the gangs that make a living by stripping cars of parts which can be sold. But instead of holding their own courts and executing their own justice. they bring them to jail and they are handled by the regular machinery that metes out justice to criminals. So the old order changes.

Chapter XI   Law on the Old Frontier

T HE ONLY LAW out on the big cattle ranges and
in the roaring mining camp was most often carried on the hips. Whichever one was quickest on the
draw won the case. But sometimes the decision given
by the six-gun didn't seem right and then the case was
decided by Judge Lynch and settled by what we called
a "necktie party."

In some of the big towns there was a United States
marshal with his deputies and I was a deputy marshal
on occasions. In other places the ranchers elected a
sheriff who, mostly always, was afraid of nothing and
a dead-shot with his Colts. Many of them didn't live
long. Now and then some two-gun badman got to be

sheriff and his deputies were bandits and killers. I have told about that kind. An outfit like that was likely to get mixed up with holdups, stagecoach robberies and taking care that their outlaw friends never got arrested. The small frontier towns often had a city marshal who had to be a good gun-fighter and sooner or later most likely was drilled by some drunken cowboy or crazy miner or maybe a quick-shooting, tinhorn gambler.

So it was that all through the frontier country the ranchers and miners made their own laws and enforced them. If a man was killed in a fair pistol fight there was no penalty on the man who killed him. The friends of the victim, if he had any, carried the body up to the town's Boot Hill and piled stones over his grave so the wolves and coyotes wouldn't dig him up, and the case was closed.

There were no lawyers—"law coyotes" we called them—to slow things up by their tricks and nobody had any law books to be looked over. Most of the towns had no jail to hold a prisoner or a condemned man for long, and so it often came that justice in those days was dealt out by a necktie party. In some cases it was decided there wasn't any need to hold a jury trial at all. The general facts in the case being known to the community, a badman was condemned by popular consent and, there being no public hangman, the citizens did the job prompt and thorough.

I was around at quite a number of "necktie parties" and no two were just alike. Sometimes the man about to be lynched had friends. This added a little spice to the party, because the gents who ran the lynching were not sure whether they would be interfered with by the gents who would like to stop it. And so it was now and then that a bunch of cowboys would be rounded up to surround the "necktie party," each one with a Colt revolver or two hanging from his belt and a rifle resting handy across the saddle, ready to see that bandit friends of the man or the men about to be elevated at the end of a rope had no chance to stop the performance.

This was the way things were done in a fairly orderly community, where no more than one man was shot each week and where cattle thieves, horse thieves or stagecoach robbers were only caught once in two or three months. But now and then a community was so tormented by rustlers or bandits, or where the sheriff or marshal, if there was any, was so lazy or crooked that the cattlemen or miners or both together lost their patience and formed what were called Vigilantes. Some angry ranchman who had lost a bunch of cattle would be elected leader and he would round up a bunch of hard-riding, quick-shooting cowpunchers. And then followed "necktie parties" on a wholesale scale, without wasting much time for formalities. Everybody knew who the thieves or the murderers were and probably very few, if any, mistakes were made by the Vigilantes. They moved quick and sudden and acted like a big dose of physic for the neighborhood. A few "necktie parties" usually cleaned up the worst of the bandits and the others got out of the country as fast as their cayuses would take them.

One of these parties, where we all felt most as bad as the cuss that got the rope, was the hanging of Russian Bill at a little town called Shakespeare. One day a young tenderfoot came to town in good new clothes that must have cost plenty in the East. All we knew about his past was that his name was supposed to be Bill and he came from Russia. That was as much as we ever knew about some men and women but he was such a good-looking, likeable young man that we didn't kid him much about his smooth manners or play many tricks on him like was always done to a tenderfoot.

Young Bill hung around saloons and dance halls quite a spell, looking for a way to make some money but he didn't seem fitted for mining, prospecting, working on a ranch, tending bar, gambling or preaching, which is about all the steady jobs there were.

Nobody noticed that Bill had been gone a few days until the Vigilantes brought him in, caught in the act of stealing a horse. To steal a horse right, so you won't probably he caught, was no easy job and had to be done with a lot of thought. It wasn't enough not to be seen doing it. You had to figure how to get out of the neighborhood without leaving tracks that could be followed. Knowing what would happen if they got caught, most horse thieves were pretty careful and smart about it.

But this job was the worst I ever saw. Bill had just untethered the first horse he saw on his way down from the hills and ridden off through the mud, leaving tracks a blind man could have followed. They caught him in less than an hour. He confessed that he had been up in the mountains to see about getting a job with

Curly Bill, the outlaw. Curly Bill was busy planning something and said:

"All right, but I reckon the first thing you better do is go steal a hoss."

Maybe Curly Bill was joking, but anyhow here was a confessed horse-thief and there was only one thing to do. So they strung him up quick, right where they were, in the dining-room of the hotel, to get it over with.

Though the lynchings had nothing to do with the law, they mostly always were done with some dignity and the local custom was followed as near as possible. I remember the hanging of Whisky Bill as about as good form as any. He was a stagecoach robber who seemed to have some sort of way of keeping sheriffs and their posses from bothering him. At last the Vigilantes caught up with him and didn't waste any time on a trial.

The leader pointed at the nearest big tree and asked:
"Bill, how do you like that one?"

Bill thought the limb too low and picked out another with a bough about twice as high as the head of a man on horseback. A rope, with the end tied to another tree, was thrown over the limb while Bill, with his hands tied behind him, was set on a horse behind another rider. The horse was brought under the limb and the noose fixed around Whisky Bill's neck. The leader then asked Bill if he had any last words and Bill guessed he hadn't. The leader then said slow and soberlike:

"Good-bye Bill."

This was the signal for the rider in front to dig in

his spurs. The horse rode off, and Bill slid over his
tail, swinging like a pendulum. At this point of the
ceremony it was often the custom for everyone to get
out his shooting irons and fill the man at the end of
the rope full of lead. If anything, it was a kind of
merciful idea because it put him right out of his
misery. In this case for some reason, members of the
"necktie party" sat on their horses silently for about
20 minutes and then rode away.

A strictly legal execution ought to be done with
more style than any lynching and I'll say that it certainly was in the case of Black Jack Ketchum, and
knowing Jack as I did it must have been considerable
comfort to him. Jack was a tall, good-looking hombre
who always liked good clothes, kept his boots and
finger-nails clean and was careful to look and act more
like a hero than a villain.

He used to claim he never robbed the poor, and that
was true enough, but then they didn't have anything
worth robbing. It was true too, that he gave the poor
a share of his plunder. This may have been because he
loved the poor and then again it may have been because
it was good business to keep them friendly so they
would be spies for him and never tell on him.

Jack got along fine until he started to rob railroad
trains in Arizona. He robbed so many that after a time
Sheriff Fly went after him with a posse of good, able
men and kept right after him though he ambushed and
killed one of them in Skeleton Canyon. At last he was
caught, tried and sentenced to hang at noon in Clayton,
New Mexico.

The sheriff wanted to have as swell a hanging as

anyone had seen in the West which just suited Jack.
When Jack heard that photographs were going to be
taken of the important stages of the performance, he
did his part by ordering a fine new suit of clothes and
shoes. You'd have thought he was going to be married
the way he fussed with the barber about the haircut
and shave he had ordered beforehand, and he stepped
up onto the scaffold without any sign of fear.

Jack listened with interest to the minister's prayer
for his soul but shook his head at the thought that he
might somehow get into heaven. Then came a wait in
the proceedings which Jack didn't like, and he asked
the sheriff what time it was. The sheriff said that there
was just one more minute before the time fixed for
him to leave this world. At this, Jack said:

"Can't you hurry up a bit? I hear they eat dinner
in hell at twelve sharp. I don't aim to be late."

When the noose was being fixed around his neck,
Jack had a lot to say about the knot being set just
right behind his left ear. The black cap was pulled over
his face and he was joking through it when the trap
was sprung.

As I have said, women were scarce on the frontier
and whether they were good or bad, they were too
precious to be killed. Usually they were above being
punished for anything they did but there was one terrible exception at Hays City in what was the Kansas
Territory, about a mile and a half from the old Army
Post of Fort Hays, where I was stationed as an army
scout. Goldie Evans, a young woman with a very good
reputation for those days, shot and killed a good-for-
nothing tin-horn gambler known as "Sleek Ear"

Evans and had enough bullets left in her gun to do the same for the woman she caught with him. This was Dance Hall Annie, a lady with a reputation so bad that she was pointed out even in that town which was about the rottenest for its size on the frontier.

Goldie proved that she was Evans' wife and everybody knew that any jury would have to let her go. Goldie walked out of the town hall meeting where the thing had been talked over, thinking that was the end of it. But I guess some other wives of gamblers must have told their husbands that they were aiming to do the same thing Goldie had done, and these crooked gents decided they ought to set the girls an example. Anyway, a big bunch of them went over to Goldie's Lucky Horse Shoe Cafe the next morning.

I was in there getting some breakfast and Goldie, a pretty girl of twenty-five was behind the counter. The first thing I knew was the sound of shuffling outside. As a scout I learned to notice a lot of things that other people wouldn't and I didn't like that sound. So I wasn't much surprised when two gamblers with Colts in their hands threw open the door and told Mrs. Evans that somebody wanted to see her outside.

I jumped off my stool, pulled my six-shooter and motioned Mrs. Evans to back into the rear, but she stood her ground. She had a sawed-off shotgun and she motioned me, being in the line of fire, to step back. I stood my ground for a few minutes, but seeing that it would do no good, I got out of the way.

I told them that if anything happened to Mrs. Evans we'd make the town wish it had never been built. And it would not take long. With that warning

I stepped back out of the way. Mrs. Evans came from behind the counter with the gun she held at full cock. She was smiling as she walked toward the men and seemed to have no fear about her safety. You see she figured they wouldn't hurt a woman.

About the time she got near the door, one of the gamblers snatched her gun away and grabbed her arms, tying them behind her back. She struggled but had no chance against that gang of murderers that piled in the door.

I couldn't do anything there to save her except to warn them again. And I rode off to the fort as fast as my cayuse would take me. Their laugh was sounding in my ears and I thought it was only a threat but, as things turned out, it wasn't. While I was gone, they rushed her down to the creek, under a tree, tied her feet and hove a rope over a limb. To fit the noose right they cut away her dress at the neck. Even at this, the meanest of all lynchings I ever heard of, and they were in a hurry too, they took time to ask the girl if she had any last words. Goldie said:

"I am not afraid to die for anything I have done, I had a right to kill them for what they were doing, and you know it."

She did, by an unwritten law on the frontier, and this one was commonly respected, but when she was through, the leader of the gang shouted:

"Lead up!"

One of the men obeyed by leading his horse forward. The other end of the rope was tied to the horn of the saddle that drew the poor woman up to the bough. The gamblers let her choke there a while and then blazed away at her. When their guns were empty they tied the rope to a lower branch and left her hanging there.

At the fort, Lieut.Col. Cummins gave me a squadron of cavalry, but it was all over long before we got there. Almost never did you hear of anything being done to members of a "neck-tie party" and these gamblers thought they had nothing to worry about. But Goldie Evans was liked and respected by her customers and I can't remember when so many people got so mad so fast about anything.

It happened that a long train of emigrant wagons was camped further down the creek, with a lot of men from Kentucky, Tennessee, Louisiana, Arkansas and a few Texans. They were stern, quiet men, hard to rouse, but when stirred up, they were dangerous. There were half a dozen soldiers from the fort and some Pawnee Indians visiting the camp. The soldiers told how three men from the post had been murdered and others robbed in that town. Just as I got there they were asking each other what ought to be done.

Quietly one rather old man said that the place should be wiped off the map like Sodom and Gomorrah in the Bible. They all agreed and started into the town to see how it was to be done. The old fellow promised that the Lord would show them how it was to be done, and sure enough I reckon God or the gamblers themselves gave them the idea.

The men who were running the dives didn't like the looks of these strangers who were staring at them and thought it might prevent trouble if they closed up early that night. The next morning the wagon train would probably move on. As soon as the lights had been out a while, the soldiers and emigrants collected a lot of dry grass and other stuff which they piled along the ground beside the flimsy wooden buildings, and under the eaves, especially of the Buckhorn Saloon, where most of the dance hall girls slept.

Around midnight the Pawnees crept up with fire-brands (grass soaked in oil and grease), and they set the buildings on fire in so many places that they seemed to catch all over at once. The sleepers woke up in a prison of flames. As they rushed out through doors and windows they were mowed down by rifle fire. The fire wiped out everything in the business end of town except Goldie's cafe which was wet down before things started.

Some got away, mostly badly wounded, but in the morning we threw the bodies of 50 men and women into a long trench and covered them with quicklime. It was a pretty thorough job, but in those days when anybody told a story it was the custom to put a moral at the end of it so that even an Indian would get some good out of it. So we stuck up a slab of wood and one of the emigrants with his trigger finger dipped in a mixture of coal oil and lamp black wrote this:

PROCLAMATION!

To cattle rustlers and horse thieves, Greetings! Keep Clear of this town, and if you don't, Judge Lynch will get you with his Court.

To others whom it may concern: Tin-horn gamblers, what-not, all bad hombres —Stay clear!

When entering the town, leave your hard-ware at the jail with our City Marshal. By orders of the Vigilance Committee.

Hays City, Kansas Territory.

You'd be surprised how much good that burning and shooting party did. From the ashes of what was about the rottenest little town on the frontier sprang up a new Hays City, one of the cleanest. Crooks hated the place.

So the hanging of poor Goldie Evans did some good.

Women weren't usually invited to "necktie parties" unless they had some special interest in seeing that things were done proper. This wasn't because anybody was afraid that the sight might be bad for them be-cause their nerves were as good as a man's. The reason was that women were scarce and we didn't want any-thing to happen to any of them.

But the "necktie party" at Sycamore Creek that I joined was run by a woman, "Poker" Nell, who not only bossed the job but did the actual hanging with her own jewel-covered hands. I was in charge of the posse of Volunteers who arrived in time to help, but about all we did was to bring Nell the only thing she needed, a couple of lengths of rope. Lack of that was the only thing that kept the show from being over before we got there.

Nell ran a string of gambling joints between Denver and Cheyenne. She was still fairly good-looking at that time, was a good gambler and a good shot, but that was about all the kinds of a good woman she was except that she wasn't afraid of anything or anybody.

On a hot day the coach from Denver to Cheyenne came slowly dragging up to stop where a row of sycamore trees marked the creek by that name. There was the driver and up on top a messenger with a shotgun, guarding $28,000 in currency for the banks at Maverick City. Also there were three or four other men passengers, with at least one six-shooter on each of them. The bandits, squinting from behind the trees, thought it was from the men that trouble would come. Inside were two women, one an ordinary soft woman from the East, the other "Poker" Nell. Nell had a small bag holding a few toilet articles and about $14,000 in gambling receipts. On her hips were a pair of Colts.

With the ladies were a couple of men, one a little, unarmed jewelry peddler from New York and the other a Baptist minister with a long coat and a Bible. The driver jumped down to water his horses and the others on top climbed down after him. Just then two bandits rose up and got the drop on them, leaving not much choice but to stick up their hands. One of the bandits then turned his face and guns toward the inside of the coach.

One of the women let go a scream and fainted, the peddler turned white and almost fainted too. The other woman had a poker face which you couldn't read, but she didn't seem to be doing anything. The

other man was a preacher who started to preach at
them, beginning with "Thou shalt not steal."

The bandits snorted at this and got kind of careless
as they ordered the four to get out of the coach. The
peddler came out with his knees knocking together
and gave up his jewel case. The Eastern girl laid where
she was in a faint on the floor. Nell and the parson
came out too, but they took the door on the far side
and made a dive for cover. Nell got behind a tree and
jerked out her two guns. The parson went down on
his knees behind a rock, not to say his prayers, but to
use two six-shooters which were tucked under his long
coat-tails. He was the kind of sky-pilot you had to
have respect for.

With these two blazing away at them, the two
bandits found themselves in a bad hole. They had to
take cover, too, and could not keep much of an eye
on their men captives, who threw themselves on the
ground and began to creep away in all directions. The
messenger got clear, found one of the bandits' horses
and brought the news to Lodgepole Creek, where I
rounded up a bunch of cowboys, miners and Indians.

As I say, it was all over before we got there. The
bandits had surrendered, after each got a small wound
and the preacher had been nicked in the knee. His
wasn't serious, but for a few days he looked funny
praying on one knee and the other stuck out in front
stiff-legged.

When we got out to the place, we saw the minister,
with one pants' leg rolled up, preaching to a short
man and a very tall man who were standing with

their wrists and ankles tied, under a tree. When they say us, the parson closed his book and said:

"Here end the last lesson."

Nell called out to us:

"Court has set and sentence been passed. Gimme that rope."

She took one away from Charley Overshole and another from Fred Wildhorse, a half-breed Sioux. She tied a neat noose around the neck of the short bandit, tossed the other end over a bough and had one of the boys tie it to the saddle of one of our ponies. The other man was too tall for her to reach, so Charley offered to fix the necktie for her.

"Nope," said Nell, "this is all my party." She tied a running knot, making a lariat of the rope and with the loop lassoed him like a steer. When everything was set, she asked if the two had anything to say before being raised at least part way towards heaven. They shook their heads and again when she asked if they needed any more consolation from the parson.

"All right, send 'em up," she ordered, "I want to see 'em kick."

The horses were led forward and up went the bandits. While they were still swinging the boys filled them full of lead, but they gave Nell the first shot. We left them hanging with this sign nailed to the tree:

"Road agents keep off or be buzzard bait, like these." The peddler gave Nell a nice pin for her work in saving the rest of his stuff and she collected a $1,000 reward that was out for the tall bandit. Nell wanted to split it with the parson but he thought maybe a parson ought not to get paid for that line of work. So she and I borrowed the peddler's derby with a bullet hole through it and took up a collection in the saloons and dance halls in town. There was enough to buy a new hat and nearly a thousand dollars in currency and gold dust for the preacher.

The presentation was made in one of Nell's own joints and I guess it was a mistake because the preacher had too much to drink. He said mournfully that it was the first time he had ever been drunk in his life. This did not seem possible to one of the gamblers who called him a liar. Quick as lightning the parson knocked him down. Other gamblers yanked out their guns but Nell's were out first and nothing more happened. Of course they wouldn't think much of a minister who behaved that way today, but that was the kind they believed in and respected on the old frontier.

One day I was standing in front of the Palo Verde Saloon in Red Gap, Arizona talking to sheriff Limestone McCarthy, when a stranger rode in and hollered:

"Got any long pine boxes—we call 'em coffins back East."

Limestone said he reckoned the town could accommodate him with a couple of dozen maybe, but wanted to know who was going to be put in them. The stranger said he thought three would be enough because that was the number of bandits that had just held up the Denver-Cheyenne coach.

"We don't waste wood shirts on that buzzard bait," said Limestone as he went into the saloon and collected a posse from the bar. There was only one Bible in town and that was locked up in the church, so he swore them in over a deck of cards. The crowd was mostly gamblers, so it was just as good. While he was doing this I packed my burro with coffee and water which is better than whisky for posses.

When we reached Sycamore Springs, there was a man hanging from a tree, plenty dead, which made us think at first that the Vigilantes had been there ahead of us but the bandis had had an argument and two of them had hanged the other. We were right pleased to see that it was "Picketwire" Collins, with $500 reward on him, dead or alive. The boys were so tickled that they stopped to dig "Picketwire" a regulation six-foot grave and laid a pint of liquor under his head for a pillow.

Being a scout I was sent ahead to locate the other two. I supposed they would be at least 20 miles away by that time and started circling around, looking for their trail. It was nothing but luck that I saw their fire before I ran into them. Looking over a ridge, I could see two men, through my glasses, playing cards for a big pile of money. When I got back to the sheriff with the news, he thought of a scheme to take them alive without any shooting. This idea was for me to ride up on my burro, say I was a prospector and keep them interested in my fool conservation until the rest of them could creep up and get the drop on them.

The pair listened to me for a while but I could see that one of them didn't like my talk. Pretty soon he walked over to me and growled:

"You say you're a prospector. Well, I'm going to see what you've got."

Just before he reached me I whisked out my six-

shooter and told him to go back to his game. I had
him covered all right but the other man jumped up
and started reaching for his Colts, which was bad, because while I would be shooting one the other was
pretty certain to plug me. Just then Limestone poked
two six-shooters over the top of the sage brush and
said:

"Stick 'em up. I've got the winning hand, a pair
of sixes."

The rest of the boys came in, walked the pair over
to the nearest mesquite tree, which was quite a ways,
and were fitting the lariats around their necks when
one of them complained:

"You ain't aimin' to hang us without sayin' what
fer—are you?"

"Why, no, not if you are curious," said Limestone.
One reason is because we reckon you just stuck up a
coach back yonder."

The pair said the sheriff ought to prove it but
Limestone said rather than do that they'd hang them
over another count. Digging in his saddle-bags he
showed them two notices of men wanted.

"Now," said Limestone, "we figure that these ain't
yore pictures and it is all a mistake and that money
over there didn't come from the stagecoach. But anybody who looks so damn much like the pictures of
these two gents as you do we reckon ought to be
hanged on general principles."   --

They didn't argue any more after that and only
asked us not to put their names on the graves. We
didn't and just left a notice that they had come to

their deaths through strangulation and signed it "Vigilance Committee."

The stranger that rode in and asked us for the pine boxes said his name was Cyclone Johnson, but that didn't tell us who he was. Some of the old-timers thereabouts speculated on his being a peace officer. No one was sure of his identity, but there were several bets put up as to who he was.

I figured that he was either a detective of the Cattlemen's Association or a special agent employed by the Wells Fargo people. But it was never proved who he was. This man was what was called in those days, "a mysterious rider." He had seen the hanging of the one robber. He spread the alarm and gave the warning that there had been trouble on the road but he did not join the posse. He knew the Red Gap citizens would follow his tip and fix up a little "necktie party" for the other two. The reward money was always divided among the men. We all got a little whack at it.

That rider had some reason for wanting those bandits caught and strung up but he wanted to keep out of it himself.

Another day a prospector named "Coyote" Collins (no relation to "Picketwire" Collins) staggered into town and fell on the doorstep of the first saloon, which was a good place to fall. When they rolled him over, he whispered weakly:

"I've been robbed. I'm dying of hunger and thirst—but I'm thirsty first."

It took about four fingers of red-eye to give him strength enough to explain that a bandit had robbed him of his gold dust and kept him prisoner in a cave

for three days. Even Limestone couldn't make anything out of his description of the badman, but I
thought it might be George Francis Skinner, one of
Quantrell's old gang, who hadn't been doing anything for so long that most everybody had forgotten
that there was still $1,000 reward for him.

Without saying anything, I just loped out of town
next morning for Cactus City. At Tin Cup Post
Office I heard that somebody had robbed one of the
camps of its dust and from the descriptions I thought
it must be the same man. I kept right on to Cactus
City, where I figured he would most likely be spending his money. When I got there I found he wasn't
spending anything but his time, which he was doing
in jail, but they didn't know who he was or that there
was a reward on him.

After taking a peek through the bars to make sure,
I told the jailer, Ed McKeever, about the reward and
asked how he would like to split it with me. He asked
if it was dead or alive, and when I told him they were
not particular he shook hands on it and asked me to
sit into a poker party on the opposite side of town.
From one thing and another I suspected that he was
aiming to get himself and me out of the way so the
boys could take Skinner out for a "necktie party" so
as soon as I could get away from the game I hurried
back to the jail. Just as I had feared, the door was wide
open, the place empty and a man swinging from the
nearest tree.

But I took a look at the dead man's face and it
wasn't Skinner at all. My reward money was gone
and I was sore, but the boys were all celebrating

the hanging and it would be a dangerous time to tell them they had made a mistake. It wouldn't do any good to tell Ed either. So I started back to Red Gap wondering how such a mistake could have happened.

Just as I was riding through a gulch, looking for a place to camp for the night, I heard a voice:

"Put 'em up high."

I did, and from behind a rock stepped Skinner. He looked me over for a long time and at last asked if I hadn't been in the Arizona Rangers once. When I nodded he said:

"Reckoned I knew your face. What you aimin' to do down here, lookin' for me?"

"Yep," I answered.

"Well," said he, "you've got me. I'm sick and tired of all this. If you'll take me where they will try me before they hang me, I'll go peaceable and you can collect the reward." I took him to Prescott, but Ed McKeever made me pay him $500 just the same.

The queer thing was how the other man came to be hanged in his place. One of Skinner's old pals, George McCurtney, had been bothered with headaches so long that he was just going to shoot himself when he heard that Skinner was caught and George decided he might as well get some use of his own death.

He got there just as the boys were prying open the jail. He told them they had an innocent man, and George himself confessed to all the crimes that had been committed for 100 miles during the last ten years. They took him at his word, strung him up and let Skinner go. Skinner was right smart in giving himself up because the jury wouldn't convict him for crimes another man had confessed to and had been hanged for. He reformed after that and made a first-rate peace officer.

All my life I had wondered how decent people stand so much deviltry from crooks before they get mad and put a stop to it. Most parts of the West at one time or another got so the bandits and thieves ran things. You could hardly blame the sheriffs, even if they were honest, for not working too hard to round up the badmen. Everybody knew they would break jail or if they didn't bother to escape would be turned loose by juries who were afraid of being shot by their gang if they didn't let them loose.

In Indiana it got so bad that the law was a joke and the honest people seemed to have given up struggling with the crooks. Then, all of a sudden, vigilance committees sprang up and things began to happen. The first blow-up came after a train robbery at Marshfield.

It was a sort of mild stickup because though they got away with $96,000 in cash and bonds, I don't remember that anybody was killed. For a few weeks it looked as if nothing was going to be done about it. But this was because a new band of Vigilantes hadn't gotten any clue about just what outfit had done it. Then, in Syracuse, N. Y., a man was picked up trying to sell some of the stolen bonds.

He said he had gotten them from Frank Reno and Charles Anderson, who were arrested a little later, at Sandwich, Canada. Following out this clue, Simeon and William Reno were jailed at New Albany, Indiana and three more of the Reno gang named Elliot,

Clifton and Jarrell were arrested within the State and were being taken to that same jail. But on the way, a Vigilance committee pounced on them and hanged the three with no delay.

The Vigilantes then did a little better, making the arrest and the hanging at the same time for three more of the gang, Moore, Sparks and Rosenberg. These six stringings brought general approval, but the three Renos and Charley Anderson were meanwhile safely in jail waiting, as everyone supposed, another of those joke trials.

But at 3:30 one December morning, seventy well-dressed men, each wearing a red flannel mask and heavily armed, appeared suddenly on the streets of New Albany and marched on the jail. Breaking in the door, they wounded the sheriff, hanged the four men they were after and scattered. It was one of the quickest jobs on record I ever knew about, some people saying that they were in the jail only five minutes.

There were some howls from Canada, which had allowed Frank Reno and Anderson to be extradited on the promise of a fair trial. This was too bad but the effect of these and a few more neck-stretchings was beautiful to see. Dishonest sheriffs resigned, honest ones took heart and went after the badmen with confidence because the juries now dared to convict. Soon none of them had much to do because the crooks ran like rats from a state that was so mean to them, to other places that were more kind.

Here and there throughout the West are grim relics and reminders of the work of the Vigilantes. Some spots are marked with signs telling of lynchings.

giving the names of the victims and explaining why the outraged had to take action. In a good many of the old Boot Hill Cemeteries slabs are set up with the name of the outlaw and the date that he was made to dance at the end of a rope.

The Hangman's Tree for a long time was quite a famous place in Helena, Montana. The historical society there have records of ten badmen who dangled from the limbs from time to time and how many more there were, I don't know. The tree used to be on what was known as Dry Gulch, but was cut down a few years ago.

CHAPTER XII   Stagecoach Robberies

IN THE OLD days the stagecoaches handled the
    mail and the express and sometimes there was quite
a fat load of gold dust and nuggets. Here and there
in one of the big towns was a bank and the money
coming and going went in stagecoaches, mostly always in the Wells Fargo Express Company box.

Bandits didn't have much trouble holding up the
stages. A couple of robbers could step out from a
bunch of chaparral and get the drop on the driver and
the armed guard that sat up with him; this guard was
called the "shotgun."

More than once a stagecoach was held up and rob-

bed by a lone bandit. It didn't take long to line up
the passengers, if there were any, clean up their wal-
lets and watches, gather up the gold dust and nuggets,
and smash open the express box. By the time the stagecoach got to the next town and told the sheriff, and
he rounded up a posse, the robbers had a good start.

The Indians decided that holding up stages was a
pretty good game and some of them took to this for
a while. The redskins added a few frills of their own
by killing and scalping everybody in the coach and
tipping it over and riding off with six or eight horses.

Later on when the railroad began to push across
the plains, of course they put most of the stagecoaches
out of business.

The Indians figured the "iron horse" was bad
medicine and they didn't bother the railroads much.
But the old stagecoach bandits tackled the railroad
trains and made some big hauls.

In some of the stagecoach jobs the robbers took
time to add little touches that people talked about
more than the robbery itself. Quite often as a bandit
emptied a passenger's pockets he would ask his name,
address and business. Some explained that they wanted
to know in case they should meet up again somewhere.
Sometimes the passengers were told that the money
was only being borrowed and would be sent back as
soon as the "borrowers" got out of their jam. It looked
like they never did get out, but some victims kept
hoping to the end of their days.

When the James boys were robbing a coach in
Texas, they were tickled to find that some of the
passengers had more money on them than they had

figured was likely. Among these was Bishop Gregg, a rich and important sky-pilot of the Episcopal Church in San Antonio. The Bishop stood with hands stretched toward heaven while Jesse James went through his pockets, at the same time asking a lot of questions that sounded like it was a minister talking.

The Bishop knew enough not to make any fuss when the masked bandit lifted his fat roll of paper money and a money belt full of gold coins, but when he also helped himself to a fine gold watch and heavy gold chain, the Bishop put up a kick in his best pulpit voice:

"I beg of you to spare that watch. It was a gift to me from my beloved flock." But Jesse replied:

"Reckon the Savior wouldn't never worn such an expensive time-piece."

As the Bishop stood sticking the linings of his emptied pockets back in place, Jesse turned to the next passenger in line who happened to be a widow. She answered the bandit's questions and handed over a purse that had a daguerreotype of her dead husband in it, a lock of hair of her dead baby, but only five dollars.

"Look, Bishop, the widow's mite," said Jesse, and then imitating the preacher's voice said: "This poor widow hath cast more in, than all they which have cast into the treasury: for all they did cast in of their abundance; but she of her want did cast in all that she had, even all her living. Reckon I quoted the Scripture right, didn't I?"

"I believe so," answered the Bishop and then could

not keep from adding, "The devil can cite Scripture for his purpose."

"The devil ain't always so bad," said Jesse James, as he returned the widow's five dollars and added to it twenty dollars from the Bishop's own pockets.

"The first shall be last and the last shall be first," Jesse James called back as the bandits waved their sombreros and rode away. It was true, the poorest passenger had become the richest. At Austin, the next town, the widow grub-staked them to a meal and lent them enough to send telegrams home for more money. They were a long time getting in because the bandits had left the stagecoach just three horses, which meant walking all the way and everyone getting out to push on some of the hills.

Every trip afterward, the driver used to pull up at the same spot and say to the passengers:

"It was right here at this bend in the road where a man with a black mask and a couple of Colts stepped out from behind that rock yonder." And then he'd tell the whole story.

He did that for about two years and then one day, just as he was telling about the man and the mask, one did step out from that very rock and the coach was robbed all over again in just the same way except that there was no poor widow and rich sky-pilot to liven things up. Again the sheriff never caught sight of the bandits but the driver was sure they were a different bunch because he didn't recognize any of the voices. Nobody would have known that the James boys did the first job if some of the gang hadn't talked about it.

The reason that posses in these and so many cases never got near the bandits is easy to see. The important part of stick-ups was not the robbery itself because three or four well-armed men could do that part safely; it was the get-away. The robbers always knew the trail they were going to follow and rode it hard till some time after dark when they would come to a place where fresh horses were waiting for them. On these they would keep on riding hard all night. Before daylight they would get to some hide-out where grub and beds would be all ready. By riding at night and sleeping in the daytime, they would be out of the State unseen before the posses would be fairly on the trail.

Another important part of holding up stages was knowing which one to rob and when. At first the bandits were right smart about finding out somehow when the Wells Fargo would be sending a box of money. As far as I know the express company never did find out where the leak was, but they got around it by a neat trick which used to make the bandits cuss them. The express company would make its plans as usual to ship the money and then, just as the stage was leaving, snatch it off to go the next day. Or sometimes they sent it the day before and on the regular day shipped an "April fool" box with nothing but junk in it.

Most robbers don't steal from the poor for the good reason that the poor are not worth robbing, but the James boys were extra good at sizing up where money people were traveling. Jesse James was troubled with rheumatism from some of his many wounds and tried the baths at Hot Springs, Arkansas.

There he met most everyone and told them the water
had done him a lot of good. Every day he went down
to see the coach came in from Malvern and took note
how many workmen rode on it as compared with
people carrying enough money for a few weeks' stay
at the hotels while they took the cure. He took a trip
on the coach one day and when he came back to the
gang, he told them he had figured out a nice spot for
a hold-up, about five miles from the city of Hot
Springs. But Jesse did not go with them on this job,
probably he was afraid some of his new friends he had
made in town might be on the coach and recognize
his voice.

It was brother Frank who rose up from behind a
bush and drew the driver's attention by putting a
bullet within a few inches of his head. When he told
the driver to stop the coach and get down, the man
was not slow in doing it. The passengers stuck heads
out and saw revolvers pointed at them from behind
five horsemen. They agreed afterwards that they were
the meanest bunch of cuthroats they had ever seen,
which if they referred to their looks seems strange to
me, because Cole Younger was among them and he
was as handsome a man as I ever met.

Another of them, said to have been Clel Miller,
warned the passengers that he would count five and
then begin shooting anyone who had not gotten out
of the coach by that time. They were all out except
one man who cried that he was so crippled by rheumatism that he had to be carried out for he had had to
be carried in. It was the truth as several of the passengers assured the bandits, but Jesse had ordered

them to act fierce and as bloodthirsty as possible, so Clel roared out:

"Orders is orders. I reckon I got to shoot you just the same."

As part of the bluff, Clel fired a shot near the poor devil. To everyone's surprise, his own most of all, the cripple jumped to his feet and scrambled out of the coach as spry as anybody. A few minutes later when Clel and Jim Younger were taking about $200 out of his pockets, the man said he didn't mind a bit and would gladly give him as much more if he had it with him and was sure that the cure would last. The story is that it did.

But the others, especially former Governor Burbank, of Dakota, who had to give up $1,500, were not so happy. In all, they were shaken down for more than $4,000. Noticing that one of the passengers was scared white, Frank James and Cole Younger made a bet in a loud voice as to which could shoot the smallest piece out of the trembling man's ear. They had a noisy argument as to who should have the first shot, which was supposed to be an advantage because the blood might interfere with the aim of the man who was to shoot second.

At last, they agreed that each should shoot at a separate ear. Both aimed their guns at the poor wretch until he dropped in a faint. As the bandits rode away, Frank James called back:

"Tell them robbers who run the hotels that we got to you first."

Nobody tried to follow the band, which was probably just as well. The surrounding country was bar-

ren, mountainous and full of natural ambushes. The
few people who lived there were more or less outlaws
who would be sure to side with the bandits against the
sheriff.

The James boys studied travelers carefully, and
found out that while some men move from place to
place on business, without taking more than perhaps
a dollar or two with them, sight-seeing tourists
whether poor or not, always had quite a little sum
of money on them, even if it was the savings of several years. So they figured to stick up the stage between
Cave City, Kentucky and Mammoth Cave. In the
early 80's tourists used to go by train to Cave City
and the rest of the way by stagecoach.

Probably to fool the sheriff, Frank James, who
bossed this job, did everything as different as he could
from the Hot Springs hold-up, doing it with only one
man, Jim Cummings. The two horsemen, with guns
in each hand, rode out of the woods and told the
driver to stop. Then Frank in a polite, soft voice, said
to the passengers:

"Get out of the coach, please—and hurry, if you
don't mind."

They hurried because Cummings with a shaggy,
black beard and wild eyes, looked as if it would not
take much to make him forget his manners. But before they were out, Frank said:

"Oh, pardon me. I see there is a lady. She may re-
main seated."

The seven men climbed out and reached for the
stars. Under the guns of Cummings, who also held
Frank's horse, Frank soon went through the pockets

of the men, taking money and jewelry, but returning pocketbooks and tickets. First, he stepped into the coach and asked Miss Elizabeth Rountree to give him her rings, explaining that he had to attend to her first because he would not like to have her hide the jewelry about her and make him search her.

In cash the haul was disappointing, amounting to little more than $400, but the jewelry is said to have been worth about $2,000 more. As the pair rode off, Frank told his victims that he had just held up the coach going the other way and done rather better, collecting $700 from one passenger, alone.

The posse that pretended to follow them was little more than a bluff. I wouldn't want to hunt bandits in the Kentucky Mountains, even now, and I don't blame them. As I said before, the important parts of a stage hold-up are getting to the scene and away again. For these old time hold-ups the bandits needed plenty of empty land to make a safe get-away. The West has filled up so much since then that even the James boys, if they could come back, would have a hard time to get away with their old tricks, except in a very few places.

This was proved in 1899 when Pearl Hart came from Canada to Arizona and did not see why one more stagecoach robbery could not be done. There is no reason why a woman couldn't have held up a coach just as well as a man bandit. Calamity Jane, my aunt Belle, Cattle Annie or Little Breeches could have done it right, if they had liked the idea. But they never would have tried it in any such careless way as Pearl and her dumb boy-friend, Joe Boot, did.

Pearl Taylor, when she was sixteen years old, eloped from a girls' boarding school, in Ontario Canada, with a man named Hart, the kind of a man we used to call a tin-horn sport, who lived by his wits, wore a big diamond, made of glass, and carried a big gun he didn't dare use. He brought the girl to Arizona where she soon found out what a cheap sort of hero he was, and left him to be a saloon and dance hall friend of the miners.

From time to time she reformed and made good wages as a restaurant cook. Nobody ever said she was a good cook but women cooks were so scarce they didn't have to be good. Just as other people were giving up prospecting, Pearl took her small savings and tried it. All she found was why they were giving it up.

Just then came a letter from her mother in Toledo, Ohio, saying that she was dying and if her daughter wanted to see her again, had better come in a hurry. Pearl, who had been growing tougher and meaner all the time, was sure that the world had cheated her. When this letter found her without enough money to buy a round trip ticket to Toledo, she made up her mind to make the world stand and deliver. She and Joe Boot, dumb, but good-natured, talked it over. Joe had no ideas but seeing the coach from Benson to the Globe Mining Camp, he said jokingly that probably the only way would be to stick it up. Pearl took it seriously. Each had a gun and horse and next day they did it.

It had been some years since a road agent had stopped a coach, but everybody knew what to do when two riders, one a man and the other what seemed to be a boy, pointed guns and told them to stop and get out. Joe held the guns on them while Pearl went through their pockets. A traveling salesman had $380 on him, another $36, the driver gave up $20 and a Chinaman was found to have $5. Pearl generously handed back a dollar each for their first meal. They sent the coach on its way and then came the question of what to do next.

Joe guessed they had better get off the road which they did, getting lost in the bad lands and coming out three days later, hungry, thirsty and their horses hardly able to walk, about where they had gone in. They slept that night near a camp of Mexicans and hardly three miles from the place of the hold-up. Next morning they were waked up by the sheriff. The lady bandit and her boy-friend hadn't been able to spend a cent of the loot and even the Chinaman got his money back. Pearl was sentenced to ten years, but was pardoned out in two.

That's how things worked out for a couple of amateur road agents, and now let me tell you of the doings of a very different bunch. Jim Reynolds had been a captain in the Confederate army and came from a tough town in northern Texas. But he got tired of army life and figured there was more excitement and a lot more money raiding around the western cow country and mining camps. So Jim, who was called Captain, rounded up a bunch of badmen and they started out from Texas to ride the cattle ranges to Denver.

Captain Reynolds and his outfit robbed everybody

they met and helped themselves to food, liquor and ammunition at the ranches along the way. There were twenty-three men in the gang, all well armed and as wicked a crowd as ever straddled leather. Soon after they started they met up with a band of Indians on the warpath. The redskins attacked the Reynolds party but didn't know what wildcats they were tackling. All the warwhoops were killed but the bandits didn't lose a man.

A little further along they rode up to a Mexican border stagecoach. Wasting not a moment the outlaws held it up and when they came to look over the loot they were quite happy—there was $40,000 in currency, $2,000 in silver coins and $6,000 in other valuables. But Captain Reynolds stuffed most of the currency in his own saddlebags and this made the outfit sore. So fourteen of them quit right there and went back to Texas.

That left Reynolds with eight men—nine in all. They figured there was enough of them to handle most anything that turned up, so they went right along with their plans. One night a few days later the outfit stopped at a town called Fairplay. They heard that the stagecoach from Buckskin that goes on down to Texas usually carried quite a lot of gold from the smelters and gold dust from the miners. Captain Reynolds told his outfit that it sounded good to him.

Reynolds looked the ground over and planned to rob the coach at a lonely spot about ten miles from Fairplay. He decided that they would hide at a ranch, owned by Major Demere and another man by the name of McLaughlin until the coach came along. The ranchmen didn't like their self-invited guests but they had to do what the gang told them to. McLaughlin, at the point of a gun, treated the men to some whisky and Reynolds ordered his wife to rustle up dinner for the gang.

When the Buckskin coach pulled up at the ranch, Reynolds stepped out, fired his Colts twice in the air and ordered the driver, Abe Williamson, and Billy McClelland, the superintendent of the stage line who sat on the seat alongside the driver, to throw up their hands. Their hands went up quick, and after being disarmed by another member of the gang, Reynolds ordered them to get down, at the same time taking their money.

Williamson was good and sore at the idea of his having any money. He said that it was the first time in all his travels that a stage driver had ever been accused of having anything worth taking. Hold-up men never robbed the driver, he insisted. But his talk didn't go with these bandits, and after searching him carefully they found fifteen cents, which they took. Williamson had a lot to say to the bandits and promised to teach them a lesson some day. They shook down McClelland with much better results, taking from him $400 in money and a fine gold watch. Then they got busy with the express trunk as there happened to be no passengers on this trip.

One of the gang found an axe on the coach and broke the trunk open. They took out $6,000 worth of gold dust and $2,000 worth of gold bars that John W. Smith was sending East from his Orphan Boy mine. Then they ripped open the mailsack and letters were torn open and money taken out, so that all in all the loot amounted to $10,000.

After gathering up all the valuables Captain Reynolds told his men to smash up the coach. They went to work chopping the spokes out of the wheels, ripping out the seats and hacking at the sides with the axe. The horses were driven away, and then the men were ordered to go inside the ranch house and eat the dinner Mrs. McLaughlin had been told to get ready for them.

Before leaving, Reynolds told Williamson and McClelland, his captives, that they would be killed if they should try to follow the gang and that the best thing they could do would be to stay quietly at the ranch for a day or two.

After the gang had left, McLaughlin decided to alarm the mining camps about Reynolds and his outfit. He mounted a mule and spread the news and arrived in due time at Buckskin. From there he sent runners to California Gulch and other camps. He stayed in the saddle almost night and day for over a week and by that time had the whole country on the lookout. His efforts most likely saved many lives and thousands of dollars worth of property.

The countryside was pretty well stirred up by now and plans were made for the capture of the bandits. Armed bodies of miners and ranchmen started on their trail.

Reynolds and his band of men had meanwhile been stopping at various ranches taking whatever they wanted and robbing everybody they came across. Just a few miles beyond Deer Creek they met a posse of twenty-two men who had been following their trail. Reynolds took a spy-glass and hastily surveying the situation and the surrounding country decided to put up a fight. He strung his men out in single file in order to make a plain trail, and after going about a mile, doubled back and hid his men at the side of the trail to ambush the pursuing party. For some reason the posse turned back before they were in gunshot of the bandits. Whether they scented danger or were tired of following what they thought was a cold trail, I don't know. Reynolds feared that he and his gang were likely to be captured and thought it was a good plan for them to scatter as much as possible, hoping to be able to arrange a round-up later on down near Greenhorn.

He also decided to hide the greater part of their spoils until the excitement had died down. So Captain Reynolds and his brother John found a prospect hole near Elk Creek which they figured would answer the purpose. They took $40,000 in currency and three cans of gold dust, about $63,000 in all, leaving one large can of gold dust and considerable currency to be divided among the band before separating. They wrapped the money up in a piece of oil cloth and put it and most of the gold dust in the hole, about the length of a man's body.

Going back to the camp Captain Reynolds told his men that he reckoned it was best to disperse the band temporarily, as he believed there was no chance of escape if they remained together.

He described the place of rendezvous mentioned and told them that it would be safe to move on down to a grove of large trees in Geneva Gulch, a short distance below, and camp for dinner, as there was no one in sight. As they were getting dinner a dozen guns roared from behind some large rocks about 200 yards from the outlaws' camp. One of the men fell dead and Reynolds, who was at the time dividing some gold dust from a can with a dinner spoon, was wounded in the arm. The outlaws at once broke for the brush, some of them leaving their horses behind.

The attacking party were twelve men from Gold Run, under the leadership of Jack Sparks, and they had crawled around the mountain without anybody seeing them until they reached the rock and then pumped a volley into the robber band. If they had been a bunch of cowboys more of the robbers would have been killed, but miners are not such good shots. When the robbers took to the brush the posse seized the gold dust and the horses and after searching the gulches for a while in vain, they cut off the dead robber's head which they took back with them to Fairplay as a trophy of the fight. Some of the men were caught later on and were brought to Denver under a heavy guard and locked up in jail. They were given a trial by a miners' jury, and as it could not be proved that they had killed anybody they were sentenced to imprisonment for life, although a great many claimed they ought to be hanged anyhow.

That being the feeling around town the prisoners in the jail were taken to Fort Lyon for safe-keeping. Their guard was under orders to shoot any bandit making any attempt to escape.

The prisoners knew that they would be shot if the

guard could find the slightest excuse for doing so. For
the guard was made up mostly of citizens of Denver,
and some of them had suffered at the hands of the
gang. One of the posse was Abe Williamson who was
driving the Buckskin coach when it was robbed at
McLaughlin's ranch.

The prisoners were given all kinds of chances to
escape, but they were afraid to try it. Part of the guard
returned to Denver and Williamson was left in charge,
and he laughed in his beard as he planned his revenge.

He marched his prisoners to an abandoned log cabin
some five miles from Russellville, where he had intend to stay for the night. He told the gang that they
were to be shot, that they had violated not only the
civil but the military law, and that he had orders to
execute them. Captain Reynolds, who was in the
group, pleaded with Williamson to spare their lives,
reminding him of the time when the robbers had him
in their power and left him unharmed.

Williamson replied that they had better use what
little time they had on earth to make their peace with
their Maker.

They·were then blindfolded, the posse stepped back
ten paces and Williamson gave the order "Fire!"

The sight of the six unarmed, blindfolded, manacled
prisoners being stood up in a row to be shot down
like dogs unnerved the guards, and at the command to
fire they raised their rifles and fired over the prisoners
so that but one man was killed, Captain Reynolds, and
he was at the head of the line opposite Abe Williamson.

Williamson was disgusted and remarked that they

''were mighty poor shots'' and ordered them to reload. Several of the men flatly said that they would
not have a hand in any such cold-blooded murder and
threw down their rifles while two or three fired over
their heads again at the second "Fire!" and just Williamson killed his second man. Seeing that he had to
do all the killing himself, Williamson began cursing
his men, and taking a gun from one of them shot his
third man. At this moment one of the guards spoke up
and said he would help Williamson finish the job and
he raised his gun and fired. The fourth man fell dead.
Williamson had to finish the other two with his revolver. The bodies of the dead men were left on the
prairie and their bones were picked clean by the coyotes.

Several hours later one of the prisoners, John
Andrews, that they had left for dead, recovered consciousness. Although shot through the chest he managed to crawl to the cabin and dress his wound as best
he could. He found some dried buffalo meat left there
by the former occupants, and he managed to live on it
for a couple of days. A horseman traveling through
took a note from Andrews to his friend, Cochran, who
in a few days came for him in a wagon.

John Reynolds, a brother to Captain Reynolds, had
escaped from the posse and had gone south to Santa
Fé. When Andrews recovered he went South looking
for Reynolds with the hope that together they could
dig up some of the hidden loot. Andrews was killed
a little while later in a fight with some Mexicans that
he and Reynolds had stolen horses from. Reynolds
had escaped and returned to Santa Fé where he had
changed his name to Will Wallace, making his living as

a gambler. His reputation grew until the time he joined up with another desperado by the name of Albert Brown and the two of them started a hold-up business. It wasn't long before the country was too hot to hold them.

Reynolds was mortally wounded on the way to Denver and Brown had to carry on alone seeking the treasure which the Reynolds gang had given their lives to get hold of. Brown made the acquaintance of Andrew's friend, Cochran, and showed him the map which John Reynolds had roughly sketched as he lay dying. They went to Geneva Gulch but they could not find any signs of where that $60,000 of loot was buried. They ran out of provisions and in trying to steal them, both men were killed.

So the outfit that started out to rob everybody and everything in sight died, one after another, with their boots on and their big cache of plunder never did them any good.

CHAPTER XIII   Train Robberies

IT DIDN'T TAKE many to hold up a stage; one
bandit could do it. It usually took four or five to
handle a train and, with that number, it was just as
easy. But there was one train robber who worked all
alone and held up twenty-five or thirty trains single-
handed.

  The Missouri Pacific train robbery in 1876 shows
how neatly the James and Younger boys worked. One
July evening old Henry, the watchman, saw five well-
dressed men walk across the Otter Bridge, some distance out of Otterville, Missouri. When one of them
asked him for a drink of water, Henry went into the

pump-house under the water tank to get it. But when he stepped out, Henry let the glass fall.

The strangers had put on black masks and drawn revolvers. The man who wanted the drink had changed his mind and now told Henry to take his red lantern and come with them. Turning a sharp bend, the watchman saw that somebody had piled a lot of ties on the track. The bandits looked at their watches until a far away train whistle was heard. Then Henry was told:

"Now you go up on the track with your lantern and you stop the train or five bullets will go through your back at the same time."

The old man swung his lantern and the engine stopped just as it reached the ties. Of the eight men in the gang, two climbed into the cab to keep the engineer and fireman quiet, five others attended to the rest of the train and one was off somewhere guarding the horses. The bandits did not bother with the passengers except to keep them quiet. What they wanted was locked in the two safes in the express car.

The express messenger did his best in the short time he had. Giving the key to the United States Express Company safe to a brakeman who hid it in his boot, he sat down among the passengers. When the bandits found nobody in the express car, they grabbed the baggage man in the next one. He told them that he was not the messenger and was advised to shwo them that man, if he wanted to live. The baggage man led them to the messenger who also wanted to live and showed them the brakeman. The brakeman felt the same way and pulled off his boot in a hurry.

This key opened the safe of the United States Express and everything was dumped into a big canvas bag. The other safe belonged to the Adams Express and was a through safe and the passengers didn't have the key to it. The bandits came within a hair of killing him before he made them believe it. Those old safes were flimsy things because one of the masked men, with the train crew's hammer soon beat in one side of it. Through the hole they fished out everything and added it to the other stuff in the bag and rode away.

Just as they were leaving, the train boy became a rash sort of hero by emptying his little .32-calibre revolver after them. Everyone threw themselves on the floor of the train expecting a rain of lead in return, but the bandits only laughed at the little "pop gun."

The loot, all in cash, amounted to a little less than $16,000, not quite $2,000 apiece, but money was worth more than twice as much in those days. Posses went out from three different towns, did all that could be done, but never caught sight of any of the robbers.

A few weeks later Charlie Pitts, one of the band, broke his promise to marry a widow, Mrs. Lillie Reamer. Charles soon wished he had done right by the widow because as soon as she heard that he had married another woman she told the sheriff what he had told her about the job. They caught Pitts on his honeymoon, with $1,800 of the stolen money in his pocket.

Charlie confessed and got a four-year sentence. He said that those who worked with him were Jesse and Frank James, Bob and Cole Younger, Hobbs Kerry, Clel Miller and Bill Chadwell. The others put up alibis and escaped being punished except Kerry, who drew a four-year sentence.

Jesse James was always proud of a Kansas-Pacific job he did outside of Wyandotte, Kansas. Somehow he knew that $30,000 in gold dust and $25,000 in cash was to be sent on a certain train. This time there was no flagging of the train or placing stuff on the track because the train stopped of its own accord at the water tank. The two James boys with Cole and Bob Younger, Clel Miller and a couple of others, including Bill McDaniels, walked out from behind the tank and took charge. In less than ten minutes, they had made the express messenger hand over his $55,000 worth of treasure and off they went.

It was the same old story of posses galloping around and not finding anybody. But McDaniels was careless and unlucky, getting arrested for a drunken row in Kansas City. Finding the prisoner loaded down with about $5,000 worth of money and gold dust the police knew pretty well that he had something to do with the big robbery that had just happened. No amount of questioning would make him talk. Later he was fatally wounded when he tried to escape, but died still refusing to say anything about the robbery.

Bob Dalton was jealous of the James boys' reputation and had the idea he could beat it by doing double jobs. It was trying to rob two banks at once in Coffeyville that finished him and his gang, but he did manage to rob two railway trains at once. While the Daltons were going through a Santa Fé train which they had flagged at midnight in the middle of the Cherokee Strip, a wild piece of territory where nobody but Indians ever lived, another train came along in the other direction.

Bob ordered that flagged and robbed too. It was done and though the profits of both together were not very big, Bob always bragged that it showed he was a smarter leader than Jesse or Frank James. A queer thing about this double hold-up was that about 200 Indians were allowed to watch the whole thing from start to finish. The Indians stayed neutral, neither helping nor hindering either side. The Daltons paid no more attention to these witnesses than if they had been so many cows. Warwhoops were no good in court, as everybody knew, because they always said they were not there, didn't see anything and didn't remember anything. Even if they did tell anything, no jury believed them.

Jesse James and his brother were better planners and got away with most of the big money. They stopped a Rock Island Express 14 miles east of Council Bluffs by piling ties on the tracks, without bothering to flag the train. Raffery, the engineer, did not see the pile quite in time to come to a full stop and was killed by the shock and several passengers were injured. They got away with $125,000 that time.

Gratton and Bill Dalton were so careless about robbing a train in California that Gratton was tried, convicted and sentenced to 20 years in jail, but escaped before reaching its doors. Bill was tried and acquitted and both were named in a $6,000 reward offered for them by the Southern Pacific Railroad. This offer made Bob the leader so proud of his two brothers that he figured to take in some more members and work in

a bigger way. It was then that he took in Ol Yountis,
Charley Bryant and Bill Doolin.

The careful James brothers not only took pains to
make sure that there would be a good haul in the
express cars but that no such unpleasant surprises as
a company of soldiers or police were on any train they
intended to work on. The careless Daltons often found
poor pickings and once when they held up a Missouri,
Kansas and Texas passenger train near Adair, Texas,
they didn't know that a company of Indian police
were riding on it.

When the police began shooting out the windows at
them the Daltons, instead of running away, returned
such a hot fire at the car that the police stopped firing
and let the bandits finish the job of robbing the mail
and baggage cars.

Of course, the James boys and the Daltons and the
Youngers were not the only train robbers in those
days. They made a business of it, but now and then
a bunch of badmen would make a try at the game.
Not being so cool-headed and lacking experience, they
sometimes made a mess of it and the train they planned
to clean up pulled into the next station without losing
anything out of the express car, but with a little extra
express on the floor in the shape of four or five dead
bodies of masked bandits.

There was one quite prosperous train robber that
almost matched up with the James boys. He was Sam
Bass and his outfit worked mostly in Texas. In those
days the cars were built of wood and a rifle bullet
would go right through the side. If the express agent
and his shotgun guard inside the door wouldn't open

up the car, the robbers could put a couple of sticks of dynamite under it and blow it up. If they didn't have the dynamite handy, they could throw a quart or two of kerosene on it and set it afire.

The first train job Sam Bass did, if I remember right, was on the old Houston & Texas Railroad, not many miles out of Dallas. Bass liked to get his work done and get to bed early, so he mostly picked between nine and ten o'clock in the evening for his hold-ups.

This first job of Bass and his outfit was at Allen Station, a small stop. Four masked men came out of the dark and one jumped into the cab of the engine, holding a Colt on the surprised engineer and fireman. That took care of that end of the train.

The other three ran up to the express car and tried to get in. But a man named Thomas saw the masked men and as Sam Bass yelled, "The money or your brains!" Thomas ducked back and pulled his gun.

All hands began shooting and, at last, the gang got into the car, tied up the express agent, took his keys, opened the safe and helped themselves to more than $5,000. Of course, the outfit didn't know whether there might be a bunch of soldiers or some Texas Rangers back in the passenger cars. So they cut the bell cord, uncoupled the express car and made the engineer pull ahead down the line where nobody would disturb them. There was a fifth member of the gang in charge of their horses and when the job was finished they signaled for their cayuses and rode off. They didn't bother the passengers at all.

The express company was sore at losing the money and a posse was started on the trail of the robbers. The gang had divided up the cash and separated, but they caught one of them, Tom Spotswood, at a ranch on Little Elm Creek. They yanked him into court right quick and, Thomas, the express agent, swore that he recognized Spotswood as he was the man who held a six-gun in his face while the others robbed the safe. Spotswood either didn't have a mask or had lost it and Thomas said he specially noticed Spotswood's glass eye. He was convicted and got ter years.

This was the first train robbery in Texas and the express company thought that Spotswood was the leader of the gang. So they were pretty pleased at getting him and reckoned they would be bothered no more by the outfit. Nobody knew at that time that Sam Bass was the leader, because Spotswood kept his mouth shut. But it wasn't long before there was another hold-up and on the same railroad, and this time about ten miles outside of Dallas at a small station called Hutchins. It was a well-planned job, like a Jesse James piece of work.

They figured everything out in advance and as the train slid to a stop, one rounded up the station agent and another covered the engineer and fireman with his Colts. Curious to know what was going on, a couple of tramps that had been stealing a ride on the cow-catcher of the engine peeked around and were seen by the bandits. These were grabbed, the engineer and fireman were made to climb down from the cab and the station agent was added to the little round-up. This innocent squad of five were marched up to the express car ahead of the robbers. They thought the express agent wouldn't fire into that bunch but they were wrong.

It happened that the man in charge of the express car was named Thomas, a brother of the agent they had run into on the first robbery. He barred the car doors, but the bandits broke open one of them. Thomas fired into the crowd and hit one of the tramps, but a bullet from Sam Bass' Colts hit the express agent in the face. As Thomas fell the robbers pushed into the car, broke open the safe and tore open the registered mail sack. They got away with several thousand dollars. A posse was collected, but couldn't follow the trail of the robbers; maybe they weren't hungry to meet up with them anyway.

Pretty soon Sam Bass and his gang tackled another train. This time it was at Eagle Ford, not far outside of Dallas. It was about ten o'clock in the evening and the bandits used the same method they did in the Hutchins hold-up.

As the station master came out of the depot he was faced by a man who came around the corner, wearing a mask and holding a couple of guns. This robber was followed by two men, masked and armed. One of them brought the engineer and fireman out of the cab and another went along to the passenger cars to keep the passengers from horning in. The robbers went up to the express car, pushing their prisoners along ahead of them and soon were in the car and had $12,000 in their saddlebags as they rode away in the darkness. Quite a neat, quick job with good profits.

Sam Bass and his outfit kept right busy robbing

trains and between jobs gambled away or drank up their easy money.

During this series of robberies, the robbers had made their headquarters at a deserted ranch in Denton County, where most of the hold-ups had taken place. Like a bunch of fools, they were rounded up by the sheriff's posse. During the capture of the gang Bass managed to escape, severely wounded. The sheriff swore he would get Bass himself. He knew that the leader of the gang could not get very far in his condition.

As the sheriff was riding out on the prairie, he met some men on railroad construction work and asked them if they had seen a wounded man in the vicinity. The workers replied that there was a man lying under a tree nearby who was hurt and who said that he was a cattleman from one of the lower counties and had been shot in some gambling difficulties. The sheriff saw some mules grazing near the spot and thought that the man could not possibly be Bass, and so he rode away. On his return home that night after a wasted day searching for Bass, he rode very close to the spot where the man had lain earlier in the day. As he came near the tree a voice called out, "Don't shoot, I ain't armed. I am the man you're looking for. I'm Sam Bass."

The sheriff took Bass to the hospital where it was soon found that he had no chance of getting better. In his statement to the sheriff, he said that he was twenty-seven years of age and told of some of his hold-ups. His biggest robbery was the Union Pacific train at Big Spring, Texas, where the haul amounted to $60,000 in gold. Like the others in his line of business, he spent the money as fast as he got it, so when he died, the town had to bury him. Over his grave the people of Round Rock, where he is buried, raised a monument which reads:

"Samuel Bass

Born July 21st, 1851

Died July 21st, 1878

A BRAVE MAN REPOSES IN DEATH HERE WHY

WAS HE NOT TRUE"

Funny kind of epitaph, wasn't it?

There was a lone bandit; one who worked all alone. This was a man known as "Black Bart." I have heard that "bart" is a German word and means "beard." Anyhow, nobody knew the name of that busy, lone, black-bearded bandit until he was caught and then he turned out to be Charles Boles of California.

"Black Bart" started in as a stagecoach robber, like most of the train robbers, and then began to tackle railroad trains. He was a comical cuss and must have got quite a lot of fun out of his business besides the money he stole. I never knew Bart, never saw him, but I heard about his doings from friends of mine who were deputy sheriffs and possemen that tried to get him.

He always wore a long linen duster with a jute bag wrapped around his body like an Indian's blanket. A tall, cone-shaped hat, such as clowns in the circus wear, completed a costume as outlandish as a stage comedian would wear, if he was playing the part of a burlesque bandit. But the people he robbed didn't think he was funny.

"Black Bart" picked the place for each of his robberies with the greatest care. His favorite spot was a sharp curve at the foot of a hill where the road ran through a strip of forest or between high cliffs.

A few yards from this point in the road but close enough to be plainly seen from the halted stagecoach, the robber rigged a cute decoy which made his victims believe that he was not alone but had with him quite a bunch of outlaws.

With jute bags or pieces of tent canvas he fixed up a screen about three feet high between two piles of rocks or two trees. The outside of this ambush he carefully masked with branches of trees or chunks of sod. Behind the ambush he stuck in the ground a half dozen sticks and on each stick he hung an old sombrero, such as every cowboy and miner in those days wore. These hats showed above the ambush just as they would have if there had been real men underneath them. Below each hat "Black Bart" stuck a piece of broomstick painted black, that looked like rifle barrels. The stagecoach people never doubted that six men were crouching there with rifles in hand ready to fire on them at the first sign of resistance.

After planting his dummies and when it came almost time for the coach to be due the lone highwayman would climb to the top of a tree or a neighboring cliff and watch for it with the powerful field-glasses he always carried. If there was anything he didn't like the looks of, he would quickly dismantle his dummies

and lay them aside to wait for a more favorable time.
But if everything looked all right, "Black Bart"
climbed down and took up his position at the bend of
the road where he could not be seen from the coach
until it was almost upon him. He carried the shotgun,
which he afterward said was never loaded, and behind him there were the hats of his six dummy confederates with their rifle barrels.

"Hands up!" shouted the highwayman, stepping
out into the road right in front of the horses and
leveling his shotgun at the driver's head.

The driver tugged on the reins, jammed the brake
down hard and the heavy stage came to a stop. Everybody looked at the comical figure in the road—not
quite sure whether to laugh or to cry.

But any hopes that it might be a joke were quickly
spoiled by the business-like way the highwayman
handled his gun and by the meaning nod of his head in
the direction of the sombreros and rifle barrels, which
made such a threatening background for the little
drama.

"Don't shoot until I give the word, boys," he called
over his shoulder to his supposed confederates—the
scarecrow imitation bandits who looked very dangerous in the bushes beside the road.

Whatever idea of putting up a fight the driver or
any one else on the stage might have had was dropped
at sight of the dummy desperadoes that were right in
plain sight to back up "Black Bart."

"I'll have to trouble you to step out of that stage
for a moment," said "Black Bart," with a pleasant
smile.

As the men, women and children left the stage he lined them up by the roadside, right in range of the ambushed riflemen, whose painted broomstick guns kept the little group constantly covered. From under his duster he drew out a neat canvas bag. With this in one hand and his shotgun in the other, he passed along the line and gently but firmly made his victims toss in their watches, pocketbooks, scarf-pins and everything else of value.

This job over, he would make the driver open the mail bags and the strong-box where the valuable shipments were carried. From their contents he selected all the money and gold dust and stowed it away in his bag, which by this time was likely to be bulging with plunder.

"Now drive on," said "Black Bart," motioning his victims back to their places on the coach, "and if you value your lives don't look back. My men and I are dead shots and will fire at the first head we see lookin' around."

Anything that would take them out of the range of those guns was welcome to the frightened people on the coach. The driver would crack his whip and away the stage would roll at a great pace—with never a person bold enough to look back at the scene of the robbery.

"Black Bart" was something of a poet and took a great deal of pride in his verses. Quite often after robbing a stagecoach, he would hand one of his victims a bit of paper on which were scrawled some of his rhymes. Here is a "poem" which the driver of a Wells-Fargo stage received from "Black Bart" as souvenir of the time when the highwayman robbed the strong-box of $6,000 in gold and diamonds.

> *Here I lay me down to sleep,*
> *To wait the coming morrow—*
> *Perhaps success, perhaps defeat*
> *And everlasting sorrow.*
> *Yet come what will—I'll try it,*
> *My condition can't be worse,*
> *And if there's money in that stage,*
> *'Tis money in my purse.*

> "Black Bart."

When railroads began to take the place of stage routes "Black Bart" proved to his satisfaction that the scheme by which he had robbed so many stages single-handed and without taking a life, would work just as well in holding up trains. Time and again fast express trains on the Western roads would be stopped just at dusk in some lonely spot by the frantic waving of a red flag.

When the engineer jumped down to see what the trouble was, he was faced by "Black Bart" dressed as usual in the clownish outfit which was so different from every other train robber. At the point of his shot-gun the robber forced the engineer and fireman to un-couple the engine and run it a few hundred feet down the track.

By this time the passengers and trainmen were pour-ing out of the cars to find out what had happened. "Black Bart" wasted few words on them. Nodding his head in the direction of his "riflemen" whose hats and "gun barrels" showed from the usual ambush at the side of the track, he said loud enough for all to hear:

"Don't fire unless I give the word, boys!"

The hint was enough. Everybody looked at those sombreros and broomstick rifle barrels and decided they were at the mercy of a band of desperate men. Passengers, trainmen and express messengers quickly handed their valuables over to "Black Bart." When he had got all the plunder he could, he yelled his usual threat about looking back on penalty of being shot if they did and allowed the train to move on.

After dodging the police and express companies for years, "Black Bart" finally lost his nerve in a way that seemed strange because he had always shown cool-headedness on so many occasions. He had held up a Southern Pacific train in the usual way. As he was packing up the last of the plunder a rancher's boy came walking down a mountain trail toward the train.

The boy had been hunting and carried a rifle. He hadn't any notion to interfere with "Black Bart"—if he had had any idea that a train robbery was going on he would have taken to his heels. Strangely enough the sight of this lone boy with the rifle scared the robber. Hurriedly throwing his bag of booty over his shoulder, he started off in the opposite direction as fast as he could run.

The passengers and trainmen were dumbfounded. Why should this robber run away when he had six armed men to protect him?

Just then a passing gust of wind blew two of the sombreros off the "heads" of "Black Bart's" dummies. That laid bare for the first time his clever trick—the dummy desperadoes that had made it easy for him to steal thousands of dollars from trains and stages single-handed.

The express messenger was the first of the victims to come to his senses. Grabbing the rifle from the astonished ranch boy, he fired several shots at the fleeing robber. But none of them hit the mark and "Black Bart" soon disappeared in the woods high up on the mountainside.

Detectives who visited the scene of the robbery found that in his hurried flight "Black Bart" had dropped his first clue to an identity they had never been able to find. It was a handkerchief, and in one corner was the initial "B" and the mark of a San Francisco laundry.

A close watch was set in the vicinity of this laundry. When, a few weeks later, "Black Bart" left his lonely cabin in a wilderness of the Sierras and came to San Francisco to dispose of the proceeds of his latest robberies, he was arrested. His panic at the sight of the ranch boy and his rifle had wound up his career.

"Black Bart" pleaded guilty. At his trial he amused the court by telling how on his visits to San Francisco he had often discussed his crimes with some of the very detectives who were searching for him.

Bart hadn't killed anybody so the judge gave him only four years behind the bars. When his term was served, would he go back to robbing trains?—that's what had the express company worried. So the Wells-Fargo Company put Bart on their payroll for $125 a month, not to rob any more express boxes. He went straight, I heard. There was another road agent who

also went by the name of "Black Bart." He was a bad
hombre and his name was Holzhay. While in prison in
Michigan they cut a tumor out of his brain. He became a different man, was pardoned and is now leading an honest life.

"Old Bill" Miner was another famous train robber
who generally worked alone and who, like "Black
Bart" never posed as a bad man and never took a
human life. He was one of the first train robbers to
work on the Pacific Coast, and is said to have invented
the expression, "Hands up!"

Later on he figured in a daring series of robberies
along the Canadian Pacific Railway—hardly a week
passed that he didn't hold up some fast train and make
his escape with large sums in currency and gold dust.

The reward of $15,000 which the Canadian Gov-
ernment offered for his capture didn't seem to worry
Miner. One May evening when the search for him was
at its height, he stopped a fast train near Furrer,
British Columbia, on almost the exact spot of one of
his previous robberies.

At the point of his revolver, Miner forced the engineer to uncouple the combination mail and express
car from the rest of the train and take it a mile or so
down the track. As Miner knew, a heavy shipment
of gold dust had been made on this train and he expected to make a rich haul. But to his surprise, when
he came to rob the car, he found not one of the express
company's strong boxes. The only thing of value on
the car was a small bunch of registered mail.

The frequent robberies had made the express messenger wide-awake for the safety of his treasure. Just

before reaching the point where Miner had waved his
red lantern across the track he had taken the boxes of
gold dust out of the express car and hidden them in a
vacant state-room in a sleeping car at the rear of the
train. Disgusted at his failure to find the gold dust
where he had expected and fearing some trap if he attempted to search the rest of the train, Miner abandoned the robbery and rode off.

But again he was to be foiled by the quick wits of
this same express messenger. As the train robber
jumped on his horse and rode away, the messenger
climbed a telegraph pole, cut a wire and with an emer-
gency key, flashed the news of the robbery to the
nearest post of the Canadian Mounted Police.

As a result, several armed posses were soon hot on
Miner's trail. They surrounded him five days later,
and after a gun fight, made him prisoner, and he did
a long stretch in a Canadian prison.

"Black Bart" always said he had never killed anybody in his hold-ups and the people I talked with
who know about his jobs said that was true. And I
never heard that Bill Miner ever killed anybody. But
there was a different kind of train robber.

Late one stormy night, a track-walker named Kel-
ley was speeding along the track on a lonely stretch
near Davisville, California, on his track tricycle.

Suddenly two men leaped out of the underbrush
at the side of the track and stood directly in his path.
To avoid running them down he brought his tricycle
to a stop.

At once they jumped on him, dragged him to the
ground, bound and gagged him so tight that he could

neither move nor speak. After emptying his pockets
of a little money and taking his red lantern and a box
of railroad torpedoes, they broke up the tricycle by
pounding it with stones and threw the broken pieces
of the machine down underneath a culvert. Then
they disappeared in the darkness.

These two men were Browning and Brady and their
attack on the track-walker was the first step in a long
series of robberies which finally brought one of them
to a sudden death and sent the other to prison for life.

A few minutes later the whistle of a fast overland
train sounded in the distance. As it drew near the spot
where the helpless track-walker lay bound and gagged
the engineer was surprised to see a red lantern waving
across the track and to hear at the same instant the
sharp report of two torpedoes on the track—signal
that there was danger ahead.

As the train slowed down, the robbers—wearing
black masks and carrying revolvers—climbed up on
either side of the cab. They made the astonished engineer and fireman hold up their hands and walk
back to the third car from the engine—a Wells-Fargo
express car.

"Uncouple that," said Browning, shoving his revolver into the fireman's face, and pointing to the
coupling between the express car and the one behind
it. The fireman, with trembling hands, did what he
was told.

Still covered by the robbers' guns, the engineer and
fireman were marched back to the engine and ordered
to pull three cars several miles down the track. When
at last they came to a stop the engineer and fireman

to pull the three cars several miles down the track. When at last they came to a stop the engineer and fireman were again taken out of the engine and made to go back with the masked men to the express car.

But Paige, the express messenger, had suspected what the trouble was and had locked the door and barricaded the windows as well as he could with packages of freight. When the robbers pounded on the door and told him to open it he refused and yelled that he would shoot the first man who tried to come in.

"Tell him that if he doesn't open the door we're going to shoot you full of holes," said one of the bandits and he emphasized his words by firing a bullet so close to the engineer's head that it ploughed through the visor of his cap.

The engineer was in terror of his life. With shaking knees, he added his pleas to the swearing threats of the robbers.

"Think of my wife and babies, Paige," he begged, "and let these men in before they kill me."

The express messenger was between two fires. If he did his duty to his employers and kept the robbers out he would be bringing death to his friend, the engineer. Was it worth sacrificing a man's life to protect the company's property? And if he did not open the door, would they really carry out their threat?

Just then the engineer cried out in terror as another bullet whistled by his ears. The robbers were going to keep their word, thought the messenger, and he unbarred the door and slid it open.

The contents of the safe—$53,000 in bags of gold —were quickly emptied into their sacks, and the robbers made the engineer and fireman carry the plunder to the engine. Then the engine was uncoupled and with a few parting threats the robbers entered the cab, pulled the throttle wide open and rode away into the night.

After going about three miles they reversed the engine and jumped to the ground. The wild engine ran backward until it crashed into the cars it had left. making such a bad wreck that pursuit of the robbers was delayed for hours.

The loot taken from the express car was so heavy that it could not have been taken any great distance without attracting attention and the detecives maintained that it must have been buried near where the robbers abandoned the engine. A careful search failed to reveal its hiding place until years later.

But these robbers played their game once too often. The end of their career came when they tackled the robbery of an express train near Marysville, California—and all, as I will tell you, through the presence of mind of a Negro sleeping-car porter.

The train was stopped in the usual way. Several well-aimed shots frightened the messenger into letting them into his car.

But the safe was locked and the msesenger swore that he did not have the combination. After bullying and threatening him for several minutes the bandits decided that he was telling the truth, and, not having any dynamite and being no experts at working combination locks, they saw there was nothing of value they could get in the express car.

"Well," said Browning, "By G— we've got to

pay expenses, and if there's nothing here for us we'll have to see what the passengers have to offer."

Seizing an old pair of overalls he tore off the legs, and, by fastening the ends together, made two rough bags. One of them he handed to the fireman, the other to the engineer. Revolver in hand he led the way to the smoking car. "Hand over everything you've got or you're dead men."

Behind him came the engineer and fireman, holding out their bags to receive the watches, pocketbooks and pieces of jewelry which the passengers produced. Brady brought up the rear, threatening with his revolver any who hesitated and making sure that no victim escaped. When one man refused to part with his wallet, Brady hit him over the head with the butt of his revolver and snatched his valuables from his pockets as he fell over senseless.

After stripping every man in the smoking car of his valuables, Browning led the way into the first of the sleeping cars. At sight of the masked men and their weapons several of the passengers started to run out of the rear door but quickly returned when Browning fired a shot over their heads.

Right here something unexpected happened—one of those chances which even the smartest criminals can't see coming, and just such a one as I have often seen spoil the most carefully planned robberies. It turned out to be the one thing that was needed to bring the careers of Browning and Brady to an end.

The first person they met as they entered the sleeping-car was a Negro porter, his teeth chattering with fright. Browning shoved him down into a seat and took away his gold watch.

That was what proved a fatal mistake. Had Brady not taken the darkey's watch he and Browning might have gone on looting the train without any hitch and made their escape just as they had so many times before.

But that watch was the Negro's dearest treasure—he had been saving for a year to get it, and this was the first time he had worn it. Frightened, as he was, he began to turn over in his head plans for getting back that watch.

Suddenly he remembered that J. J. Bogard, the sheriff of Tehama County, was a passenger on the train. He was a frequent traveler on this train, and the porter had seen him board a rear sleeper at San Francisco on this trip.

If anybody could recover his watch, thought the darkey, Sheriff Bogard was the man. He had a reputation all over the Pacific Coast for bravery, and the porter had once seen him single-handed round up a party of cowboys who were shooting up a railroad station.

Thoughts of his lost watch made the Negro bold. When the robbers reached the middle of the car he slipped out of the front door and ran alongside the train to the last car, where the sheriff lay in his berth knowing nothing of the trouble ahead.

"Oh, Mr. Sheriff, Mr. Sheriff," the excited darkey called, "the train is full of robbers, and they've stolen my new watch!"

The sheriff hastily dressed, and pistol in hand,

rushed through the train and boldly faced the robbers. His first shot pierced Browning's heart, killing him instantly.

The next instant Brady fired—killing the sheriff and seriously wounding the fireman. Without stopping to gather up any of the booty he backed out of the car, emptying his revolver right and left as he went and injuring several passengers.

Brady escaped on the bicycle on which he had ridden to the scene of the robbery. The wheel Browning had used was found hidden under some brush nearby. With this bicycle as a clue the detectives identified the dead bandit as Browning and finally tracked down Brady. He got a life sentence at San Quentin Prison.

* * * * * *

Well, the lively days of the old Wild West are gone. The world will never see anything like them again. America has come a long ways since then, but I hope my readers have enjoyed going back with me over the old trails and meeting some of the men and women of the frontier as I have introduced them. To me, it doesn't seem so long ago; only a few yesterdays when I was a part of it all.

The End.

INDEX

INDEX

INDEX

311

INDEX

INDEX

INDEX

INDEX

CPSIA information can be obtained
at www.ICGtesting.com
Printed in the USA
BVHW051103090421
604510BV00003B/106